PhoneGap Essentials

Building Cross-Platform Mobile Apps

John M. Wargo

Addison-Wesley

Upper Saddle River, NJ • Boston • Indianapolis • San Francisco

New York • Toronto • Montreal • London • Munich • Paris • Madrid

Capetown • Sydney • Tokyo • Singapore • Mexico City

The publisher offers excellent discounts on this book when ordered in quantity for bulk purchases or special sales, which may include electronic versions and/or custom covers and content particular to your business, training goals, marketing focus, and branding interests. For more information, please contact:

U.S. Corporate and Government Sales
(800) 382-3419
corpsales@pearsontechgroup.com

For sales outside the United States, please contact:

International Sales
international@pearson.com

Visit us on the Web: informit.com/aw

Library of Congress Cataloging-in-Publication Data

Wargo, John M.
  PhoneGap essentials : building cross-platform mobile apps / John M. Wargo.
    p.   cm.
  Includes index.
  ISBN 978-0-321-81429-6 (pbk. : alk. paper)—ISBN 0-321-81429-0 (pbk.
: alk. paper)
  1. PhoneGap (Application development environment) 2. Mobile
computing. 3. Application software. I. Title.
  QA76.59.W37 2012
  004—dc23
                                                          2012010042

ISBN-13: 978-0-321-81429-6
ISBN-10:   0-321-81429-0
Text printed in the United States on recycled paper at RR Donnelley in Crawfordsville, Indiana.
First printing, June 2012

PhoneGap Essentials

To my wife, Anna.
This work exists because of your outstanding support.

Contents

Foreword by Bryce A. Curtis   *xiii*
Foreword by Jim Huempfner   *xv*
Preface   *xvii*
Acknowledgments   *xxiii*
About the Author   *xxiv*

Part I   PhoneGap **1**

Chapter 1   Introduction to PhoneGap **3**
A Little PhoneGap History   4
Why Use PhoneGap?   5
How PhoneGap Works   6
Designing for the Container   11
    The Traditional Web Server (Web 1.0) Approach   11
    The Web 2.0 Approach   11
    The HTML 5 Approach   12
Writing PhoneGap Applications   13
Building PhoneGap Applications   13
PhoneGap Limitations   17
PhoneGap Plug-Ins   18
Getting Support for PhoneGap   19
PhoneGap Resources   19
Hybrid Application Frameworks   19
    Appcelerator Titanium   20
    AT&T WorkBench and Antenna Volt   21
    BlackBerry WebWorks   21
    Strobe   22
    Tiggr   22
    Worklight   22

Chapter 2   PhoneGap Development, Testing, and Debugging **23**
Hello, World!   23
PhoneGap Initialization   25

Leveraging PhoneGap APIs   28
Enhancing the User Interface of a PhoneGap Application   30
Testing and Debugging PhoneGap Applications   35
    Running a PhoneGap Application on a Device
    Simulator or Emulator   35
    Running a PhoneGap Application on a Physical Device   36
    Leveraging PhoneGap Debugging Capabilities   37
    Third-Party PhoneGap Debugging Tools   43
Dealing with Cross-Platform Development Issues   49
    API Consistency   50
    Multiple PhoneGap JavaScript Files   51
    Web Content Folder Structure   51
    Application Requirements   52
    Application Navigation and UI   52
    Application Icons   53

Part II   PhoneGap Developer Tools 55

Chapter 3   Configuring an Android Development Environment
             for PhoneGap. 57
Installing the Android SDK   58
Eclipse Development Environment Configuration   64
Creating an Android PhoneGap Project   66
    New Eclipse Project   67
    Using Command-Line Tools   74
Testing Android PhoneGap Applications   77
    Using the Emulator   78
    Installing on a Device   78

Chapter 4   Configuring a bada Development Environment for
             PhoneGap 79
Downloading and Installing the Correct PhoneGap bada Files   80
Creating a bada PhoneGap Project   82
Creating a bada Application Profile   86
Testing bada PhoneGap Applications   95

Chapter 5   Configuring a BlackBerry Development Environment
             for PhoneGap. 97
Installing the BlackBerry WebWorks SDK   98
Creating a BlackBerry PhoneGap Project   99
Building BlackBerry PhoneGap Applications   103
    Configuring the Build Process   104
    Executing a Build   107

Testing BlackBerry PhoneGap Applications   109
    Testing on a BlackBerry Device Simulator   109
    Testing on a Device   111

**Chapter 6   Configuring an iOS Development Environment
for PhoneGap** 113
Registering as an Apple Developer   113
Installing Xcode   114
Creating an iOS PhoneGap Project   116
Testing iOS PhoneGap Applications   122

**Chapter 7   Configuring a Symbian Development
Environment for PhoneGap** 125
Installing the Nokia Web Tools   125
Installing the Make Utility   126
Creating a Symbian PhoneGap Project   128
Configuring Application Settings   129
Modifying HelloWorld3 for Symbian   130
Packaging Symbian PhoneGap Projects   131
Testing Symbian PhoneGap Applications   132

**Chapter 8   Configuring a Windows Phone Development
Environment for PhoneGap** 135
Installing the Windows Phone Development Tools   135
Creating a Windows Phone PhoneGap Project   136
Testing Windows Phone PhoneGap Applications   139

Chapter 9   Using PhoneGap Build 141
The Fit   142
Getting Started   142
Configuration   143
Creating an Application for PhoneGap Build   145
Creating a PhoneGap Build Project   146
    Upload Options   146
    New Project   147
    The Build Process   148
    Project Configuration   148
Dealing with Build Issues   150
Testing Applications   152
    OTA Download   152
    Via Camera   152
Debug Mode   153

Part III **PhoneGap APIs** **155**

Chapter 10 **Accelerometer** 157
Querying Device Orientation 158
Watching a Device's Orientation 162

Chapter 11 **Camera** 165
Accessing a Picture 165
Configuring Camera Options 176
quality 177
destinationType 178
sourceType 179
allowEdit 180
encodingType 181
targetHeight and targetWidth 181
mediaType 181
Dealing with Camera Problems 182

Chapter 12 **Capture** 185
Using the Capture API 186
Configuring Capture Options 189
duration 190
limit 190
mode 190
Capture at Work 191

Chapter 13 **Compass** 205
Getting Device Heading 205
Watching Device Heading 209
watchHeading 210
watchHeadingFilter 213

Chapter 14 **Connection** 217

Chapter 15 **Contacts** 223
Creating a Contact 224
Searching for Contacts 236
Cloning Contacts 242
Removing Contacts 242

Chapter 16 **Device** 243

Chapter 17 **Events** 249
Creating an Event Listener 249
deviceready Event 250

	Application Status Events	251
	Network Status Events	254
	Button Events	256

Chapter 18 File **263**
	Available Storage Types	263
	Accessing the Device's File System	264
	Reading Directory Entries	267
	Accessing FileEntry and DirectoryEntry Properties	269
	Writing Files	272
	Reading Files	274
	Deleting Files or Directories	275
	Copying Files or Directories	276
	Moving Files or Directories	276
	Uploading Files to a Server	277

Chapter 19 Geolocation **279**
	Getting a Device's Current Location	280
	Watching a Device's Location	284
	Setting a Watch	285
	Canceling a Watch	289

Chapter 20 Media **293**
	The Media Object	293
	Creating a Media Object	294
	Current Position	297
	Duration	297
	Releasing the Media Object	298
	Playing Audio Files	298
	Play	298
	Pause	299
	Stop	299
	Seek	299
	Recording Audio Files	299
	Start Recording	300
	Stop Recording	300
	Seeing Media in Action	300

Chapter 21 Notification **307**
	Visual Alerts (Alert and Confirm)	307
	Beep	310
	Vibrate	310
	Notification in Action	310

Chapter 22   Storage 315
              Local Storage   316
              SQL Database   317

Appendix A   Installing the PhoneGap Files 327
              Preparing for Samsung bada Development   329
              Preparing for iOS Development   329
              Preparing for Windows Phone Development   330

Appendix B   Installing the Oracle Java Developer Kit 333
              Downloading the JDK   333
              Installing the JDK   335
              Configuring the Windows Path   335
              Confirming Installation Success   336

Appendix C   Installing Apache Ant 337
              Macintosh Installation   337
              Windows Installation   338

              Index   *341*

Foreword

by Bryce A. Curtis

Everywhere you go, people are using mobile devices to keep in touch with family and friends, to find a nearby restaurant, or to check the latest news headlines. Their phones have become an indispensable part of their lives with applications that bind them closer to each other and the world around them. It's these applications that make their phones truly useful. Most users aren't aware of the underlying technology used to develop their favorite app or how much time it took to write. Instead, they view an application in terms of the benefit it provides them. Therefore, as developers, we are free to select technologies that deliver this benefit in the most efficient manner.

One technology decision that must be made early on when developing an application is whether it is to be written using native or web APIs. Depending upon the application, native APIs may be required to meet the user's expectations. However, for most applications, web technologies consisting of HTML 5, JavaScript, and CSS provide equal user experiences. The advantage of using web APIs is that they are written using web technologies familiar to many developers, thus providing an easier and quicker development process. In addition, since web technologies are standardized, they exhibit fairly consistent behavior across the many different mobile platforms available today, such as Android and iOS phones and tablets.

One significant difference between native and web applications is that the native applications provide extensive access to device features such as the camera and accelerometer, while the web applications are limited to what the device's web browser supports. To bridge this gap between native and web, a new type of application called the **hybrid application** was created. A hybrid application is written using the same web technologies—HTML 5, JavaScript, and CSS—but includes additional code that enables native APIs to be called from JavaScript. It works by wrapping your web code with a web browser and packaging both together to create a native application.

This book focuses on how to develop mobile applications using PhoneGap, which is a popular open source toolkit for building hybrid applications. You investigate the extensive PhoneGap API and learn how to include many of the device features in your applications. It will become apparent that PhoneGap delivers on the promise of a simplified, cross-platform mobile development by enabling you to write your application using web technologies and then packaging it up so that it can be distributed throughout the various app stores and markets. With any luck, your application may even become someone's favorite app.

BRYCE A. CURTIS, PH.D.
Mobile & Emerging Technologies
IBM Master Inventor
IBM Software Group

Foreword

by Jim Huempfner

There is no doubt that everything is going mobile—not just because everything can but because it is having a transformational impact on how we live, work, and communicate. Mobile applications have become critical solutions for both businesses and consumers.

As a result, many companies are gravitating toward mobile web as their primary mobile app development technology. If not done correctly, defining, designing, building, and maintaining mobile applications for both evolving multiple OS platforms and the ever-changing device landscape can be difficult, time-consuming, and expensive. Numerous commercial and open source products and frameworks that can potentially simplify mobile application creation and development are coming to the marketplace.

PhoneGap is proving to be one of the most popular solutions in this space, allowing users to quickly and easily build applications that will run on multiple platforms, leveraging your existing web development skill sets (tweaked for mobile development, of course). Because of the emergence of this solution as a front-runner and the challenges customers face in implementing the technology, John Wargo has written this book to aid developers in the process.

After a decades-long career in various computing technologies, John started to focus on mobile development platforms in 2006 when he began working for RIM, the makers of the BlackBerry handheld devices. When I first met him, he was teaching a group of colleagues and me the ins and outs of BlackBerry development. John has a passion for teaching that is surpassed only by his passion for mobile development, which was demonstrated both loud and clear during the class. You'll see that passion and depth of understanding clearly demonstrated in this book as well.

We were fortunate to hire John to work in AT&T's Mobility Group in 2009. He quickly became my team's go-to expert on mobile development, constantly evaluating technologies and learning new options in this rapidly changing mobile environment. John is a particularly valuable resource in helping our customers define their mobile application strategy and understand their options for mobile development, whether they are using the mobile web, native, hybrid frameworks (such as PhoneGap), or mobile application platforms such as MEAP or MCAP.

Mobile technology professionals will benefit from this book because it provides experienced mobile web developers with everything they need to know to transition their mobile web applications into native mobile applications using PhoneGap. This book walks you through configuring and using the development environments you need to work with PhoneGap plus shows you how to use each of the APIs provided by the framework; it's everything you need to get started developing with PhoneGap.

Success in the rapidly evolving and ever-changing mobility space should not cause fear and frustration of inaction. Rather, we should embrace technology enablers like PhoneGap and resources like this book to bring truly winning solutions to reality.

JIM HUEMPFNER
Vice President
Industry Solutions Practice
AT&T

Preface

This book is about PhoneGap—a really cool technology that allows you to build native mobile applications for multiple mobile device platforms using standard web technologies such as HTML, CSS, and JavaScript. I'd been looking at PhoneGap for several years, and when I finally got a chance to start working with it, I quickly found it to be a really simple and compelling way to build a single application that can run across multiple device platforms.

I knew Java from my work at RIM and from building Android applications. I'd poked around at Objective-C for iOS development and even did some work for Windows Mobile using Visual Basic. The world, however, is no longer focusing on applications for single mobile platforms but instead expects that mobile applications are available simultaneously for all popular mobile device platforms. PhoneGap helps solve that particular problem.

This book is for web developers who want to learn how to leverage the capabilities of the PhoneGap framework. It assumes you already know how to build web applications and are looking to understand the additional capabilities PhoneGap provides. The book highlights the PhoneGap API capabilities and how to use the tools provided with PhoneGap.

To understand the topics covered in this book, you will need to have some experience with one or more of the most popular smartphones. Some experience with smartphone SDKs is a benefit, but I'll show you how to install and use the native SDKs as I discuss each supported platform.

The book is organized into three parts:

- **Part I, PhoneGap**: Includes a very thorough introduction to PhoneGap: what it is, how it works, and more

- **Part II, PhoneGap Developer Tools**: Includes instructions on how to install and use the SDKs and PhoneGap tools for each of the supported smartphone platforms

- **Part III, PhoneGap APIs**: Includes a detailed description of each PhoneGap API plus sample code that illustrates how to exercise the API

Additional information, downloadable code projects, and errata can be found on the book's web site at www.phonegapessentials.com.

When I first proposed this book to my publisher, it had a completely different structure than the book you're reading now. As I started writing, I realized that the structure I'd picked didn't work for people learning PhoneGap. So, I quickly reordered it and broke it into the parts listed earlier. I've tried to take you step-by-step through the things that matter for PhoneGap development. I also tried to make it as complete as possible—and not skip anything related to the topic at hand. This means, for example, that when you get to the chapters on configuring development environments for PhoneGap, you'll see that I cover each supported platform in detail (with the exception of webOS since at the time HP indicated it was going to kill the platform). If you need to write PhoneGap applications for any of those platforms, you'll find the information you need here. If you are focusing on a subset of the supported platforms, you'll find that you will need to skip some chapters, but they'll be there later if you expand the scope of your development efforts. The other PhoneGap books that preceded this one focused primarily on Android and iOS, and that didn't seem right to me.

If you're looking for a no-nonsense, complete guide to PhoneGap, this is it.

Inside the Book

As I worked through the manuscript, I deliberately assessed each topic against the book's title and my goals for the publication. I kept my focus on PhoneGap and eliminated any topic that didn't directly relate.

What you'll find in the book:

- Lots of detailed information about PhoneGap and how PhoneGap works

- Lots of code examples

What you won't find in this book:

- Mobile web development topics (this is a book about PhoneGap, not mobile web development)

- Complete listing of the `phonegap.js` source file

- Expressions or phrases in languages other than English

- Obscure references to pop-culture topics (although there is an obscure reference to Douglas Adams' *Hitchhiker's Guide to the Galaxy* and one blatant reference to Monty Python)

- Pictures of my cats (I have no cats, but a picture of one of my dogs did make it into the book)

As you look through the example code provided herein, it's important to keep in mind that the code was deliberately written to clearly illustrate a particular PhoneGap-related topic or concept. While there are many things a developer can do to write compact and/or efficient code, it's distracting to readers when they have to analyze every line in order to be able to tell what's really going on therein. In this book, the code is expanded to make it as readable as possible. There are, for example, very few instances where JavaScript anonymous functions are used in the sample applications. Although using them would have made the code samples smaller, I deliberately eliminated them (in all but one chapter) for readability purposes.

No effort whatsoever has been made to optimize these examples for speed or compactness. They've been created to teach you the nuances of the PhoneGap APIs, not best practices for web development.

The Challenges in Writing a PhoneGap Book

Writing a book about PhoneGap (and many other mobile technologies) is hard. The writing isn't hard, but keeping up with the changes that occur as you write is hard. For this book, a lot of important and interesting things happened during the writing process, and I found myself regularly rewriting chapters to accommodate recent changes. The good news is that most of the PhoneGap-specific content in here will remain valid for a very long time. It was industry changes and developer tool changes that gave me the most trouble.

Let me give you some examples:

- **Six (or more) versions of PhoneGap**: When I started the book, version 1.0 of PhoneGap had just been released. It seemed that I'd picked the perfect time to start work on a PhoneGap book. It took me just about four-and-a-half months to write the manuscript, and during that time three additional versions of PhoneGap (1.1, 1.2, and 1.3) were released. During editing and all of the post-production work that needed to be done on the manuscript, versions 1.4 and 1.5 were released. I expect that by the time this book makes it onto paper, yet another version of PhoneGap, version 1.6, will have been released.

- **HP killing and then resurrecting webOS**: As I started the manuscript, HP announced it was discontinuing its webOS devices and would be seeking someone to acquire the technology. For that reason, I decided to omit any webOS-related topics from the book. Of course, HP then changed its mind and announced it would be releasing webOS as an open source project. Unfortunately, the announcement was made after I'd finished the manuscript, so you will not find much information about webOS development for PhoneGap in this book. After the book is published, I will try to publish an update that includes information on webOS support.

- **Nokia changed the way it supported web development**: Immediately after I completed the chapter on Symbian development, Nokia released a new version of its Symbian SDK that removed support for testing web applications on the simulator. Readers of this book will need to make sure they deploy an older version of the SDK in order to build and test PhoneGap applications for Symbian.

- **Adding Windows Phone support to PhoneGap**: With the release of PhoneGap 1.2, the development team added partial support for Windows Phone development. This was fortunate since it allowed me to replace the webOS chapter with one on Windows Phone. With PhoneGap release 1.3, the team added full API support for Windows Phone development.

- **Adding BlackBerry PlayBook support to PhoneGap**: In PhoneGap 1.3, the development team added support for the BlackBerry PlayBook. This, of course, completely changed the way the Ant scripts used to build BlackBerry applications worked, and the chapter had to be completely rewritten. The BlackBerry stuff stayed basically the same, but the command-line options changed, and a whole new suite of tools was added to support the PlayBook.

- **Deprecating support for the Symbian OS**: Beginning with version 1.5, the PhoneGap project has removed support for Symbian from the PhoneGap download. You will have to download the code from a separate location if you want to continue to work with Symbian applications.

- **PhoneGap donated to the Apache project**: One of the biggest changes that occurred during this process was Nitobi's announcement that the project was being donated to the Apache Foundation. While not a huge change for the development community, what was difficult was that the project was supposed to get a name change. It was first donated to Apache as DeviceReady, but then because of a conflict with a company with the same name, it was quickly changed to Callback, which was for some bizarre reason later changed to Apache Cordova (named after the street where Nitobi's offices were located). We've been told that the commercial product will keep the PhoneGap name while the open source project will have a different name, but I'm really not sure how that's going to work out.

- **Nitobi Acquired by Adobe**: Immediately following the previous announcement (actually the next day), Adobe Systems Incorporated (www.adobe.com) announced it was acquiring Nitobi, the company responsible for the PhoneGap project. That meant big changes for PhoneGap since the folks at Nitobi could now focus entirely on the PhoneGap project instead of working on it in their spare time. A while later, Adobe announced it was ceasing development of its Flash product for mobile devices. This was huge news and clearly indicated that PhoneGap now had a very important place in Adobe's mobile strategy.

One of the biggest problems I faced was getting the help I needed when things didn't work or didn't make sense. As an open source project run by volunteers, many of my forum questions went unanswered (and to this day are still unanswered). You can try to get help there, but usually you're on your own (all the more reason to pick up this book).

Code Conventions

I put a few notes and sidebars in the manuscript, but for the most part I kept the manuscript as clean and simple as I could. I did, however, illustrate sample code in two ways.

A code snippet, a section of a complete application, will be represented in the manuscript in the following manner:

```
var d = new Date(heading.timestamp);
hc.innerHTML = "Timestamp: " + d.toLocaleString();
```

The code could stand alone, like a complete function that you could use in your application, but in many cases this type of listing illustrates a piece of code that simply affects one small part of an application.

On the other hand, complete code listings will look like this:

HelloWorld Example

```
<!DOCTYPE HTML>
<html>
<head>
  <title>HelloWorld</title>
</head>
<body>
```

```
    <h1>Hello World!</h1>
    <p>This is a very simple web page.</p>
</body>
</html>
```

In this example, the code shown is a complete, functional application that you can copy into your IDE and use.

Web Resources

I've created a web site for the book: www.phonegapessentials.com (see Figure P-1). The site contains information about the book's chapters but will also contain any errata (ideally none!), reader comments, and more. I will also make the book's source code available so you can test the applications yourself and use the code from this book in your own projects.

I also regularly publish mobile development–related articles to my personal web site at www.johnwargo.com. Check out the site when you get a chance.

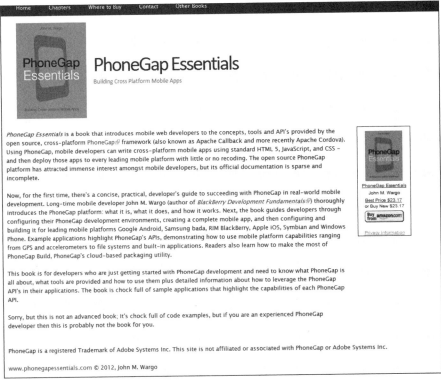

Figure P-1   PhoneGap Essentials web site

Acknowledgments

I want to thank Bryce Curtis for his excellent technical review of the manuscript and his help clarifying some of the issues that cropped up as I worked through the manuscript. There were quite a few places where Bryce added important clarifications that ultimately made this a better book.

Thanks also to the folks at Nitobi (now Adobe) for their help with this book.

Thanks to my managers at AT&T: Abhi Ingle, Jim Huempfner, Shiraz Hasan, and Vishy Gopalakrishnan for supporting me in this endeavor.

Finally, thanks to Greg Doench and the rest of the editorial staff at Pearson Education for their continued support and for letting me do another mobile development book.

About the Author

John M. Wargo has been a professional software developer for most of his career. He spent many years as a consultant and has created award-winning enterprise and commercial software products.

His involvement with mobile development began with a stint at Research In Motion (RIM) as a developer supporting a large U.S.-based carrier and its customers. After leaving RIM, he wrote one of the first books dedicated to BlackBerry development called *BlackBerry® Development Fundamentals* (Addison-Wesley, 2010; www.bbdevfundamentals.com).

He is a technical advisor for *The View*, a magazine for IBM Lotus Domino developers and administrators, and has penned a series of articles on mobile development for that publication.

Until recently, he worked for AT&T as a practice manager in AT&T's Advanced Mobile Applications Practice, specializing in cross-platform development tools and working with customers designing and building both enterprise and consumer mobile applications. He is now part of SAP's Mobile Solution Management team, focusing on the developer experience for SAP's mobile development tools.

Part I

PhoneGap

This part of the book provides an introduction to PhoneGap and a complete study of what makes a PhoneGap application a PhoneGap application. If you're new to PhoneGap, then this is the place to start. If you've been working with PhoneGap for a little while, the material in this part of the book might be a repeat of what you already know, but you might learn something as well.

1

Introduction to PhoneGap

PhoneGap is an open source framework for building cross-platform native applications using standard web technologies such as HyperText Markup Language (HTML), Cascading Style Sheets (CSS), and JavaScript. This type of mobile application is called a **hybrid application**. A group of developers created PhoneGap as a way to simplify mobile development, and adoption of the framework has grown significantly over time.

As described on the PhoneGap web site (www.phonegap.com), "PhoneGap is an open source implementation of open standards." The project's development teams work to implement relevant web development standards (from the World Wide Web Consortium [W3C] and others) into the PhoneGap framework. There are a robust suite of application programming interfaces (APIs) included in the framework today, and there's a solid road map for implementing additional capabilities over time. There's much more detail about what PhoneGap is and what makes a PhoneGap application in this and the following chapter.

PhoneGap currently supports the following mobile device operating system platforms:

- **Apple iOS (both iPhone and iPad)**: http://developer.apple.com
- **Google Android**: http://developer.android.com
- **HP/Palm webOS**: http://developer.palm.com
- **Microsoft Windows Phone 7**: http://create.msdn.com/en-us/home/getting_started

- **Nokia Symbian**: www.developer.nokia.com/Devices/Symbian

- **RIM BlackBerry (devices running BlackBerry Device Software 4.6 and newer)**: www.blackberry.com/developers

- **Samsung bada**: http://developer.bada.com

The PhoneGap project has plans for adding other platforms as they become popular in the market (and popular with mobile developers). With Hewlett-Packard's announcement of its discontinued support for webOS, development for that platform, although supported by PhoneGap, will not be covered in this book. With Nokia's announcement that it is adopting Windows Phone over its own Symbian OS, it's possible that PhoneGap will drop support for Symbian in the future, but the Symbian OS is still covered in this book.

The framework is available under an open source license; as a user of PhoneGap, you can choose to use either the modified BSD license or the MIT license. The software is free to use, and the PhoneGap team will not accept any external contributions that are incompatible with either license (either through inclusion of proprietary code or license under a more restrictive license). As the project finishes the process of migrating to the Apache Software Foundation community, the license will change to an Apache license. To contribute code to the project, you will need to sign a contributor agreement.

A Little PhoneGap History

PhoneGap was started at the 2008 iPhoneDevCamp by Nitobi (www.nitobi.com), which started the project as a way to simplify cross-platform mobile development. The project began with a team of developers working through a weekend to create the skeleton of the framework; the core functionality plus the native application container needed to render web application content on the iPhone. After the initial build of the framework, the PhoneGap project team quickly added support for Android, with BlackBerry following a short time thereafter.

In 2009, PhoneGap won the People's Choice award at the Web 2.0 Expo Launch-Pad competition. Of course, being a project for geeks, the conference attendees voted for the winner by Short Message Service (SMS) from their mobile phones.

Over time, PhoneGap has added support for additional hardware platforms and worked to ensure parity of API features across platforms. The project team continues to add support for new devices and APIs over time and has a very robust road map for future versions of the framework.

IBM has recently become more involved in the project. You can now find IBM's copyright alongside Nitobi's in the source code for new PhoneGap projects. When

IBM got involved in the Eclipse project (an open source integrated development environment [IDE]; www.eclipse.org), Eclipse quickly became integral to IBM's product strategy and became the core of several IBM projects. It's likely that IBM's involvement in the PhoneGap project indicates where IBM could be taking its mobile development or mobile product strategy.

After this section of the chapter had been written, PhoneGap applied to become part of the open source Apache project (www.apache.org), first as Apache Callback and later (beginning with version 1.4) as Apache Cordova (the name of the street where the Nitobi offices are located). At the same time, Nitobi announced that it had been acquired by Adobe (www.adobe.com).

Right before the book went to press, the PhoneGap project team changed the name of the PhoneGap JavaScript file (`phonegap.js`) to `cordova.js`. Throughout all of this, the commercial name for PhoneGap should remain PhoneGap, so all references in the book will refer to its commercial name, not the Apache project name. Sample project source code included herein will be updated with the correct file name and posted to the book's web site at www.phonegapessentials.com.

The move to the Apache Software Foundation helps to reassure companies wishing to use PhoneGap that the framework will remain a stable, available tool to use. The acquisition of Nitobi by Adobe (and Adobe's subsequent announcement that they're discontinuing support for Adobe Flash on mobile devices) clearly indicates that Adobe sees PhoneGap as an important part of their product portfolio. The folks at Nitobi who were working on PhoneGap in their spare time as a labor of love should now find themselves in a position where they can work full-time on the project. Expect regular and frequent updates to the framework.

Why Use PhoneGap?

You would use PhoneGap to build mobile application for several reasons:

- Your mobile application was already built using web technologies, and you want to be able to deploy the application through one or more mobile application stores (such as the Android Market, the Apple App Store, or BlackBerry App World).

- You want to build a mobile application leveraging your web development skills but need to leverage device-side features (such as the camera or the calendar), which are not supported by the mobile browser.

- You want to build a quick prototype of a mobile application and don't have time to learn Java or Objective-C.

- You think PhoneGap is cool.

A lot of commercial applications are available today that were built using PhoneGap; you can find a list of many of the applications on the PhoneGap web site at www .phonegap.com/apps. The framework is used primarily for consumer applications (games, social media applications, utilities, productivity applications, and more) today, but more and more enterprises are looking at PhoneGap for their employee-facing applications as well.

How PhoneGap Works

As mentioned previously, PhoneGap allows a developer to build native applications for mobile devices (both smartphones and tablets) using web technologies such as HTML, CSS, and JavaScript. A developer builds a web application for the mobile device, and special tools provided by PhoneGap package the web application into a native application for each supported mobile platform. Figure 1-1 illustrates the packaging process, which will be described in greater detail later in the chapter.

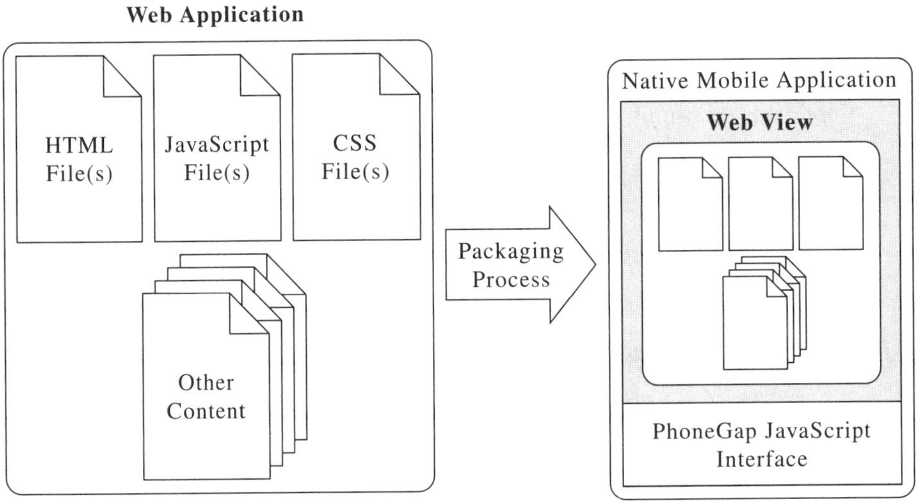

Figure 1-1   PhoneGap application architecture

Within the native application, the application's user interface consists of essentially a single screen that contains nothing but a single web view that consumes all of the available space on the device's screen. When the application launches, it loads the web application's startup page (typically `index.html` but easily changed by the developer to something else) into the web view and then passes control to the web view to allow the user to interact with the web application. As the user interacts with the application's content (the web application), links or JavaScript code within the application can load other content from within the resource files packaged with this application or can reach out to the network and pull content down from a web or application server.

For some mobile device platforms such as bada, Symbian, and webOS, a native application is a web application; there's no concept of a compiled native application that is deployed to devices. Instead, a specially packaged web application is what is executed as an application on the device. You'll learn more about this in subsequent chapters.

Web Views

A **web view** is a native application component that is used to render web content (typically HTML pages) within a native application window or screen. It's essentially a programmatically accessible wrapper around the built-in web browser included with the mobile device.

For some examples, on the BlackBerry platform, it's implemented as a `Browser Field` object (using `net.rim.device.api.browser.field2`). On Android, it's implemented using a `WebView` view (`android.webkit.WebView`), and on iOS, it's a `UIWebView` (`System/Library/Frameworks/UIKit.framework`).

The web application running within the container is just like any other web application that would run within a mobile web browser. It can open other HTML pages (either locally or from a web server sitting somewhere on the network); JavaScript embedded within the application's source files implements needed application logic, hiding or unhiding content as needed within a page, playing media files, opening new pages, performing calculations, and retrieving content from or sending content to a server. The application's look and feel is determined by any font settings, lines, spacing, coloring, or shading attributes added directly to HTML elements or implemented through CSS. Graphical elements applied to pages can also help provide a theme for the application. Anything a developer can do in a web application hosted on a server can be done within a PhoneGap application.

A typical mobile web browser does not have access to device-side components such as any of the other applications running on the device (such as the Contacts application) plus device-specific hardware (accelerometer, camera, compass, microphone, and more). The typical native mobile application, on the other hand, may make frequent use of those components. To be able to build an interesting mobile application (interesting to prospective application users anyway), a mobile application may need access to those native device components outside of the typical web container. PhoneGap accommodates this need by providing a suite of JavaScript APIs that a developer can use to allow a web application running within the PhoneGap application container to access device components that are outside of the web context. Figure 1-2 illustrates how this works at a high level.

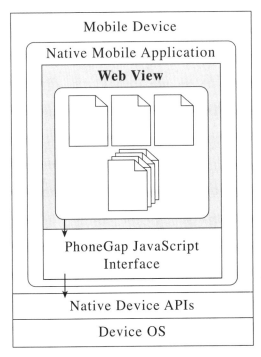

Figure 1-2   PhoneGap application: device interaction

When a developer implements a feature in an application that uses one of the PhoneGap APIs, the application calls the API using JavaScript, and then a special layer within the application translates the PhoneGap API call into the appropriate native API for the particular feature. As an example, the way the camera is accessed on a BlackBerry is different from how it's done on Android, so this API common layer allows a developer to implement a single interface that is translated behind the scenes (within the container application) into the appropriate native API for each supported mobile platform. To take a picture in a mobile application using PhoneGap, the JavaScript code would look like this:

```
navigator.camera.getPicture( onSuccess, onFail );
```

As parameters, the application passes in the names of two callback functions: onSuccess and onFail (callback functions will be described in detail in subsequent chapters).

On BlackBerry, the code being executed behind the scenes might look like this:

```
Player player = Manager.createPlayer("capture://video");
player.realize();
player.start();
VideoControl vc = (VideoControl) player.getControl(
  "VideoControl");
viewFinder = (Field)vc.initDisplayMode(
  VideoControl.USE_GUI_PRIMITIVE,
  "net.rim.device.api.ui.Field");
scrnMain.add(viewFinder);
vc.setDisplayFullScreen(true);
String imageType =
  "encoding=jpeg&width=1024&height=768&quality=fine";
byte[] theImageBytes = vc.getSnapshot(imageType);
Bitmap image = Bitmap.createBitmapFromBytes(
  imageBytes, 0, imageBytes.length, 5);
BitmapField bitmapField = new BitmapField();
bitmapField.setBitmap(image);
scrnMain.add(bitmapField);
```

On Android, the code being executed by the function might look like this:

```
camera.takePicture( shutterCallback, rawCallback,
  jpegCallback );
```

And on iOS, the code might look like this:

```
UIImagePickerController *imgPckr =
  [[UIImagePickerController alloc] init];
imgPckr.sourceType = UIImagePickerControllerSourceTypeCamera;
imgPckr.delegate = self;
imgPckr.allowsImageEditing = NO;
[self presentModalViewController:imgPckr animated:YES];
```

The code samples listed here don't cover all aspects of the process of taking a picture (such as dealing with errors or processing the resulting image), but the examples illustrate how PhoneGap simplifies cross-platform mobile development. A developer makes a single call to a common API available across all supported mobile platforms, and PhoneGap translates the call into something appropriate for each target platform. This eliminates the need for the developer to have intimate knowledge of the underlying technologies, instead allowing them to focus on their application rather than how to accomplish something on multiple devices.

PhoneGap currently supports the following APIs:

- Accelerometer
- Camera
- Capture
- Compass
- Connection
- Contacts
- Device
- Events
- File
- Geolocation
- Media
- Notification
- Storage

Additional APIs are added as the PhoneGap project team gets to them and as new standards evolve. The PhoneGap project's efforts around API implementation are partially guided by the W3C's Device APIs and Policy (DAP) Working Group (www.w3.org/2009/dap/). This group is working to "create client-side APIs that enable the development of Web Applications and Web Widgets that interact with device services such as Calendar, Contacts, Camera, etc." You'll find that the PhoneGap project will implement the DAP APIs as they become standardized.

Over time, as mobile device browsers implement the DAP APIs in a consistent manner, PhoneGap will find itself obsolete. When mobile browsers all support these APIs, there won't be a need for the capabilities PhoneGap provides, and essentially the project will just disappear.

Apple and PhoneGap

As restrictive as Apple is about what you can and cannot do within an iOS application, in October 2009, Apple began approving PhoneGap applications built with version 0.80 of the PhoneGap framework. Currently, many applications in the Apple App Store were built using PhoneGap.

Designing for the Container

PhoneGap applications are web applications running inside a client-side native application container. Because of this, web applications running within a PhoneGap application leverage an HTML 5 application structure rather than that of a traditional server-based web application. Let's talk about the different options.

The Traditional Web Server (Web 1.0) Approach

With old-school, traditional web applications, a web server serves up either static HTML pages or dynamic pages to the requesting user agent (the browser). With dynamic pages, a server-side language or scripting language is used to retrieve dynamic content (from a database, for example) and format it all into HTML before sending it to the browser. When the browser makes a request, the server retrieves the containing page and content, massages it all into HTML (or some variant such as XHTML), and sends it to the browser to be displayed.

In this example, the browser doesn't need any intelligence with regard to the content; it merely requests a page, and the server does most of the work to deliver the requested content. On the browser, the application can leverage client-side JavaScript code to allow the user to interact with the content on the page, but in general, most of the work is done by the server.

The Web 2.0 Approach

With the advent of Web 2.0, a reduced load is placed on the web server; instead, JavaScript code running within the browser is responsible for requesting and presenting data. The web server delivers an HTML-based wrapper for the web application, and JavaScript code delivered with the page dynamically manages the content areas of the page, moving data in and out of sections of the page as needed.

What allowed Web 2.0 applications to be successful was the addition of the XMLHTTPRequest (XHR) API in JavaScript. This API allowed a web application to submit asynchronous requests to a server and process the data whenever it returns from the server, without interrupting the user's activity within the application. You'll find that many PhoneGap applications make heavy use of XHR to interact with a remote server.

This approach allows for much more interesting web applications—applications that can easily look and feel like native desktop applications. The web server is still involved, serving up the pages and the content to the browser, but it does less direct manipulation of the data. Google Maps (http://maps.google.com) or Google Gmail (http://mail.google.com) are good examples of Web 2.0 applications available today.

The HTML 5 Approach

Mobile devices need a slightly different approach. Web 1.0 and 2.0 technologies work great on smartphones, but Web 1.0 apps caused a lot of data to be transmitted between server and device, and Web 2.0 apps were cooler but still required constant network connectivity to operate. Google even created a technology called Google Gears (http://gears.google.com), which included a client-side SQL database and other capabilities that web applications could use to allow an application to run, even if the web server was not available. They later stopped work on the project and instead shifted their efforts to helping craft the HTML 5 standard.

With HTML 5, web applications can make use of new capabilities that allow an application to operate more efficiently on a mobile device (or devices with limited connectivity). With HTML 5, web applications can make use of a client-side database to store application data. This makes it easier for mobile devices to operate as they go in and out of wireless coverage. Additionally, HTML 5 supports the addition of a manifest file that lists all of the files that comprise the web application. When the web application's index file loads, the browser will read the manifest file and retrieve all of the files listed in the manifest and download them to the client device. If a mobile device were to lose network connectivity, if the files listed in the manifest were available on-device, then the application can continue working, using any data that may be stored locally.

To leverage these HTML 5 capabilities, though, a web application must be written so it is able to run completely within the browser container (or in the case of PhoneGap applications, within the PhoneGap application container). The index.html file is typically the only HTML file in the application, and the application's different "screens" are actually just different `<div>` containers that are switched in and out as needed. HTML 5 applications will still reach out to a server for data as needed, using XHR to request data asynchronously and store it locally as needed.

Web developers must rethink their approach to web development to leverage these capabilities. Instead of having access to everything on the web server, the HTML 5 application running on a mobile device should try to be self-sufficient, making sure it has the files and data it needs to run whenever possible.

The web applications running within a PhoneGap application are HTML 5 applications.

Writing PhoneGap Applications

As mentioned previously, PhoneGap applications are built using normal, every-day web technologies such as HTML, CSS, and JavaScript. Whatever you want your application to do, if you can make it work using standard web technologies, you can make it work in a PhoneGap application. PhoneGap applications can do more than standard web applications, through the specialized JavaScript libraries provided with the framework.

To build PhoneGap applications, you'll need to dig out your editor of choice and get coding. To keep things simple, you could use Notepad on Windows or TextEdit on a Macintosh. You could even use something more sophisticated such as Adobe Dreamweaver or Eclipse. Aptana Studio (www.aptana.com) is a good option for web developers; it's an open source Eclipse-based IDE tailored for web development. The PhoneGap project doesn't currently offer or support any special editor for coding your PhoneGap applications.

Building PhoneGap Applications

Once you have a completed web application, whether it uses any of the PhoneGap APIs or not, it has to be packaged into a native application that will run on-device. Each of the mobile device platforms supported by the PhoneGap project has its own proprietary tools for packaging or building native applications for its platform. To build a PhoneGap application for each supported mobile platform, the application's web content (the HTML, CSS, JavaScript, and other files that comprise the application) must be added to an application project appropriate for each mobile platform and then be built using the platforms proprietary tools.

What's challenging about this process is that each mobile platform uses completely different tools and the application projects for each use different configuration files and a different folder structure. To make it even worse, the PhoneGap JavaScript libraries are different for each mobile platform; the API calls are consistent across all platforms, but the internal JavaScript code used to interact with the native container differs depending on the platform (Android, BlackBerry, or iOS, for example).

As you can see, there is no direct way for developers to configure development system so they can create one project and use it to create PhoneGap applications for multiple platforms.

What happens is that a developer will create a project for one platform (Android, for example), write the appropriate web content, and then package and test the application using the tools Google provides for Android developers. Once the application is working correctly on Android, the web content is copied into a new Xcode project (for iOS applications) or a new BlackBerry WebWorks project, and the process repeats. Figure 1-3 illustrates the process; the figure doesn't show all of the PhoneGap-supported platforms, but you should get the point.

If that weren't bad enough, tools for creating new PhoneGap projects for each of the target platforms place the PhoneGap JavaScript libraries in a different location depending on the project type. For example, in a BlackBerry project, the PhoneGap JavaScript library is placed in the /JavaScript folder, where for iOS it's placed at the root folder of the project. As an application's web content is copied from one mobile platform's project to another, the code may have to be adjusted since the JavaScript resource files may be in a different location on each.

Some platforms, such as webOS, require that their framework library (called mojo) be the first JavaScript library loaded in your web project. So, in this case, there's special code that will be in only one flavor of your application: the version for webOS.

What this means is that for developers to be able to build mobile applications for multiple mobile platforms, they must install a complete development environment for each and manually copy and adjust the web source files between each project.

Part 2 of this book contains information on how to configure each of the supported development environments for PhoneGap.

You probably read the last few paragraphs and said to yourself that there must be a better way. Fortunately, there is. The PhoneGap project team has been hard at work building a cloud-based packaging service for PhoneGap applications called PhoneGap Build, shown in Figure 1-4. This service should dramatically decrease the complexity of maintaining a development environment for PhoneGap.

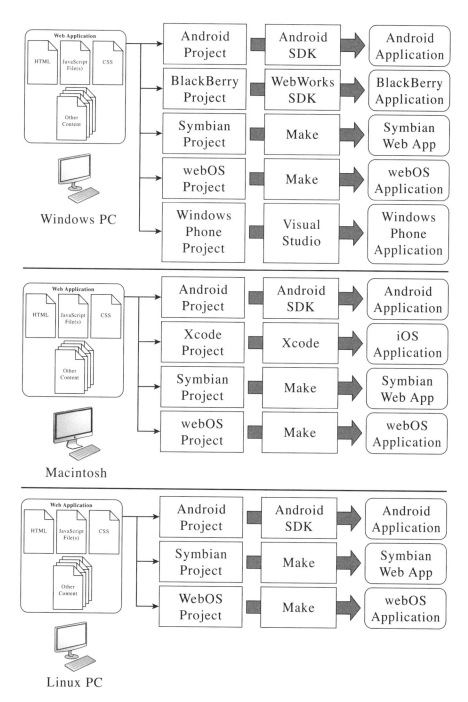

Figure 1-3 PhoneGap application build process

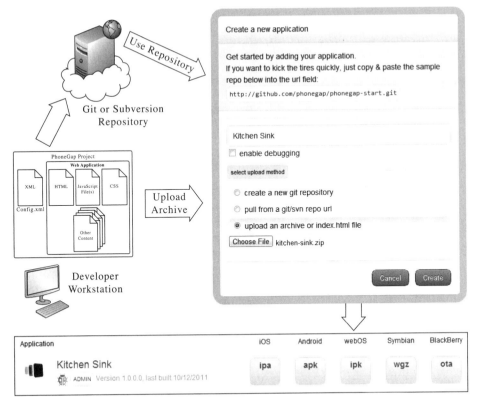

Figure 1-4 PhoneGap Build build process

With PhoneGap Build, a developer creates a configuration file called `config.xml` that describes settings for the mobile application. The format of the file is defined in the W3C widget specification (www.w3.org/TR/widgets). The configuration file and the application's web content (the application's HTML, CSS, and Java-Script files) are uploaded to the PhoneGap Build server and packaged into native mobile applications for each supported mobile device platform. A developer will interact with PhoneGap Build using a standard desktop web browser.

PhoneGap projects can be loaded into PhoneGap Build as a `.zip` file or pulled from a Git (http://git-scm.com) or svn (http://subversion.apache.org) repository. Developers can even store their PhoneGap projects in a Git repository hosted by the PhoneGap project. The PhoneGap build process is described in detail in Chapter 9.

PhoneGap Limitations

There are some limitations with using PhoneGap for your mobile application projects. As an open source project, its ability to deliver new features and bug fixes in a timely manner is controlled mostly by volunteers.

Even though the project has a robust road map, it can deliver on that road map only if it has enough resources, with relevant skills for each supported mobile platform, to do the work. What happens then is that features and bug fixes for more popular platforms (such as Android and iPhone) get more attention while less popular platforms languish. As an example, take a look at Figure 1-5, which shows the API documentation for the PhoneGap Device API. This API, described in more detail in Chapter 16, allows a PhoneGap application to access information about the device the application is running on. A developer would use this feature, for example, to enable or disable features or capabilities within an application based on the capabilities of the device.

Figure 1-5   PhoneGap API documentation example

As you can see from the figure, even though PhoneGap supports a wide range of mobile devices, this simple API to obtain the name of the device, device.name, is supported by only three platforms. As a developer working with PhoneGap, you're going to have to constantly assess availability of a particular API against the target audience for your application and possibly adjust the features of your application accordingly.

That being said, I know that one of IBM's goals is to help enforce a more consistent implementation of the supported APIs across all of the supported platforms. In this particular example, it's a documentation omission; the device.name property is available on all PhoneGap-supported mobile platforms. Someone just needs to update the documentation to reflect the current supported devices for the API. The differences in implementation of a method or property of a particular API are listed in the PhoneGap documentation under a "Quirks" section of the document.

As with most open source software projects, a limited amount of documentation is available for many topics. Even though the API documentation is excellent and there are source code examples of most API functions (something that isn't very common even for commercial software packages), a lot of things related to PhoneGap are just not documented or not documented in detail. When you go to the PhoneGap web site, you can very quickly get to the API documentation, but except for some quick-start guides for most of the supported mobile platforms, there's very little information available about how to actually "use" PhoneGap or do cross-platform development using PhoneGap.

Fortunately for you, this book should fill in many of the gaps.

PhoneGap Plug-Ins

As with any developer tool, often there are times when the base functionality provided by the solution just isn't enough for your particular needs. For those, cases, PhoneGap supports the ability to extend PhoneGap applications with additional functionality. You can find more information about plug-ins at http://wikiphonegap .com/w/page/36752779/PhoneGap%20Plugins.

The PhoneGap project has a very active developer community. When a developer sees a gap in a product, especially an open source project like PhoneGap, it doesn't take long before someone builds an enhancement (whether it is a plug-in or some other mechanism) to "fix" the problem. Here are just a few examples of what's available from the PhoneGap community:

- PhoneGap Facebook Platform Plug-in (www.phonegap.com/2011/08/30/ get-the-new-phonegap-facebook-platform-plugin)

- PhoneGap Android development plug-in for Eclipse (www
.mobiledevelopersolutions.com)

- PhoneGap iOS Plugin for Drupal (www.jefflinwood.com/2011/07/
announcing-phonegap-ios-plugin-for-drupal-v0-1/)

Getting Support for PhoneGap

One of the things corporations worry about is getting support for the software products they use for their business applications. Open source products such as Open-Office.org (http://openoffice.org) and Linux wouldn't be as popular with companies if there weren't support options available to them. Since commercial support for OpenOffice.org is available from Oracle and Linux is supported by a wide range of companies including Red Hat, Canonical, SUSE, and others, organizations are much more willing to run their businesses on these open source software products.

The PhoneGap project is no different. As more and more companies look at PhoneGap for their mobilization needs, their willingness to select the platform is influenced partially by the availability of commercial support for the framework. In early 2011, Nitobi announced availability of commercial support options for PhoneGap. Support is offered at different levels (from Basic, currently at $249US per year, up to Corporate and Enterprise at $20,000US or more per year), and a wide range of support options are available at each level. You can find information on support options for PhoneGap at www.phonegap.com/support.

PhoneGap Resources

You can find detailed information about how to work with the PhoneGap framework in several places:

- **PhoneGap web site**: www.phonegap.com

- **PhoneGap wiki**: http://wiki.phonegap.com

- **Google Groups**: http://groups.google.com/group/phonegap

- **Blogs**: www.phonegap.com/blog

Hybrid Application Frameworks

The hybrid application approach PhoneGap uses is not unique to the market. The PhoneGap project may have started the trend, but now several other products on the market use a similar approach, as shown in the following sections. The following products are only a subset of the available options in the hybrid mobile application space.

Appcelerator Titanium

Titanium is another open source hybrid application framework. Appcelerator (www.appcelerator.com) launched Titanium right about the time that PhoneGap started to gain popularity with mobile developers. Titanium works very similarly to PhoneGap in that developers build mobile applications using web technologies, but with Titanium, applications are built entirely in JavaScript. The native application running on a mobile device is just a container executing JavaScript code, as shown in Figure 1-6. The application's user interface and application logic are all coded entirely in JavaScript.

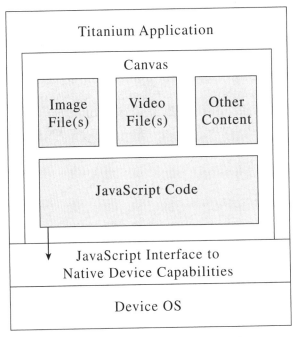

Figure 1-6 Appcelerator Titanium application structure

AT&T WorkBench and Antenna Volt

These two products provide managed containers for running multiple HTML 5 applications. The solution is implemented as a native application container that is provisioned remotely by a management server. When a user first launches the application, they must authenticate against the back-end infrastructure, and the web applications provisioned for the user are downloaded over the air into the container. What users see is a single application icon on their mobile device screen, but when they launch the application, the list of the provisioned applications appears on the screen, and the user can easily switch between the applications.

This solution is designed primarily for enterprise customers, but there are many use cases for consumer use as well.

Like Worklight, described shortly, WorkBench and Volt are part of an enterprise mobile application platform that includes additional server components (with management and reporting capabilities as well as the ability to provide connectors to back-end data sources).

You can find additional information on these solutions at www.wireless.att.com/businesscenter/built-for-business/AMEAP.jsp and www.antennasoftware.com/resource-center/volt.

BlackBerry WebWorks

The Research In Motion (RIM) developer community complained that it was too hard to build native mobile applications for the BlackBerry platform (in Java), so RIM responded with the BlackBerry WebWorks platform. WebWorks (originally called BlackBerry Widgets, which I think is a much better name) is a hybrid application framework for BlackBerry applications. Developers build mobile applications using HTML, CSS, and JavaScript and use tools from RIM to package the web application into a native Java application container just like PhoneGap does.

When you build a PhoneGap application for BlackBerry, you're actually using the BlackBerry, a WebWorks SDK to package the web application into a BlackBerry native application. In essence, and there are certainly more technical details behind this, a BlackBerry PhoneGap application is simply a BlackBerry WebWorks application with the custom PhoneGap JavaScript libraries added in.

Note: If you want to learn more about BlackBerry development, there's a great book on the subject called *BlackBerry® Development Fundamentals* (see www.bbdevfundamentals.com) written by yours truly (me!). Unfortunately, the book was released while the BlackBerry WebWorks tools were still in beta, so that topic is not covered.

Strobe

Strobe (www.strobecorp.com) is a mobile application delivery network that utilizes PhoneGap Build (described in Chapter 9) to package native applications built using their frameworks. There's a free test version of Strobe and additional paid options depending on the size of your development needs. The solution is currently in private beta.

Tiggr

Tiggr (www.gotiggr.com) is a web-based IDE for building mobile applications. It includes a visual editor and jQuery Mobile interface components that can just be dragged onto a web application. Tiggr integrates with PhoneGap to provide native mobile applications built with its IDE. Currently, the Tiggr Mobile Apps Builder is free for a 15-day trial but then costs $45US per month thereafter.

Worklight

Worklight (www.worklight.com) is a commercial mobile application platform built on top of PhoneGap. Worklight provides its own Eclipse-based IDE for building Worklight applications and special server infrastructure for connectivity to provide management and reporting capabilities as well as a mobile optimized conduit to back-end or external applications and application data. Worklight applications are simply PhoneGap applications with some additional capabilities provided by the Worklight platform (implemented through some additional JavaScript libraries). Worklight was acquired by IBM in early 2012.

2

PhoneGap Development, Testing, and Debugging

As mentioned in the previous chapter, a PhoneGap application can do anything that can be coded in standard, everyday HTML, CSS, and JavaScript. There are web applications and PhoneGap applications, and the distinction between them can be minor or can be considerable. In this chapter, we'll analyze the anatomy of a PhoneGap application, identifying what makes an application a PhoneGap application and then highlighting ways to make a PhoneGap application...better.

The following sections will highlight different versions of the requisite Hello-World application found in every developer book, article, and training class. For the purpose of highlighting aspects of the applications' web content, rather than how they were created, the steps required to create the applications are omitted. Refer to the chapters that follow for specific information on how to create and test PhoneGap projects for each of the supported mobile platforms.

Hello, World!

As with any developer book, we're going to start with the default HelloWorld application and then build upon it to highlight different aspects of a PhoneGap application. The following HTML content describes a simple web page that displays some text on a page.

HelloWorld1 Application

```
<!DOCTYPE HTML>
<html>
<head>
  <title>HelloWorld1</title>
</head>
<body>
  <h1>Hello World</h1>
  <p>This is a sample PhoneGap application</p>
</body>
</html>
```

If you package that page into a PhoneGap application and run it on a smartphone or device emulator (in this case an Android emulator), you will see something similar to what is shown in Figure 2-1.

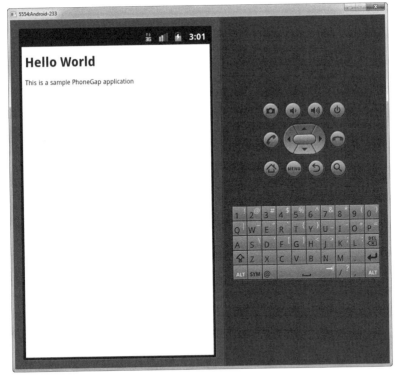

Figure 2-1   HelloWorld1 application running on an Android emulator

This is technically a PhoneGap application because it's a web application running within the PhoneGap native application container. There is, however, nothing

PhoneGap-ish about this application. It's running in the PhoneGap native container, but it isn't leveraging any of the APIs provided by the PhoneGap framework.

Therefore, any web application can be built into a PhoneGap application; there's nothing forcing you to use the PhoneGap APIs. If you have a simple web application that simply needs a way to be deployed through a smartphone app store, then this is one way to accomplish that goal.

PhoneGap Initialization

Now let's take the previous example application and add some PhoneGap-specific stuff to it. The HelloWorld2 application listed next has been updated to include code that recognizes when the PhoneGap application has completed initialization and displays an alert dialog letting you know PhoneGap is ready.

HelloWorld2 Application

```
<!DOCTYPE html>
<html>
  <head>
    <meta http-equiv="Content-type" content="text/html;
      charset=utf-8">
    <meta name="viewport" id="viewport"
      content="width=device-width, height=device-height,
      initial-scale=1.0, maximum-scale=1.0,
      user-scalable=no;" />
    <script type="text/javascript" charset="utf-8"
      src="phonegap.js"></script>

    <script type="text/javascript" charset="utf-8">

      function onBodyLoad() {
        document.addEventListener("deviceready",onDeviceReady,
        false);
      }

      function onDeviceReady() {
        navigator.notification.alert("PhoneGap is ready!");
      }
    </script>

  </head>
  <body onload="onBodyLoad()">
    <h1>HelloWorld2</h1>
    <p>This is a sample PhoneGap application.</p>
  </body>
</html>
```

On the iPhone simulator, the application will display the screen shown in Figure 2-2.

Figure 2-2   HelloWorld2 application running on an iOS simulator

Within the <Head> section of the web page are two new entries: meta tags that describe the content type for the application and viewport settings.

The content-type setting is a standard HTML setting and should look the same as it would for any other HTML 5 application.

The viewport settings tell the web browser rendering the content how much of the available screen real estate should be used for the application and how to scale the content on the screen. In this case, the HTML page is configured to use the maximum height and width of the screen (through the width=device-width and height=device-height attributes) and to scale the content at 100% and not allow the user to change that in any way (through the initial-scale=1.0, maximum-scale=1.0, and user-scalable=no attributes).

Note: The viewport and associated attributes are not required; if they're omitted, the browser will revert to its default behavior, which may result in the application's content not consuming the full screen area available to it or zooming beyond it. Because there's not much content in the HelloWorld2 application, it could, for example, consume only the upper half of the screen on some devices.

You may find that on some platforms the settings have no effect. On the BlackBerry Torch simulator, the height and width attributes are respected; on the BlackBerry Storm simulator, the application doesn't consume the entire height of the screen no matter how the attributes are set.

There's also a new script tag in the code that loads the PhoneGap JavaScript library:

```
<script type="text/javascript" charset="utf-8"
  src="phonegap.js"></script>
```

This loads the PhoneGap API library and makes the PhoneGap APIs available to the program. In this example, and all of the examples throughout the rest of the book, I'll load the PhoneGap JavaScript library using this standard snippet of code. In reality, the PhoneGap file being loaded by your application will include version information in the file name. As I wrote the chapter, PhoneGap 1.0 had just been released, so the code in reality looked like this when I wrote the application:

```
<script type="text/javascript" charset="utf-8"
  src="phonegap-1.0.0.js"></script>
```

As I wrote subsequent chapters, the PhoneGap team released three additional versions of the framework. Rather than have inconsistent PhoneGap JavaScript file names in the book, I chose to just show `phonegap.js` as illustrated in the first example. In reality, many of the example applications used throughout the book were actually built using PhoneGap Build, which requires only the simple `phonegap.js` reference (or no reference at all), which is then replaced with the appropriate JavaScript file version PhoneGap Build is currently using.

Beginning with PhoneGap 1.5, the project team changed the name for the open source project to Cordova and changed the JavaScript file (for most but not all of the supported platforms) from `phonegap.js` to `cordova.js`. So, even though you're working with PhoneGap, the JavaScript file name no longer matches the commercial name for the project.

JavaScript code in a PhoneGap application does not have immediate access to the PhoneGap APIs after the web application has loaded. The native PhoneGap application container must complete its initialization process before it can respond to calls JavaScript made using the PhoneGap APIs. To accommodate this delay in

API availability, a web developer building PhoneGap applications must instruct the container to notify the web application when the PhoneGap APIs are available. Any application processing that requires the use of the APIs should be executed by the application only after it has received its notification that the APIs are available.

In the HelloWorld2 application, this notification is accomplished through the addition of an onload event defined in the page's body section, as shown here:

```
<body onload="onBodyLoad()">
```

Within the onBodyLoad function, the code registers an event listener that instructs the application to call the onDeviceReady function when the device is ready, when the PhoneGap application container has finished its initialization routines:

```
document.addEventListener("deviceready", onDeviceReady, false);
```

In this example application, the onDeviceReady function simply displays a PhoneGap alert dialog (which is different from a JavaScript alert dialog), letting the user know everything is OK:

```
navigator.notification.alert("PhoneGap is ready!")
```

In production applications, this function could update the user interface (UI) with content created through API calls or do whatever other processing is required by the application. You'll see an example of this in the next sample application.

The PhoneGap Navigator

Many of the APIs implemented by PhoneGap are instantiated from the Navigator object. Unfortunately, it's not consistent; some do and some do not. Be sure to check the API documentation before calling an API.

Leveraging PhoneGap APIs

Now that we know how to configure an application to wait until the PhoneGap APIs are available, let's build an application that actually uses the PhoneGap APIs as shown in the following HelloWorld3 application.

HelloWorld3 Application

```
<!DOCTYPE html>
<html>
  <head>
    <meta http-equiv="Content-type" content="text/html;
      charset=utf-8">
    <meta name="viewport" id="viewport"
      content="width=device-width, height=device-height,
      initial-scale=1.0, maximum-scale=1.0,
      user-scalable=no;" />
    <script type="text/javascript" charset="utf-8"
      src="phonegap.js"></script>

    <script type="text/javascript" charset="utf-8">

      function onBodyLoad() {
        document.addEventListener("deviceready", onDeviceReady,
        false);
      }

      function onDeviceReady() {
        //Get the appInfo DOM element
        var element = document.getElementById('appInfo');
        //replace it with specific information about the device
        //running the application
        element.innerHTML = 'PhoneGap (version ' +
          device.phonegap + ')<br />' + device.platform + ' ' +
          device.name + ' (version ' + device.version + ').';
      }
    </script>

  </head>
  <body onload="onBodyLoad()">
    <h1>HelloWorld3</h1>
    <p>This is a PhoneGap application that makes calls to the
    PhoneGap APIs.</p>
    <p id="appInfo">Waiting for PhoneGap Initialization to
    complete</p>
  </body>
</html>
```

Figure 2-3 shows a portion of the application's screen when running on the Black-Berry Torch 9800 simulator.

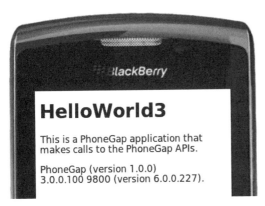

Figure 2-3   HelloWorld3 application running on a BlackBerry simulator

In this version of the HelloWorld application, the code in the onDeviceReady function has been updated so the program updates a portion of the application's content with an ID of appInfo with information about the device running the application and the version of PhoneGap used to build the application. Device-specific information is available via the PhoneGap device API (http://docs.phonegap.com/phonegap_device_device.md.html), and this sample application uses only a subset of the available methods in this API.

Figure 2-3 highlights one of the problems with the PhoneGap APIs: inconsistent implementation of an API across different mobile device platforms. The call to the device.platform API is supposed to return the name of the mobile device platform the application is running on. In this case, the call should return "Black-Berry," but instead it returns "3.0.0.100" for some bizarre reason. For iOS devices, the call returns "iPhone" when in reality it should be returning "iOS." It's important to keep in mind that any function call might not return what you expect depending on the mobile platform the application is running on. Be sure to test your application on each platform you plan on supporting and make adjustments to your code as needed to deal with inconsistencies with the PhoneGap APIs. Expect the values returned by this property to change over time as well.

Enhancing the User Interface of a PhoneGap Application

As you can see from the application examples highlighted so far, the PhoneGap framework doesn't do anything to enhance the UI of a PhoneGap application. The framework provides access to device-specific features and applications and leaves it up to developers to theme their applications however they see fit. Web developers should use the capabilities provided by HTML, CSS, and even Java-Script to enhance the UI of their PhoneGap applications as needed; we're not going to cover mobile web UI design here.

As Android and iOS-based smartphones became more popular, web developers found themselves needing to be able to build web applications that mimic the look and feel of native applications on these mobile platforms. To accommodate this need, many open source and commercial JavaScript mobile frameworks were created to simplify this task such as jQuery Mobile (www.jquerymobile.com), Dojo Mobile (www.dojotoolkit.org/features/mobile), and Sencha Touch (www.sencha.com/products/touch).

Although not directly related to PhoneGap development, the use of these frameworks is very common for PhoneGap applications, so it's useful to highlight them here. In this section, we'll discuss how to enhance the UI of a PhoneGap application using jQuery Mobile (jQM), an offshoot of the popular jQuery project. The jQuery and jQM libraries work together to provide some pretty useful UI elements and theming for any mobile web application.

 Note: jQM currently supports most of the mobile platforms supported by PhoneGap. As of this writing, the Samsung bada OS has not been tested but is expected to work, and support has not yet been added for the Windows Phone OS.

In the following HelloWorld4 application, we'll take the HelloWorld3 application and apply an enhanced UI using the jQuery Mobile framework.

HelloWorld4 Application

```
<!DOCTYPE html>
<html>
  <head>
    <meta http-equiv="Content-type" content="text/html;
      charset=utf-8">
    <meta name="viewport" id="viewport"
      content="width=device-width, height=device-height,
      initial-scale=1.0, maximum-scale=1.0,
      user-scalable=no;" />
    <link rel="stylesheet" href="jquery.mobile-1.0b3.css" />
    <script type="text/javascript" charset="utf-8"
      src="jquery-1.6.4.js"></script>
    <script type="text/javascript" charset="utf-8"
      src="jquery.mobile-1.0b3.js"></script>
    <script type="text/javascript" charset="utf-8"
```

```
      src="phonegap.js"></script>

  <script type="text/javascript" charset="utf-8">

    function onBodyLoad() {
      document.addEventListener("deviceready", onDeviceReady,
        false);
    }

    function onDeviceReady() {
      //Get the appInfo DOM element
      var element = document.getElementById('appInfo');
      //replace it with specific information about the device
      //running the application
      element.innerHTML = 'PhoneGap (version ' +
        device.phonegap + ')<br />' + device.platform + ' ' +
        device.name + ' (version ' + device.version + ').';
    }
  </script>

</head>
<body onload="onBodyLoad()">
  <div data-role="page">
    <div data-role="header" data-position="fixed">
      <h1>HelloWorld4</h1>
    </div>
    <div data-role="content">
      <p>This is a PhoneGap application that makes calls to
      the PhoneGap APIs and uses the jQuery Mobile
      framework.</p>
      <p id="appInfo">Waiting for PhoneGap Initialization to
      complete</p>
    </div>
    <div data-role="footer" data-position="fixed">
      <h1>PhoneGap Essentials</h1>
    </div>
  </div>
</body>
</html>
```

Figure 2-4 shows the application running on the Android simulator.

Figure 2-4   HelloWorld4 application running on an Android emulator

Notice that the `device.platform` call is working correctly on the Android emulator; in Figure 2-4, it lists "google_sdk" as the platform for the emulator.

Notice how jQM has a problem rendering the "PhoneGap Essentials" text in the footer. Just so you can see how this looks on a different mobile platform, Figure 2-5 shows the exact same web content running within a PhoneGap application on the BlackBerry Torch simulator. This isn't an issue with PhoneGap but instead is an issue related to available screen width and how jQM renders content leaving space on the left and right for buttons (which aren't used in this example).

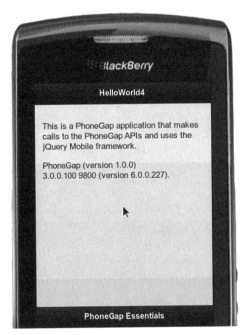

Figure 2-5   HelloWorld4 application running on a BlackBerry simulator

In this version of the application, some additional resources have been added to the page's header:

```
<link rel="stylesheet" href="jquery.mobile-1.0b3.css" />
<script type="text/javascript" charset="utf-8"
   src="jquery-1.6.4.js"></script>
<script type="text/javascript" charset="utf-8"
   src="jquery.mobile-1.0b3.js"></script>
```

The first line points to a CSS file provided by the jQM framework. It contains the style information used to render the iPhone-ish UI shown in the figure. Next come references to the jQuery and jQuery Mobile JavaScript libraries that are used to provide the customized UI plus add additional capabilities to the application. The files referenced in the example application are the full versions of the CSS and JavaScript files. These files are used during testing of the application and should be replaced with the min versions of the files, as shown in the following code snippet, before rolling the application into production.

```
<link rel="stylesheet" href="jquery.mobile-1.0b3.min.css" />
<script type="text/javascript" charset="utf-8"
   src="jquery-1.6.4.min.js"></script>
<script type="text/javascript" charset="utf-8"
   src="jquery.mobile-1.0b3.min.js"></script>
```

The min versions are compressed so comments, white space, line breaks, and so on, are removed from the files. This allows the files to take up less space within the packaged application, helping reduce the overall file size for the application, and allows these resources to load more quickly when the user launches the application.

The body of the HTML page has been updated to include several HTML `<div>` tags wrapped around the content for the application. These `<div>`s include a `data-role` attribute that is used by jQM to define specific areas of the content page that are then styled appropriately depending on which role is assigned.

In Figure 2-5, the content in the section of the page given the `header` data-role is styled with a gradient background and forced to the top of the page by the `data-position="fixed"` attribute. Similarly, the content in the section of the page given the `footer` data-role is styled with a gradient background and forced to the bottom of the page by the `data-position="fixed"` attribute. The page content defined within the `data-role="content"` `<div>` will be rendered between the header and footer, with the middle section scrollable as needed to display all of the content within the section.

These examples only lightly cover the capabilities of jQM; there's so much more you can do with this framework to enhance the user experience within your PhoneGap applications. Refer to the jQM online documentation or several of the new books on jQM for additional information about the capabilities provided by the framework.

Testing and Debugging PhoneGap Applications

Each of the mobile platforms supported by PhoneGap has a mechanism a developer can use to test and, in the unlikely event your code has bugs, debug PhoneGap applications. In general, you can load a PhoneGap application into a device simulator or emulator, provided as part of the mobile platform's SDK, or you can load an application onto a physical device. There are also third-party solutions you can use to test your PhoneGap applications within a desktop browser interface.

Running a PhoneGap Application on a Device Simulator or Emulator

Each smartphone operating system supported by PhoneGap has a device emulator or simulator (E/S) provided by the originator of the OS. In some cases, what's provided is a generic emulator that simply mimics the capabilities of the specific OS version, while for other mobile platforms there are simulators available that mimic specific devices. Either way, there's a software-only solution available that developers can use to test PhoneGap applications in an almost real-world scenario (I'll explain "almost real-world" in the following section).

An E/S is typically included with the native development tools for each mobile platform, but in some cases there are options that can be downloaded individually. Research In Motion, for example, includes a set of simulators with each Black-Berry Device Software version SDK but also provides individual downloads for specific BlackBerry Device Software versions or for older devices that have software updates available for them. Either way, there are likely options available for each and every device or device OS you want to test your application on. The chapters that follow provide detailed information on how to configure a development environment for each of the mobile devices platforms supported by PhoneGap. That's where you will find instructions on how to test PhoneGap applications on the appropriate E/S for the target platform.

Running a PhoneGap Application on a Physical Device

While the device E/S is a great option for developer and system testing of a PhoneGap application, final testing should always be performed on a physical device. As good as these options are, there is always something that doesn't work quite right on a simulator or emulator.

To run a PhoneGap application on a physical device, you will create the PhoneGap application first using the native SDK or package the application for platforms that use a widget approach. Once you have a deployable application, you will connect the device to your development computer via a Universal Serial Bus (USB) cable and transfer the application to the mobile device using some component of the native SDKs. The process varies depending on the mobile platform you are working with.

For iOS applications, for example, Apple requires a special provisioning process for every iOS device on which you want to install your application. The process requires membership in Apple's developer program and involves the Xcode development environment, Apple's developer portal, a provisioning profile, and a physical device.

For Android and BlackBerry devices, the native SDK includes command-line utilities you can use to copy an application to a target device. There's no special provisioning process; you simply connect the device to the developer computer, issue the command, and test away. In some cases, you can deploy to devices directly from the Eclipse IDE. For Android devices, there are steps you must complete to configure the device for testing applications. On BlackBerry, you'll need to secure a set of signing keys (they're free at https://bdsc.webapps.blackberry.com/java/

documentation/ww_java_getting_started/Code_signing_1977871_11.html) and sign the application before it will run on a physical device.

Regardless of the platform you use, digging into the details of on-device testing is beyond the scope of this book. Please refer to the documentation for the appropriate native SDK for additional information about how to test applications on physical devices.

Leveraging PhoneGap Debugging Capabilities

As mentioned earlier, there are two types of PhoneGap applications: PhoneGap applications that consist of a web application packaged inside of a native application container (for Android, BlackBerry, iOS, and Windows Phone) and PhoneGap applications deployed simply as packaged web applications (on bada, Symbian, and webOS).

For the mobile platforms where PhoneGap applications are simply packaged web applications, the freely available native SDK typically includes support for debugging web content running in a device emulator or simulator. In the chapters that follow, you will find instructions on how to leverage native debugging tools for these platforms when testing PhoneGap applications. You will, however, need to refer to the native SDK documentation for detailed information on how to use these tools.

The problem with the native application options for PhoneGap is that the native tools designed to help developers debug applications for each platform are designed to debug native applications; they have none or limited capabilities for debugging web content that is packaged within native applications. The BlackBerry Web-Works development tools originally supported the ability to debug web content packaged within a BlackBerry WebWorks application (which is essentially what a PhoneGap application is on BlackBerry). In 2011, RIM abandoned the Eclipse and Visual Studio IDEs and switched to an entirely command-line-driven approach.

To help debug your PhoneGap applications, you can fill your code with calls to the `alert()` function. This is what I have always called a poor man's debugger, but it works quite well for certain types of application debugging tasks. If you see an event that's not firing within your application or some variable that's not being set or read correctly, you can simply insert an alert that displays a relevant message and use that to see what's going on. There's an example of this approach in the HelloWorld2 application shown earlier with the use of PhoneGap's `navigator.notification.alert("")` function. In this case, I used the alert to help debug what was happening in the `onDeviceReady()` function. It seemed to be working on Android, but not BlackBerry, so I used the alert to help confirm my suspicion and to help test different approaches as I attempted to fix the problem.

The problem with this approach is that when you fill your buggy code with alerts, you're constantly interrupting the application flow to dismiss the alerts as they come up. For a simple problem, this approach works pretty well, but when debugging more troublesome errors, you will need an approach that allows you to let the application run and then analyze what is happening in real time or after the application or a process within the application has completed, without interrupting the application. PhoneGap applications can do this through the JavaScript `console` object implemented by the WebKit browser rendering engine.

Using the `console` object, developers can write messages to the browser's console, which can be viewed outside of the running program through capabilities provided by the native SDKs or device simulators or emulators. The `console` object has scope at the window level, so it's essentially a global object accessible by any JavaScript code within the application. WebKit supports several options; the most common ones used are as follows:

- `console.log("message");`

- `console.warn("message");`

- `console.error("message");`

Example 2-1 shows a sample application that illustrates the use of this feature.

Example 2-1

```
<!DOCTYPE html>
<html>
  <head>
    <meta name="viewport" content="width=device-width,
      height=device-height, initial-scale=1.0,
      maximum-scale=1.0, user-scalable=no;" />
    <meta http-equiv="Content-type" content="text/html;
      charset=utf-8">
    <script type="text/javascript" charset="utf-8"
      src="phonegap.js"></script>

    <script type="text/javascript" charset="utf-8">

      function onBodyLoad() {
        document.addEventListener("deviceready", onDeviceReady,
          false);
      }
```

```
    function onDeviceReady() {
      //Just writing some console messages
      console.warn("This is a warning message!");
      console.log("This is a log message!");
      console.error("And this is an error message!");
    }

  </script>
 </head>
 <body onload="onBodyLoad()">
   <h1>Debug Example</h1>
   <p>Look at the console to see the messages the application
   has outputted</p>
 </body>
</html>
```

As you can see from the code, all the application has to do is call the appropriate method and pass in the text of the message that is supposed to be written to the console.

In some cases, the browser component executing your application's web content won't throw an error if you try to do something that's not supported in your Java-Script code (calling a PhoneGap API function that doesn't exist, for example, because you've misspelled it). In this scenario, simply wrap the errant call in a try/catch block so your application will have a chance to write its error to the console, as shown in the following example:

```
try {
  console.log("Validating the meaning of life");
  somefunctioncall("42");
} catch (e) {
  console.error("Hmmm, not sure why this happened here: " +
    e.message);
}
```

Figure 2-6 shows the messages from Example 2-1 highlighted in the Xcode console window. This window is accessible while the program is running on an iOS simulator, so you can debug applications in real time.

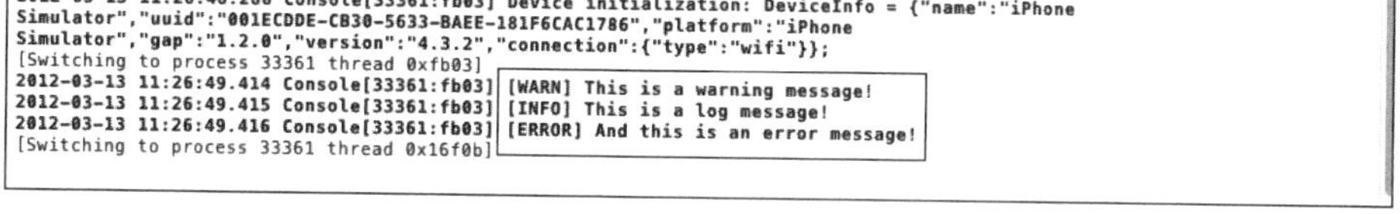

```
welcome to change it and/or distribute copies of it under certain conditions.
Type "show copying" to see the conditions.
There is absolutely no warranty for GDB.  Type "show warranty" for details.
This GDB was configured as "x86_64-apple-darwin".Attaching to process 33361.
[Switching to process 33361 thread 0x11e03]
2012-03-13 11:26:48.286 Console[33361:fb03] Device initialization: DeviceInfo = {"name":"iPhone
Simulator","uuid":"001ECDDE-CB30-5633-BAEE-181F6CAC1786","platform":"iPhone
Simulator","gap":"1.2.0","version":"4.3.2","connection":{"type":"wifi"}};
[Switching to process 33361 thread 0xfb03]
2012-03-13 11:26:49.414 Console[33361:fb03] [WARN] This is a warning message!
2012-03-13 11:26:49.415 Console[33361:fb03] [INFO] This is a log message!
2012-03-13 11:26:49.416 Console[33361:fb03] [ERROR] And this is an error message!
[Switching to process 33361 thread 0x16f0b]
```

Figure 2-6   Viewing console messages in Xcode

When working with the BlackBerry simulator, you can access the logs by holding down the simulator's Alt key and typing **lglg**. The simulator will display the Event Log, as shown in Figure 2-7.

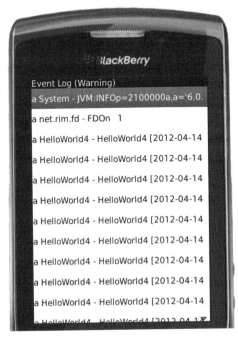

Figure 2-7 BlackBerry Event Log application

When you open an Event Log entry, you can see the details behind the entry, as shown in Figure 2-8. Press the keyboard's n and p keys to navigate to the next and previous entries in the log.

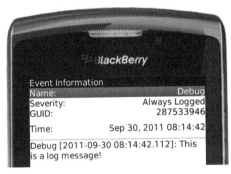

Figure 2-8 Viewing console messages on BlackBerry

Note: In my testing with the BlackBerry simulator, only the `console.log` messages appear within the Event Log application; the BlackBerry implementation of the WebKit engine doesn't seem to respond to `console.warn` and `console.error` messages.

Within the BlackBerry Event Log application, you have the ability to clear the log, filter what's displayed in the log, and copy the contents of the log to the clipboard so you can use them in another application or send them to yourself via email. Additionally, when working with a physical device, you can connect the device to your development system and use the BlackBerry Java Loader application (`javaloader.exe`) to copy the logs from the device. Many of these options are described in detail in my other mobile development book, *BlackBerry® Development Fundamentals* (www.bbdevfundamentals.com).

The Android SDK includes utilities that allow a developer to monitor log activity, while an application runs within an Android emulator. This functionality is provided by the LogCat utility, which is an integral part of the Eclipse plug-in but also available through the command line or a stand-alone utility.

To open the LogCat window in Eclipse, open the Window menu, select Show View, and then select Other. In the dialog that appears, expand the Android category and select LogCat, as shown in Figure 2-9, and then click OK. Eclipse will open a new pane in the messages area of the IDE, as shown in Figure 2-10.

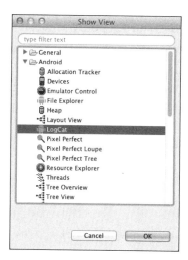

Figure 2-9　Eclipse Show window dialog

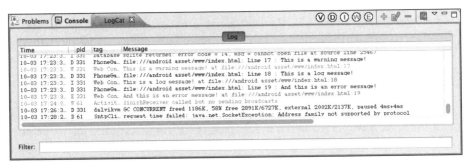

Figure 2-10 Eclipse messages area

This pane will display all messages generated by the Android device emulator as well as console messages written by your PhoneGap application; you can see the three messages written by the sample application. Use the V (verbose), D (debug), I (info), W (warning), and E (error) buttons at the top of the pane to filter the contents of the pane as needed to allow you to more quickly locate the entries you are looking for while debugging an application.

Google also offers a stand-alone utility called the Dalvik Debug Monitor Server (DDMS) that you can use to monitor the Android emulator console when testing PhoneGap applications outside of the Eclipse IDE. To launch the DDMS utility, you must first launch an Android emulator. Once the emulator is running, open a file explorer (Finder on Macintosh or Windows Explorer on Windows), navigate to the Android SDK tools folder, and execute the DDMS utility located therein. The file is called `ddms.bat` on Microsoft Windows and `ddms` on Macintosh.

When the utility launches, it will display a window similar to the one shown in Figure 2-11. At the top of the utility are windows that show the different processes running in the emulator on the left and a list of additional options on the right. The lower half of the application's window displays the same LogCat pane from the Eclipse plug-in.

To access the LogCat content from the command line on Windows, open a command prompt, navigate to the Android SDK `platform-tools` folder, and issue the following command:

```
adb logcat
```

On Macintosh, open a terminal window, navigate to the Android SDK `platform-tools` folder, and issue the following command:

```
./adb logcat
```

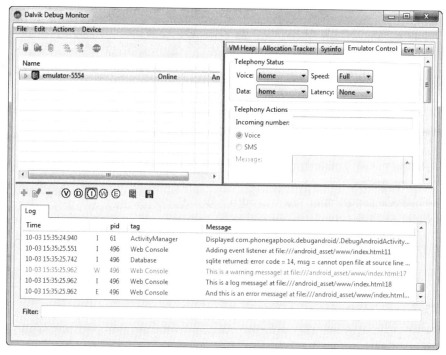

Figure 2-11   Android DDMS application window

The `adb` utility will connect to the emulator and retrieve and display in real time the contents of the logcat from the Android emulator, as shown in Figure 2-12. In the figure, the three console messages generated by the application are highlighted.

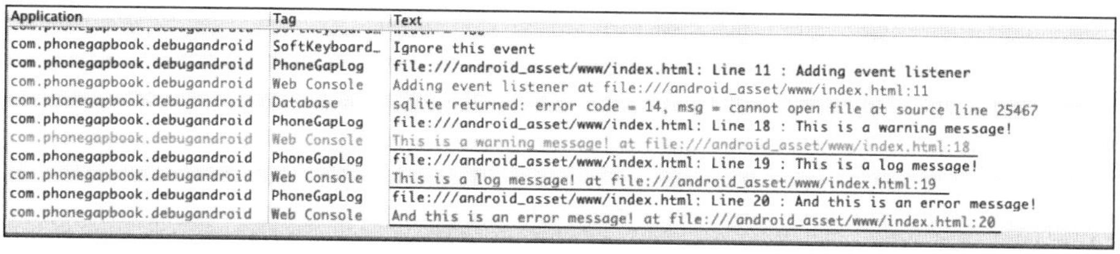

Figure 2-12   Viewing console messages on Android

Third-Party PhoneGap Debugging Tools

There's a very active partner community supporting PhoneGap with additional tools for PhoneGap developers. In this section, I'll introduce several of the available tools that help developers test and debug PhoneGap applications. This is by

no means a complete list of options; refer to the PhoneGap wiki (http://wiki
.phonegap.com) for information on additional tools that might be available.

Ripple Mobile Environment Emulator

When developing a PhoneGap application, it's quite time-consuming to build the
application and load it into a simulator or emulator for testing. The Ripple Mobile
Environment Emulator (RMEE) is a freely available tool that helps alleviate this
problem by providing a desktop browser–based interface you can use to test your
PhoneGap applications. The RMEE emulates the execution of the PhoneGap APIs
within the browser container. You should use the emulator for quick testing of
PhoneGap application features during development and then switch to packaging/
building PhoneGap applications and testing them on actual devices or device emulators or simulators for more thorough testing. The RMEE is not designed to
replace testing on real devices, device simulators, or device emulators.

RIM and the Ripple Emulator

Tiny Hippos, the company that produced of the Ripple Mobile Environment Emulator,
was recently purchased by RIM and is expected to become the default way to test
BlackBerry WebWorks applications. The emulator has supported PhoneGap for quite a
while and is expected to continue to support the project under RIM's ownership.

The RMEE is implemented as an extension to the Google Chrome browser, so
before you can start using the emulator, you must first install the latest version of
Chrome from www.google.com/chrome. Once you have Chrome up and running,
launch the browser and navigate to http://ripple.tinyhippos.com. From the Tiny
Hippos home page, click the Get Ripple link, and follow the prompts to install the
latest version of the emulator.

Before you can start emulating PhoneGap within the RMEE, you must first configure the browser to allow the emulator access to files on the local file system.
Open the Chrome browser, right-click the Ripple icon to the right of the browser's
address bar, and select Manage extensions. The browser will display a page similar to the one shown in Figure 2-13. Enable the "Allow access to file URLs" option
for the RMEE as shown in the figure and then close the page by clicking the X to
the right of the Extensions tab.

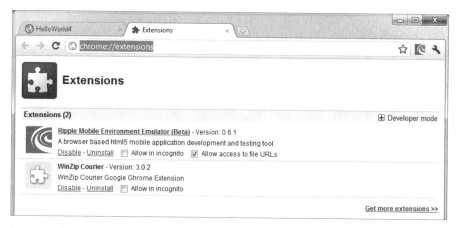

Figure 2-13   Configuring the Ripple Emulator in Google Chrome

Once the browser has been configured, open your application's `index.html` file in the browser. You can press Ctrl+O on Windows or Command+O on Macintosh to open the File Open dialog. Once the page has loaded, you need to enable Ripple for the selected page. To do this, complete one of the following options:

- Click the Ripple icon to the right of the browser's address bar to open a window, allowing you to enable Ripple for the loaded page.

- Right-click the page, open the Emulator menu, and then select Enable.

- Append `?enableripple=true` to the file URL to enable Ripple directly within the address bar when loading an application's `index.html` file.

Once the RMEE is enabled for the loaded page, the browser will display a page, shown in Figure 2-14, that prompts you to identify which type of emulation you want to enable for this page. As you can see, the RMEE supports PhoneGap plus several other platforms and frameworks. Click the PhoneGap button to continue.

Figure 2-14   Enabling PhoneGap emulation in the Ripple emulator

At this point, the RMEE will display a page with the content from the `index.html` file rendered within the boundaries of a simulated smartphone screen, as shown in Figure 2-15. Wrapped around the simulated smartphone are properties panes that can be used to configure options and status for the simulated smartphone such as simulated device screen resolution, accelerometer, network, geolocation, and more.

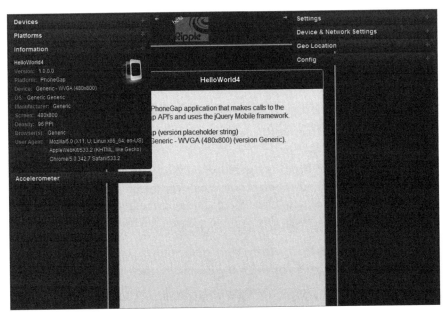

Figure 2-15   PhoneGap application running in the Ripple emulator

You can click each of the tabs to expand the options for the tab and make changes to the simulated device's configuration. At this point, you would simply click around within the simulated smartphone screen and interact with the options presented within your application. When you find a problem or a change you want to make within the PhoneGap application, simply return to your HTML editor, make the necessary changes, write the changes to disk, and then reload the page in the Chrome browser to continue with testing.

Weinre

Web Inspector Remote (Weinre) is a community-built remote debugger for web pages. It has been donated to the PhoneGap project and is currently implemented as part of the PhoneGap Build service. You can find the download files and instructions at http://phonegap.github.com/weinre. Weinre consists of a debug server, debug client, and debug target. The debug server runs on Macintosh or Windows, and the debug client runs in any compatible desktop browser.

For PhoneGap development, it allows a developer to debug a web application on physical device or a device emulator or simulator. To configure Weinre, perform the following steps:

1. Install a debug server on a desktop computer.

2. Launch the debug server.

3. Windows only: Point a compatible desktop browser at the debug server.

4. Connect the remote web application to the server.

The server component of Weinre consists of a stand-alone Macintosh executable or a Java JAR file for Windows. On Macintosh, load the debug server by double-clicking the application's executable in Finder. The debug server and debug client are packaged together in the same application, so there are no additional steps needed to launch the debug client.

On Windows, the debug server consists of a single JAR file that, assuming Java is on the Windows Path, can be loaded using the following command:

```
java -jar path/to/weinre.jar
```

There are additional command-line options that can be passed to the JAR file while it's loading to allow you to configure the host address the server will respond to, the server port number, and more. Refer to the Weinre documentation for additional information about the available command-line options. When the server starts, it will display a message indicating the URL to use to start the debug client; by default it should be http://localhost:8080. Point a compatible WebKit-based browser at the server to open the debug client.

To connect the PhoneGap application to the debug server, add the following <script> tag to the <body> section of the application's index.html file,

```
<script src="http://debug_server:8080/target/
  target-script-min.js"></script>
```

replacing the debug_server portion of the URL with the correct host name or IP address for the debug server. This provides the code needed for the PhoneGap application to upload information to the debug server. The Android emulator does not have the ability to connect to host-side resources using an IP address, so for the Android emulator, you must use the host address http://10.0.2.2, as shown in the following example:

```
<script src="http://10.0.2.2:8080/target/
  target-script-min.js"></script>
```

Note: Be sure to remove the Weinre `<script>` tag from your PhoneGap application before releasing it into production. The application will likely hang if attempting to connect to debug server that isn't available.

Figure 2-16 shows the debug server running on a Macintosh. On the bottom of the window are tabs that control the server while the toolbar on the top of the window contain options for the remote debugger client.

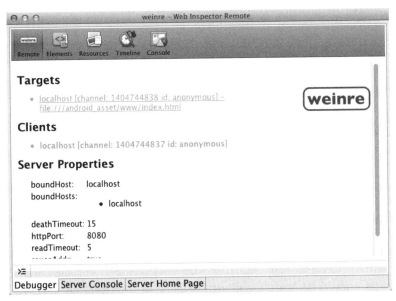

Figure 2-16   Weinre server/debug client on a Macintosh

The debug client provides the means to view and optionally manipulate many of the page elements and other aspects of your application's web content. You can view the browser console, as shown in Figure 2-17, to see console messages written by the PhoneGap application, or you can change application values or properties to tweak the application while it's running.

The available documentation for Weinre is pretty light, but since the project's capabilities are based upon the Google Chrome Developer Tools, you can find additional information on the Google Code web site at http://code.google.com/chrome/devtools/docs/overview.html.

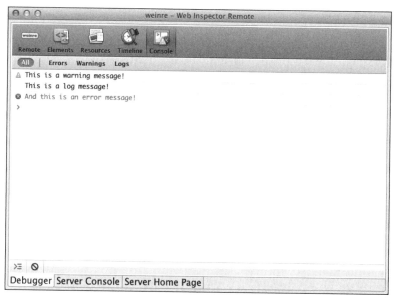

Figure 2-17   Weinre debug client console

Dealing with Cross-Platform Development Issues

As interesting as all of these PhoneGap capabilities are, there are a lot of issues that make cross-platform development tasks difficult. The PhoneGap project is supported by developers from all over the world, including developers who may have experience with only one or a small number of mobile platforms and developers who have a strong opinion about how something should be done. The problem with this is that when you take development projects written by different people and try to collect them into a single framework, you can bump up against inconsistencies. Add to this that every mobile platform supported by PhoneGap is different and has different ways of doing things, and you have a difficult task to make everything work cleanly and seamlessly.

Note: To the PhoneGap project's credit, things move pretty quickly, and the issues I'm complaining about here could very well be fixed in any subsequent release of the framework. Be sure to check the latest documentation before working around any of the issues listed in the sections that follow.

Let's look at some examples.

API Consistency

Figure 2-18 shows the supported feature matrix from the PhoneGap web site; you can find the page at www.phonegap.com/about/features. As you can see, the table is pretty complete; there are some gaps, but it's more full than empty. On the other hand, since PhoneGap is supposed to be a cross-platform framework, the gaps in this table make it very hard to truly create a cross-platform application using those APIs. If a particular feature you want to use in your application is supported on only some mobile platforms, then you'll have to make special accommodation within your application for platforms that do not support the particular API.

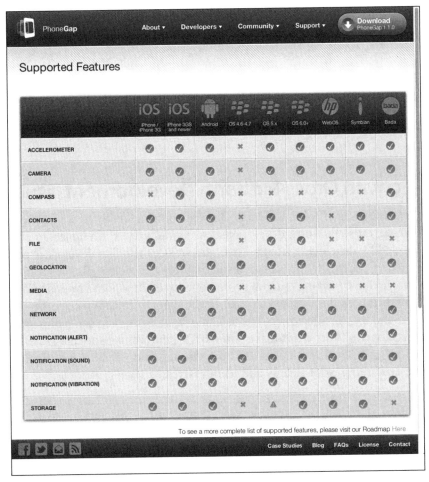

Figure 2-18   PhoneGap-supported feature matrix

Another problem arises when you look through the API documentation found at http://docs.phonegap.com/. For most of the PhoneGap APIs, the documentation lists that the APIs are supported only on Android, BlackBerry, and iOS devices. It's likely the issue here is that the PhoneGap developers are like most developers and don't like to write (or update) documentation; the impact on you is huge. Do you rely upon the API documentation? Do you instead ignore the documentation and use feature matrix as the correct reference? Or do you cover your bases and assume it is all wrong and test everything?

No matter what, this can be quite a challenge; ideally the PhoneGap project team will get more organized and make sure all of the documentation is up-to-date as each new version is released.

Multiple PhoneGap JavaScript Files

One of the first issues I bumped up against when learning to do cross-platform PhoneGap development was that the PhoneGap JavaScript library is different between mobile platforms. So, the JavaScript code within the PhoneGap JavaScript file for BlackBerry projects is different from what is found in the PhoneGap JavaScript file for Android projects. My original thought when I started was that I could just copy the web content folder between projects, build the application, and be done, but since each platform's JavaScript file is different, I would have to copy over the web content and then also make sure the correct PhoneGap JavaScript file was in the folder as well.

To make things work, with earlier versions of the PhoneGap framework, the BlackBerry and bada PhoneGap JavaScript libraries had different file names than on other platforms. This has supposedly been fixed, but you better check to make sure when building applications.

Web Content Folder Structure

As you will see in the chapters that follow, in some cases, some PhoneGap project developers have created nonstandard project folder structures for PhoneGap projects. For example, for a typical Symbian project (described in Chapter 7), the application's web content files would normally be placed in the root of the project's folder structure. The HTML, JavaScript, and CSS files should be placed right at the top of the folder hierarchy, so they can be easily accessed when working with the project. For some bizarre reason, the PhoneGap project places the files in a framework/www folder, complicating the project's folder structure and making it more difficult to get to the application's content files.

Application Requirements

One of the things you might bump into as you build cross-platform PhoneGap applications is the need to supply additional files in your application to accommodate the requirements for a particular OS version. For example, in the default PhoneGap project for iOS, you will find the following note:

```
<!-- If your application is targeting iOS BEFORE 4.0 you MUST
put json2.js from http://www.JSON.org/json2.js into your www
directory and include it here -->
```

Apparently a feature was added in PhoneGap 0.9 that requires the use of the JSON.stringify() function, so you will have to make sure you include the appropriate JSON library in your application. This further complicates a developer's ability to use an application's web content across multiple device platforms since an iOS application in this example might have additional lines of code needed to support this iOS-specific feature.

Application Navigation and UI

Mobile device platforms typically share some common elements but at the same time implement unique features or capabilities that help set them apart from competitors. The Android and iOS operating systems support many of the same features but sometimes implement them in a different way. Because of this, any mobile application designed to run on different mobile operating systems must take into consideration the differences between mobile platforms.

As you build PhoneGap applications for multiple mobile device platforms, you will need to implement different UI capabilities on different operating systems. On the Android and BlackBerry platforms, there's a physical Escape button that can be pressed to return to a previous screen; on iOS, there will need to be a back button added to the bar at the top of the application screen.

Because of this, a PhoneGap application will need to either contain additional code that checks to see what platform it's running on and update the UI accordingly or it will need to have different versions of the application's web content depending on which OS the application is running on. Neither approach is easy. There are several books on mobile web development available that deal directly with these types of issues.

Application Icons

Each mobile platform and often different versions of a particular device OS have different requirements for application icons. A developer building PhoneGap applications for multiple device platforms will need to be prepared to create a suite of icons for their application that addresses the specific requirements for each target device platform and/or device OS. The PhoneGap project maintains a wiki page listing the icon requirements for the different supported operating systems at http://wiki.phonegap.com/w/page/36905973/Icons%20and%20Splash%20Screens.

Additionally, for some devices on some carriers (older BlackBerry devices, for example), the mobile carrier applies a specific theming to the OS in order to help distinguish themselves in the market. Any application icon designed for one of these devices will need to accommodate, as best as possible, rendering pleasantly within different themes.

Part II

PhoneGap
Developer Tools

This part of the book provides complete instructions on how to set up a development environment for each of the mobile platforms supported by PhoneGap. Once you have the tools set up, each chapter will describe how to create, build, and test a PhoneGap application for each platform.

3

Configuring an Android Development Environment for PhoneGap

There are several options for PhoneGap development on Android; the tools run on Linux, Apple Macintosh OS, and Microsoft Windows. Additionally, developers have access to both an Eclipse plug-in as well as command-line tools for building applications. This chapter includes the steps to follow to install and use the Android development tools on Macintosh OS and Windows.

Refer to the Android Developer web site (http://developer.android.com) for additional or more up-to-date installation instructions including instructions for installation on a system running Linux.

To complete the steps outlined in this chapter, you must first perform several installation steps using instructions provided elsewhere in the book:

1. Install the PhoneGap framework using the instructions provided in Appendix A.

2. Install the Oracle Java Developer Kit (JDK) using the instructions provided in Appendix B.

3. If you are intending to use the command line to build Android applications, install Apache Ant using instructions provided in Appendix C.

Once those steps have been completed, you're ready to start work on PhoneGap applications for Android.

Installing the Android SDK

The Android SDK is deployed in two parts. First, you install the SDK starter package on the local system; second, SDK components are added to the existing installation via download from the Android developer web site. The starter package contains utility programs used to manage the Android software development environment on the computer and the individual Android version SDKs are installed as needed. This allows for a single installation on a developer workstation, and then needed software updates (including adding additional SDKs) are performed on the fly via software download.

To download the started package, point your browser of choice to http://developer .android.com. On the landing page, click the Download link highlighted in Figure 3-1.

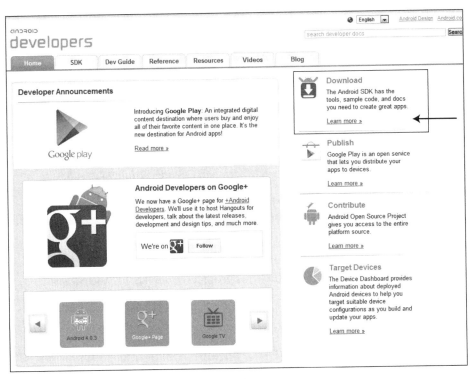

Figure 3-1   Android developer web site landing page

On the page that opens, shown in Figure 3-2, select the appropriate download for the operating system running on the computer.

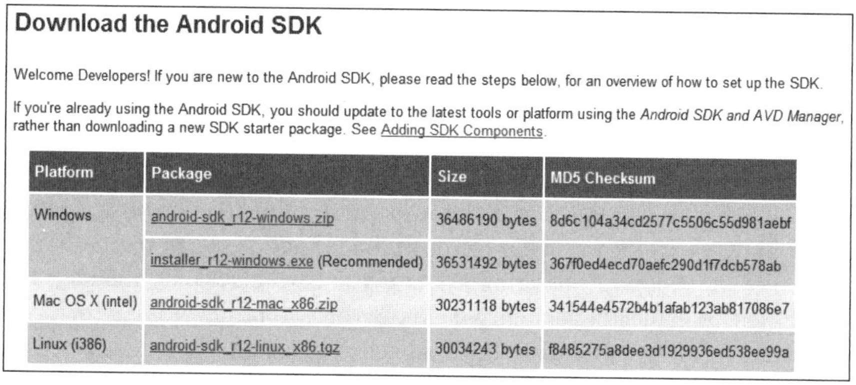

Download the Android SDK

Welcome Developers! If you are new to the Android SDK, please read the steps below, for an overview of how to set up the SDK.

If you're already using the Android SDK, you should update to the latest tools or platform using the *Android SDK and AVD Manager*, rather than downloading a new SDK starter package. See Adding SDK Components.

Platform	Package	Size	MD5 Checksum
Windows	android-sdk_r12-windows.zip	36486190 bytes	8d6c104a34cd2577c5506c55d981aebf
	installer_r12-windows.exe (Recommended)	36531492 bytes	367f0ed4ecd70aefc290d1f7dcb578ab
Mac OS X (intel)	android-sdk_r12-mac_x86.zip	30231118 bytes	341544e4572b4b1afab123ab817086e7
Linux (i386)	android-sdk_r12-linux_x86.tgz	30034243 bytes	f8485275a8dee3d1929936ed538ee99a

Figure 3-2   Android SDK download options

For Windows users, use the recommended option and download the Windows executable. Once the file has downloaded, launch the downloaded file to begin the installation. Using this option installs the software and places the appropriate shortcuts for running the Android tools onto the Windows Start menu.

Windows Installation Issues

You must pay attention to several issues related to the Android SDK Starter Package installation on Windows when installing the software.

Early versions of the Android SDK installed its files in the root of the system's hard drive. For some reason, Google changed its approach, and more recent SDK versions have installed its files in the Windows `Program Files` folder. While this is a good thing, conforming to Windows standards, there have been many bugs reported when the files are installed in that location. Google is aware of the problems and is working on fixing them, but I recommend you don't allow the installer to install in the `Program Files` folder; instead, install the files off of the root of the system's hard drive (`c:\android-sdk\`, for example).

On Windows, the installer sometimes has difficulty locating the required JDK installed on the system (described in Appendix B). When this happens, just click the Back button, and then click Next again in the installation wizard. The installer is usually able to find the JDK if you give it another chance. Repeat the process as many times as necessary depending on your experience with the installer.

For Macintosh computers, download the Macintosh version of the SDK to your system's downloads folder. The Macintosh OS may automatically extract the files within the folder; if not, manually extract the files to the location of your choice. You can either execute the tools from the `downloads` folder or open Finder and drag the Android SDK folder to the `Applications` folder or another folder of your choice.

When the installation is complete, launch the Android SDK Manager (the file is called `Android SDK.exe` on Windows and `android` on Mac OS). When the program launches, it will connect to the Android developer web site and retrieve the list of SDK packages available for download. Each package refers to a specific version of the Android operating system. You can select only the packages you need based upon the OS versions you know you will be developing for, or you can just accept the default of all packages and click the Install Selected button to begin the installation, as shown in Figure 3-3.

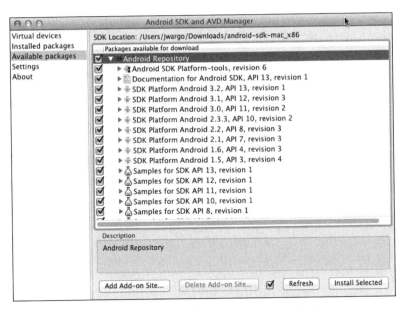

Figure 3-3 Selecting Android SDK packages for installation

A lot of files are associated with each SDK package, so the process of downloading and installing the packages will take a very long time. Make sure you're on a fast network connection before starting the installation and have other work you can do while you wait for the download and installation to complete. When the package installation completes, you may be prompted to restart the Android SDK Manager before continuing.

In the next step, you'll need to create an Android Virtual Device (AVD) to use for your testing of PhoneGap applications. The AVD is an Android device emulator representing a standard Android device. Click the "Virtual devices" option in the Android SDK and AVD Manager, as shown in Figure 3-4.

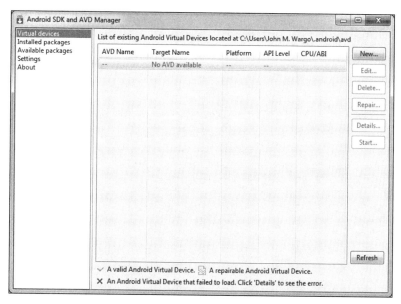

Figure 3-4 Android Virtual Devices view

Click the New button, and you will see a dialog similar to the one shown in Figure 3-5. In the dialog, give the AVD a name and select the options appropriate for your Android application development needs; then click the Create AVD button.

Most modern smartphones (excluding Apple iOS) include a certain amount of device memory plus provide the means to add memory through an extra memory card (typically a Micro SD card). More sophisticated mobile applications will make use of both types of memory, using device memory for transient values and a memory card for storing ancillary files or larger data sets or databases. It's likely that in your PhoneGap development efforts you'll someday need to write and read data from a memory card, so when you're setting up your Android AVD, be sure to allocate some space for an SD card as shown in the figure. The file option points the emulator to a local file on the development workstation, which allows you share the contents of a simulated SD card between emulators.

The Skin option is used to define the size of the emulated Android device. Keep in mind when making a selection here that the emulator can take up quite a large amount of screen real estate, so if you are working on a developer workstation with a smaller monitor, you may want to select a smaller skin so the emulator doesn't exceed the boundaries of the screen.

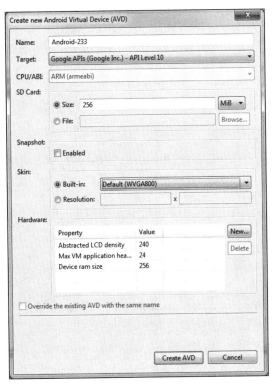

Figure 3-5   Create new Android Virtual Device (AVD) dialog

As shown in Figure 3-6, the AVD manager allows you to define many different Android emulator configurations, which allow you to more easily text your PhoneGap applications using different predefined configurations.

To launch an emulator, select the emulator definition in the AVD Manager and click the Start button. The AVD manager will display a dialog allowing you to change some emulator settings before launching, such as scaling the emulator on the screen, wiping emulator memory, or launching from a particular snapshot. Click the Launch button to start the emulator.

On many systems, the emulator will take a very long time to start, so be patient. When the emulator launches, it will display a screen similar to the one shown in Figure 3-7. There will be an image of an Android smartphone screen on one side and a keyboard with additional simulator control options on the other side.

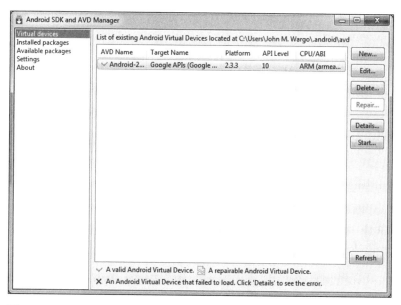

Figure 3-6   Android AVD Manager with an Android emulator defined

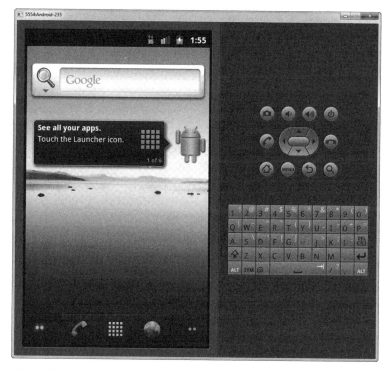

Figure 3-7   An Android emulator all ready to go

At this point, you would interact with the emulator just like you would a regular device—swiping and clicking, launching applications, and more.

Eclipse Development Environment Configuration

Google provides an Eclipse plug-in that simplifies the development of Android applications. Eclipse (www.eclipse.org) is a free, popular, open source integrated development environment (IDE) that's used primarily for Java and web development but supports many other options as well. There are several editions of Eclipse, each addressing a particular type of development or a particular suite of tools.

Google's tools support multiple editions of Eclipse and currently (although subject to change) support Eclipse 3.5 (Galileo) or greater. Since PhoneGap projects consist of both native and web technologies, I recommend installing the Eclipse IDE for Java EE Developers, which includes the Java development tools needed for Android development and the appropriate web content editors needed for PhoneGap web application development.

Applaud Eclipse Plug-In

In case you're interested, Mobile Developer Solutions (www.mobiledevelopersolutions .com) offers a free Eclipse plug-in called Applaud that helps simplify PhoneGap development for Android devices.

Point your browser of choice to www.eclipse.org/downloads/, and select the appropriate download for your developer workstation. Figure 3-8 shows a subset of options for Windows computers, the page should automatically detect Macintosh or Linux computers and display the appropriate options for the current OS. If not, simply select the OS from the drop-down list at the top of the download list to change to an appropriate list of downloads.

Be sure to select the appropriate download bit-depth for the operating system you are running. For example, select the 32-bit version of the download if your development system is running a 32-bit OS, even if the system processor is 64-bit.

Once the Eclipse files have been downloaded, extract the downloaded files to the appropriate folder (your choice, as appropriate for the target OS) on your system's hard drive and create the appropriate application shortcut needed to launch the Eclipse executable (`eclipse.exe` for Windows and `eclipse` for Macintosh OS).

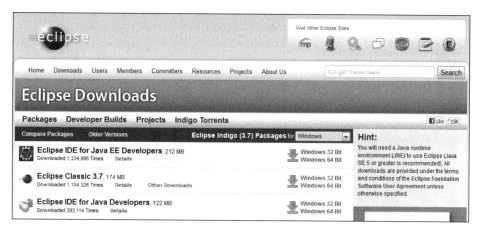

Figure 3-8   Eclipse download page

Note: Later versions of Microsoft Windows (Windows Vista and Windows 7) have implemented a security structure that by default removes a user's ability to modify the contents of the Windows `Program Files` folder. If you attempt to extract the Eclipse files to the `Program Files` folder and receive an error, just extract the files to the download folder and then copy the extracted `eclipse` folder to the `Program Files` folder afterward.

Next you'll need to install the Eclipse plug-in for Android development. Launch Eclipse and open the Eclipse Workbench. Open the Help menu, and then select Install New Software. Eclipse will display an installation wizard similar to the one shown in Figure 3-9, although the wizard page initially displayed will not have any of the data shown in the figure. Populate the "Work with" field with https://dl-ssl.google.com/android/eclipse/ and press Enter. Eclipse will connect to the Android software downloads site (represented by the URL you entered) and download information about the available options. If you encounter a problem doing this, make sure you used an https instead of http when typing in the server URL.

When the list of options appears in the dialog, place a check next to the Developer Tools option (which will accept all options) and click the Next button. Follow through the remaining options in the installation wizard including accepting the Android license agreement to complete the installation. During installation, Eclipse will prompt you to trust the software you are installing and will ask to restart Eclipse at the end of the installation process.

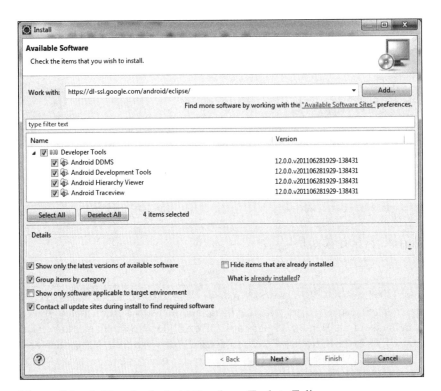

Figure 3-9   Adding the Android Developer Tools to Eclipse

When Eclipse restarts, open the Window menu, and then select Preferences. In the dialog that appears, select the Android option and Eclipse will display a blank list of Android SDK targets. In the dialog, click the Browse button, navigate to the folder where you installed the Android SDK earlier in the chapter, and then click the OK button. Once the Android SDK location has been set, click the Apply button, and Eclipse will refresh the list of the Android SDK versions available at the specified location. At this point, your Android configuration in Eclipse should look like Figure 3-10.

Creating an Android PhoneGap Project

For building PhoneGap applications for Android, two options are available to you. You can build the application using Eclipse, or you can use the Android command-line tools and your web content editor of choice. In this section, I'll show how to create a new Android PhoneGap project for each method.

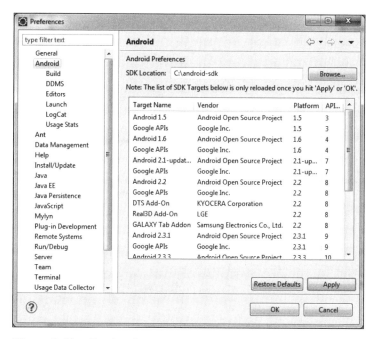

Figure 3-10   Configuring Android SDK settings in Eclipse

New Eclipse Project

To create a new Android PhoneGap project using Eclipse, open the Eclipse IDE, open the File menu, and select New and then Project. Eclipse will present a wizard similar to the one shown in Figure 3-11. Expand the Android option, select Android Project, and click the Next button. If an option for Android projects does not appear in this wizard, the Android plug-in for Eclipse (installed earlier in the chapter) must not have installed correctly.

Eclipse will then prompt for the Android-specific settings for the project, as shown in Figure 3-12. You will need to provide a name for the project, HelloWorld in the example shown, plus select the Android SDK build target for the application.

Warning: Although the dialog is presenting what appears to be a list of checkboxes, implying that you can select more than one option in the list, the checkboxes actually work like radio buttons and will allow you to select only one option.

You will also need to scroll down in the dialog shown in Figure 3-12 and provide a package name for your application (such as `com.phonegapbook.helloworld`). Set other project options as needed, and then click the Finish button to create the project.

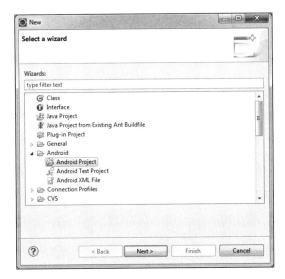

Figure 3-11   Eclipse's New Wizard: selecting project type

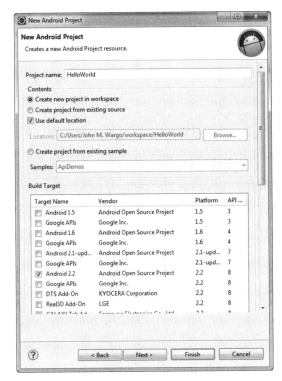

Figure 3-12   Eclipse's New Wizard: defining Android project options

The first thing you have to do is create two new folders in the project folder structure: `libs` and `assets/www`. The folders must be placed in the root directory of the project folder. To create the folders, right-click the HelloWorld project in the Eclipse Package Explorer (on the far left side of the Eclipse window shown in Figure 3-13). From the menu that appears, select New and then Folder. When prompted, enter **libs** into the New Folder dialog and click Finish.

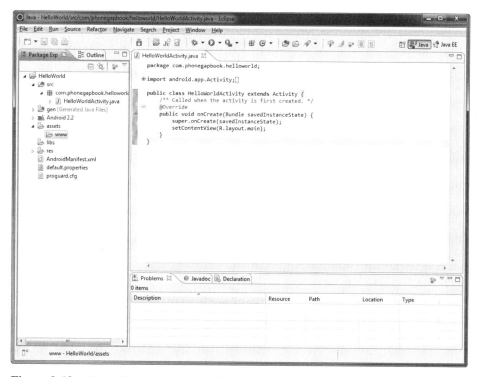

Figure 3-13   A new PhoneGap project in Eclipse

Repeat the same process for the second folder, entering **assets/www** in the New Folder dialog. For this one, Eclipse will create two nested folders; it will first create a folder called `assets` and then create a folder called www within the `assets` folder.

Next, we have some files and folders to copy from the PhoneGap software installation's Android folder. First close the Eclipse IDE, and then from the file system (Finder on Macintosh or Windows Explorer for Windows) perform the following steps:

1. Copy the `phonegap.js` file to the project's `assets/www` folder. The file will be named `phonegap-x.y.0.js` where x refers to the major version number and y is the minor version number. Example: `phonegap-1.3.0.js`.

2. Copy the `phonegap.jar` file to the libs folder. The file will be named `phonegap-x.y.0.jar` where x refers to the major version number and y is the minor version number. Example: `phonegap-1.3.0.jar`.

3. Copy the entire `xml` folder to the `res` folder (created by the Android plug-in when the project was first created).

Once all of the files have been copied to the project, it's time to modify the project's source files and convert the Android Java project into a PhoneGap project. In the Eclipse Package Explorer, expand the HelloWorld project, expand the `src` folder, and then double-click the `HelloWorldActivity.java` file. Eclipse will open the project's Java source file in the editor (as shown in Figure 3-13). Make the following changes to the Java source file:

1. Remove the `android.app.Activity` import. Since the project is no longer a standard Android activity, it's no longer needed.

2. Add an import for `com.phonegap.*`. This provides the application with access to the PhoneGap library functions in the `phonegap.jar` file you copied over earlier.

3. Change the `HelloWorldActivity` class so that it extends from `DroidGap` instead of `Activity`. This essentially changes the project from an Android activity to a PhoneGap project.

4. Replace the `setContentView(R.layout.main)` with `super.loadUrl ("file:///android_asset/www/index.html")`. This instructs the program to load the application's startup HTML file when the application launches.

When you complete the changes, the Java source file should match the following:

```
package com.phonegapbook.helloworld;

import android.os.Bundle;
import com.phonegap.*;

public class HelloWorldActivity extends DroidGap {
  /** Called when the activity is first created. */
  @Override
  public void onCreate(Bundle savedInstanceState) {
    super.onCreate(savedInstanceState);
    super.loadUrl("file:///android_asset/www/index.html");
  }
}
```

Tip: When you save the project, Eclipse may complain that it doesn't recognize the code you've entered. This is because Eclipse can't locate the `phonegap.jar` file you copied to the project folder. If this happens, in the Eclipse Package Explorer, right-click the `libs` folder and select Build Paths and then Configure Build Paths. In the dialog that appears, select the Libraries tab, and then add the `.jar` file to the project.

Once the Java source file is configured correctly, you will need to update the project's manifest file. In the Eclipse Package Explorer, right-click the `AndroidManifest.xml` file, select Open With, and then select Text Editor.

Paste the following permissions XML into the manifest file immediately following the `<manifest />` entry:

```
<supports-screens
  android:largeScreens="true"
  android:normalScreens="true"
  android:smallScreens="true"
  android:resizeable="true"
  android:anyDensity="true"
/>
<uses-permission android:name="android.permission.CAMERA" />
<uses-permission android:name="android.permission.VIBRATE" />
<uses-permission android:name=
  "android.permission.ACCESS_COARSE_LOCATION" />
<uses-permission android:name=
  "android.permission.ACCESS_FINE_LOCATION" />
<uses-permission android:name=
  "android.permission.ACCESS_LOCATION_EXTRA_COMMANDS" />
<uses-permission android:name=
  "android.permission.READ_PHONE_STATE" />
<uses-permission android:name="android.permission.INTERNET" />
<uses-permission android:name=
  "android.permission.RECEIVE_SMS" />
<uses-permission android:name=
  "android.permission.RECORD_AUDIO" />
<uses-permission android:name=
  "android.permission.MODIFY_AUDIO_SETTINGS" />
<uses-permission android:name=
  "android.permission.READ_CONTACTS" />
<uses-permission android:name=
  "android.permission.WRITE_CONTACTS" />
<uses-permission android:name=
  "android.permission.WRITE_EXTERNAL_STORAGE" />
<uses-permission android:name=
  "android.permission.ACCESS_NETWORK_STATE" />
<uses-permission android:name=
  "android.permission.GET_ACCOUNTS" />
```

The `<supports-screens />` entry tells the Android virtual machine which screen properties are supported by the application. Since we're building a web application that will scale according to the available screen real estate, we're telling Android which options are supported. For tablet applications, you could also add the following to the list of options:

```
android:xlargeScreens="true"
```

Next, add the following to the first `<Activity />` tag in the manifest file:

```
android:configChanges="orientation|keyboardHidden"
```

This tells the Android device running the application that the application will automatically handle orientation changes or when the user hides the keyboard.

Then add a second activity to the manifest using the following XML:

```
<activity android:name="com.phonegap.DroidGap"
  android:label="@string/app_name"
  android:configChanges="orientation|keyboardHidden">
  <intent-filter></intent-filter>
</activity>
```

When completed, the manifest should match the following:

```
<?xml version="1.0" encoding="utf-8"?>
<manifest xmlns:android=
  http://schemas.android.com/apk/res/android
  package="com.phonegapbook.helloworld"
  android:versionCode="1" android:versionName="1.0">

  <supports-screens android:largeScreens="true"
    android:normalScreens="true" android:smallScreens="true"
    android:resizeable="true" android:anyDensity="true" />
  <uses-permission android:name="android.permission.CAMERA" />
  <uses-permission android:name="android.permission.VIBRATE" />
  <uses-permission android:name=
    "android.permission.ACCESS_COARSE_LOCATION" />
  <uses-permission android:name=
    "android.permission.ACCESS_FINE_LOCATION" />
  <uses-permission android:name=
    "android.permission.ACCESS_LOCATION_EXTRA_COMMANDS" />
  <uses-permission android:name=
    "android.permission.READ_PHONE_STATE" />
  <uses-permission android:name="android.permission.INTERNET" />
  <uses-permission android:name=
    "android.permission.RECEIVE_SMS" />
  <uses-permission android:name=
    "android.permission.RECORD_AUDIO" />
```

```
  <uses-permission android:name=
    "android.permission.MODIFY_AUDIO_SETTINGS" />
  <uses-permission android:name=
    "android.permission.READ_CONTACTS" />
  <uses-permission android:name=
    "android.permission.WRITE_CONTACTS" />
  <uses-permission android:name=
    "android.permission.WRITE_EXTERNAL_STORAGE" />
  <uses-permission android:name=
    "android.permission.ACCESS_NETWORK_STATE" />
  <uses-permission android:name=
    "android.permission.GET_ACCOUNTS" />
  <uses-sdk android:minSdkVersion="8" />
  <application android:icon="@drawable/icon"
    android:label="@string/app_name">
    <activity android:name=".HelloWorldActivity"
        android:label="@string/app_name"
        android:configChanges="orientation|keyboardHidden">
      <intent-filter>
        <action android:name="android.intent.action.MAIN" />
        <category android:name=
          "android.intent.category.LAUNCHER" />
      </intent-filter>
    </activity>
    <activity android:name="com.phonegap.DroidGap"
      android:label="@string/app_name"
      android:configChanges="orientation|keyboardHidden">
      <intent-filter>
      </intent-filter>
    </activity>
  </application>
</manifest>
```

Depending on the nature of your development project, you will likely want to change the android:minSDKVersion element to reflect the minimum SDK version required for the application:

```
<uses-sdk android:minSdkVersion="8" />
```

Save the changes, exit the text editor, and return to Eclipse.

The final step is to create the index.html file that will be the main interface for the PhoneGap application. In Eclipse, right-click the www folder in the Package Explorer and select New and then File. In the New File dialog, enter **index.html** as the file name, and then click Finish. Double-click the newly created file, and Eclipse will load the file into the HTML editor window. Paste in the HTML from the HelloWorld3 application from Chapter 2.

Save your changes, and select Run from the Eclipse Run menu. Eclipse will launch the default Android emulator you have defined and start the application. When it loads, you should see a screen similar to what is shown in Figure 3-14.

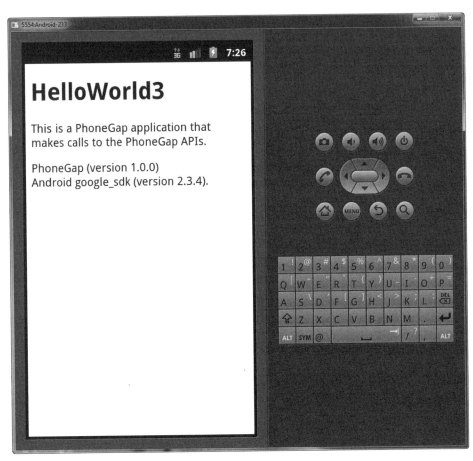

Figure 3-14 Android HelloWorld application running in the emulator

Using Command-Line Tools

For developers who want to do Android development using a different editor than Eclipse or just prefer to use command-line tools, you can manage Android projects directly from the command line. The information provided in this section covers this topic at a high level; you can find additional details on the build process at the Android Developer web site (http://developer.android.com).

To create a new Android application project, open a terminal window (Macintosh) or command prompt (Windows), navigate to the `Android SDK tools` folder, and then issue the following command:

```
android create project --target 14 --name HelloWorld --path
  c:\dev\HelloWorld --activity HelloWorldActivity
  --package com.phonegapbook.helloworld
```

The Android tools will create an Android project folder structure at the specified location and create the necessary source and configuration files for the project. Figure 3-15 shows a sample of the output from the process.

Launching Unix Applications from the Command Line

When launching applications from the command line in Unix (which applies to computers running Macintosh and Linux), when you navigate to a folder where the application resides, you must predicate the application name with a `./` in order to launch the application. For example, to launch the Android application on Mac OS, the command begins with `./android` and then includes any command-line options being passed to the application on launch.

Figure 3-15   Creating an Android project using command-line tools

Table 3-1 describes the command-line options used during this process.

Table 3-1   Android Tools Create Project Command-Line Options

Parameter	Description
Target	Identifies the Android API level used for the project. Each API version is incremented sequentially with each Android release. On my development system, the target of 14 refers to the Android 2.3.3 SDK. The available SDK targets will vary between Android SDK installations. To see a list of available SDK targets, open a command prompt or terminal window, and navigate to the Android SDK tools folder; then issue the following command: `android list targets`
Name	Optional; the name for the project. The value provided here will be used as the application's `.apk` file name. An `.apk` file is the Android executable file.
Path	The target directory path for the project's files. The folder will be created if it does not already exist.
Activity	The name of the default Activity class defined within the project; this is the activity that's launched when the application first starts.
Package	The Java package name for the application.

At this point, the project is exactly the same as the project created within Eclipse (it's actually this process that Eclipse uses behind the scenes to create new Android projects). To convert this new Android project into a PhoneGap project, complete the steps outlined in the previous section to modify the project's files with the appropriate PhoneGap components and code.

To build your new PhoneGap project using the command-line tools, you will need to install Apache Ant (the installation steps are provided in Appendix C) and then open a terminal or command prompt window, navigate to your project's root folder, and issue the following command:

`ant debug`

The Ant Build script included with the Android project will call the Java compiler and build a debug version of the Android application that can be deployed to an Android device (or Android emulator) for testing. Figure 3-16 shows an example of the build process output. The executable application file, the `HelloWorld-debug.apk` file, will be located in the project's `bin` folder.

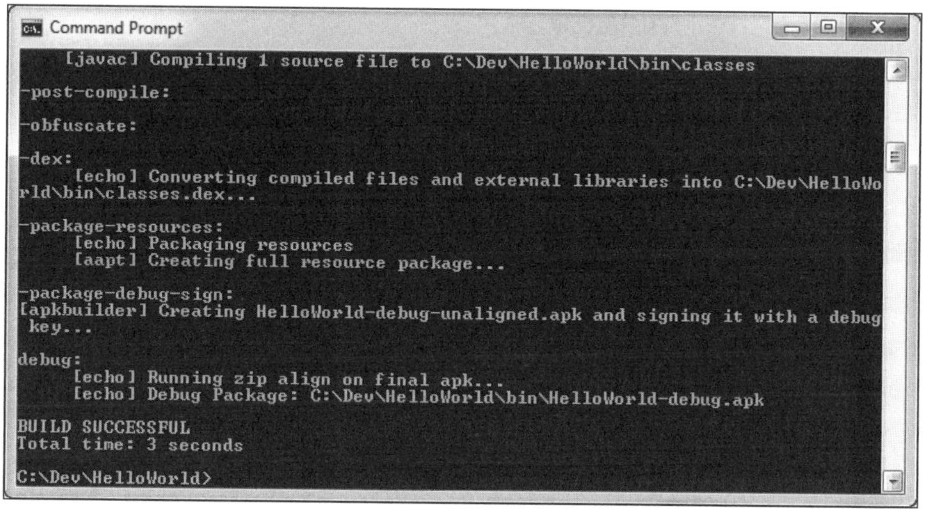

```
[javac] Compiling 1 source file to C:\Dev\HelloWorld\bin\classes
-post-compile:
-obfuscate:
-dex:
    [echo] Converting compiled files and external libraries into C:\Dev\HelloWo
rld\bin\classes.dex...
-package-resources:
    [echo] Packaging resources
    [aapt] Creating full resource package...
-package-debug-sign:
[apkbuilder] Creating HelloWorld-debug-unaligned.apk and signing it with a debug
 key...
debug:
    [echo] Running zip align on final apk...
    [echo] Debug Package: C:\Dev\HelloWorld\bin\HelloWorld-debug.apk
BUILD SUCCESSFUL
Total time: 3 seconds
C:\Dev\HelloWorld>
```

Figure 3-16   Building a PhoneGap application using the command-line tools

To build a version of the application for distribution to production devices, issue the following command:

```
ant release
```

Android applications must be signed before they can run on an Android device. The details of this part of the process are beyond the scope of this book. Refer to the Android developer web site at http://developer.android.com/guide/publishing/app-signing.html for additional information about application signatures and the signing process.

Testing Android PhoneGap Applications

When it comes to testing and debugging a PhoneGap application, developers have the option of using the Android emulator or running the application on a physical device. The information provided in this section covers this topic at a high level; you can find additional details on the debugging process at the Android developer web site (http://developer.android.com).

The ability to test and debug an application on a device or emulator is built into the Eclipse plug-in. As shown previously, simply launch the emulator or load onto a device directly from the IDE. The following sections provide information on how to test PhoneGap applications using the command-line tools.

Using the Emulator

When working with the command-line tools, you can easily deploy Android applications directly from a terminal or command prompt window.

When testing using the Android emulator, the first thing you must do is launch the Android SDK and AVD Manager highlighted in Figure 3-6; then select one of the emulators you have defined, and click the Start button. It may take a while, but the selected emulator will launch and wait for your input. Once the emulator is running, you must install the application being tested. From the Android SDK tools directory (c:\android-sdk\tools\, for example), install the application's .apk file on the emulator using the following command:

```
adb install <file_path>\<application>.apk
```

In this example, <file_path> refers to the folder where the file is located, and <application> refers to the executable file name for the application. By default, the application's executable (the application's .apk file) will be located in the project's bin folder. For the HelloWorld application highlighted in this chapter, the project was created in c:\dev\HelloWorld and the file name is HelloWorld-debug, so the command to install the application on the simulator would be as follows:

```
adb install c:\dev\HelloWorld\bin\HelloWorld-debug.apk
```

Installing on a Device

Before you can run your application on a device, you must ensure that USB debugging is enabled on the device. The setting can be located on most Android devices by launching the Settings application and selecting Applications, then Development, and finally USB debugging.

Warning: To be able to test on a live device, your computer system must be able to recognize an Android device when it's connected to the system via a USB cable. If you connect a device and it's not recognized by the system, you must resolve any connectivity issues before continuing.

Once your device is set up and connected via USB, navigate to the Android SDK platform-tools/ directory (c:\android-sdk\platform-tools\, for example), and install the .apk on the device using the following command:

```
adb -d install <file_path>\<application>.apk
```

The -d parameter passed to adb instructs the program to install the application to a physically connected device (rather than to an emulator). This process will return an error if more than one device is connected to the computer.

4

Configuring a bada Development Environment for PhoneGap

Bada is a mobile device operating system released by Samsung in 2010. Devices for this OS are not available in the United States today, but bada devices are currently popular in Europe and Asia. The current version of the bada files for PhoneGap do not support the currently version of the bada SDK; instead, it requires an older version that is not currently available for download. You will have to already have a version of the bada SDK earlier than version 2.0 installed in order to build PhoneGap applications for bada. As the PhoneGap project team adds support for the current version of the bada SDK, an updated version of this chapter will be available on the book's web site at www.phonegapessentials.com.

The bada development tools will run only on computers running Microsoft Windows, so you'll need to have a Windows PC or a Macintosh running a Windows virtual machine (VM) to install the tools. Before getting started with the bada SDK, you will need to install the PhoneGap framework, but unfortunately as of the time of this writing, the PhoneGap files installed using the instructions provided in Appendix A don't contain the project files you need to build PhoneGap applications for bada. It's possible that by the time you read this, the PhoneGap files will be updated to include the complete set of bada files. In the meantime, additional instructions are provided within this chapter for downloading and installing the correct files for PhoneGap bada development.

The free bada development tools are implemented using the Eclipse IDE, so you will also need to install the Oracle Java Developer Kit using the instructions provided in Appendix B.

According to the most current documentation for the bada components of PhoneGap, the current version provides support for only the Acceleration, Camera, Compass, Device, Geolocation and Network APIs.

Downloading and Installing the Correct PhoneGap bada Files

For PhoneGap versions up to and including version 1.4.1, the default PhoneGap download available at www.phonegap.com/download-thankyou doesn't include the project files needed to build PhoneGap applications on the bada platform. I've spoken with the developer responsible for PhoneGap's bada support, and he has indicated that he will try to get the files updated in a subsequent release of the framework.

To verify whether your existing PhoneGap framework installation (installed using the instructions provided in Appendix A) contains the necessary project files, open Windows Explorer, and navigate to the folder where the PhoneGap files have been extracted. Then navigate to the bada folder and look for the `.badaprj` and `.cproject` files shown in Figure 4-1. If the files are there, you have what you need and can skip the remainder of this section.

If you don't see these two files, you will need to download a separate package from the Apache Cordova Git repository. Open your browser of choice and navigate to https://git-wip-us.apache.org/repos/asf?p=incubator-cordova-bada.git; Figure 4-2 shows the contents of the page. This is the location for the project within the Apache Incubator; the location will likely change once the project makes it out of the Apache Incubator, or, who knows, maybe they'll change the project name yet again.

On the page, click the "snapshot" link at the top of the list of commits, as highlighted in the figure. This will start a download of the latest version of the PhoneGap bada project files. Save the file in an appropriate location, and then extract the files. The files are currently saved in `tar.gz` format, so you may have to do some additional work to extract the files since Windows may not automatically recognize the format; the files extract easily using WinZip (www.winzip.com).

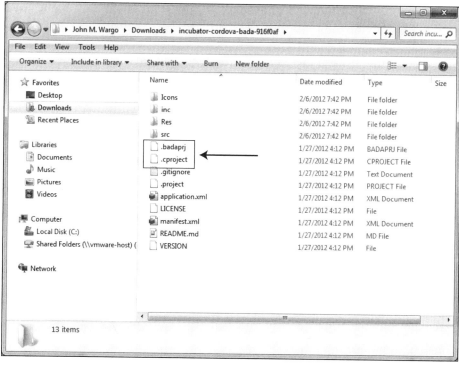

Figure 4-1   PhoneGap bada project files

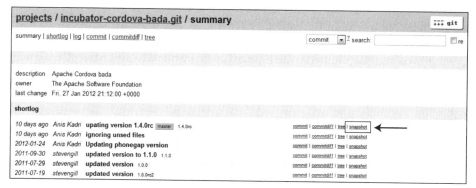

Figure 4-2   PhoneGap bada Git repository

One last step has to be completed. The bada project download includes each of the JavaScript files that make up the standard phonegap.js file, but the actual phonegap.js file is missing. Using Windows Explorer, navigate to the res\ phonegap folder shown in Figure 4-3. Double-click the phonegap.bat file highlighted in the figure, and a batch process will run that will concatenate each of the

JavaScript files into the `phonegap.js` file your PhoneGap applications will utilize.

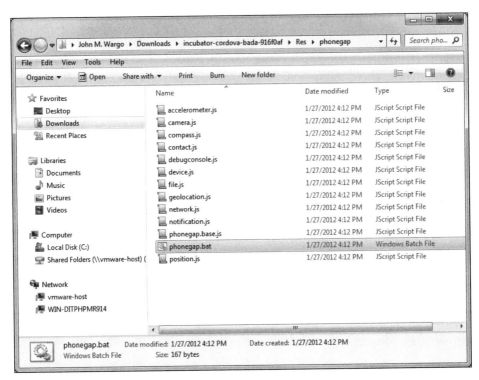

Figure 4-3   PhoneGap bada project folder

As you can see, for bada, the PhoneGap project team has broken the naming convention for the `phonegap.js` file. For most other platforms, the file name includes the PhoneGap version number; for bada, it does not.

Creating a bada PhoneGap Project

Once the PhoneGap and bada SDKs have been installed, your development environment is ready to create new PhoneGap projects. As you'll see with some other platforms, to create a new PhoneGap project for bada, instead of creating a new project in the IDE, you will instead copy an existing project and modify its contents to suit your needs.

Start the bada IDE using shortcuts installed in the Windows Start menu. When the program first launches, it will display a start page similar to the one shown in Figure 4-4. Click the Workbench icon highlighted in the figure.

Figure 4-4   bada IDE start page

As is normal with Eclipse-based IDEs, the program will prompt you to select the default location for the developer workspace used to store project files. You can either accept the default value or specify a different location as appropriate for your needs.

Once the workspace loads, open the File menu, and then select Import; the IDE will open the Import wizard shown in Figure 4-5. Expand the bada section as shown in the figure, select bada Application Project, and then click the Next button.

The bada IDE will then display the Import Projects dialog shown in Figure 4-6. Select the "Select root directory" option as shown in the figure, and then click the Browse button to the right of the input field. The standard Windows folder selection dialog will appear; navigate to the folder where you extracted the bada project files, and click the Done button to continue. When you complete this step correctly, the Import Projects dialog will list a PhoneGap project called Cordova under the list of projects, as shown in Figure 4-6.

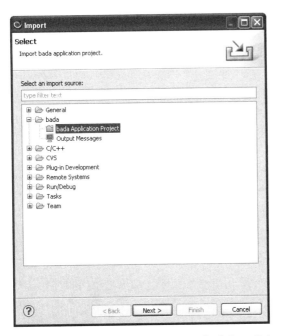

Figure 4-5   bada IDE Import wizard's Select dialog

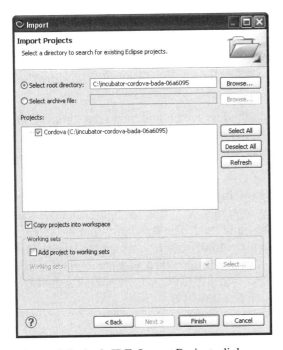

Figure 4-6   bada IDE: Import Projects dialog

Select the "Copy projects into workspace" checkbox, and then click the Finish button to continue. The IDE will copy the project files to the workspace and display a screen similar to the one shown in Figure 4-7.

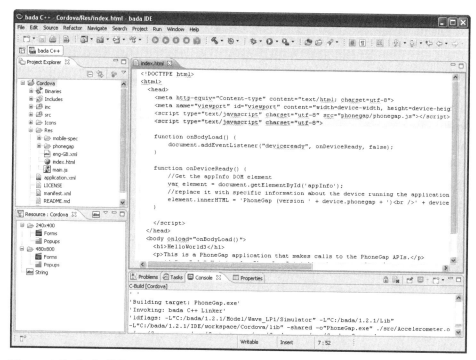

Figure 4-7   bada IDE

For PhoneGap projects, the `index.html` and associated files (such as CSS and JavaScript files plus any images and other content files) are stored in or beneath the `Res` folder. Expand the `Res` folder in the Project Explorer, and click the `index.html` file to open it in the editor, as shown in Figure 4-7. At this point, you can make whatever changes you want to the application's source files and begin testing your application.

The default project in the download includes settings related to the configuration of the IDE of the developer who created the project. Before you run the application, you will have to clean up the project files. In the bada IDE, open the Project menu and select Clean; the IDE will display a dialog similar to the one shown in Figure 4-8. Click the OK button, and the IDE will process the project folder and delete any files left over from a previous build of the project.

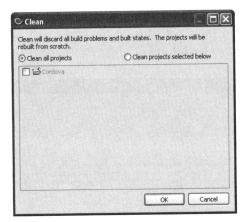

Figure 4-8 bada IDE Clean dialog

bada projects also require a manifest file; the starting project has one included with it, but you won't be able to use that manifest for your application. The process for creating a profile and its associated manifest file plus updating the project with your new manifest file is described in the following section.

Creating a bada Application Profile

bada uses an application profile to define settings for applications that are sold through their proprietary application storefront, the Samsung Apps Store. An application profile's settings are defined in a manifest file (`manifest.xml`), which must be included in the root folder of any bada application project and added to the project's properties. You can create internal use or test applications using a default manifest file created by the IDE, or you can create a separate profile for each application either within the IDE or from the bada developer web site.

For most mobile platforms, this part of the process is completed right before you submit to the appropriate application store, but with bada development, it can be part of the initial application project setup as well. For PhoneGap development, you create a new bada project by importing an existing one, so you'll need to have your own profile available to add to the new project later.

To create an application profile, log into the bada developer web site using the credentials created at the beginning of the chapter. From the landing page, select the My Applications menu (highlighted in Figure 4-9), and then select Application Manager.

Figure 4-9   Samsung bada developer web site

On the page that opens, select the Create a new Application ID button, as shown on the right side of Figure 4-10.

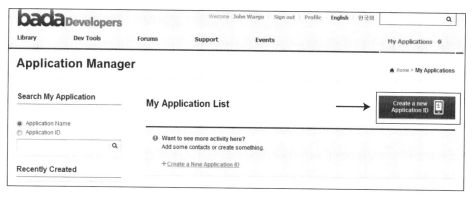

Figure 4-10   bada Application Manager

In the first step in the process, you must define a unique name for your application. The site will open a pop-up window that prompts you for the application name (as shown in Figure 4-11) and then validates the name's uniqueness against all other bada applications before allowing you to continue the process. Only after you have registered a unique name can you continue to provide a description of the application and then move to the next step. Click the OK button to continue.

Figure 4-11   bada Application Manager: checking bada application name availability

On the next page that appears, enter a description of the application, as shown in Figure 4-12, and then click the Create button to continue.

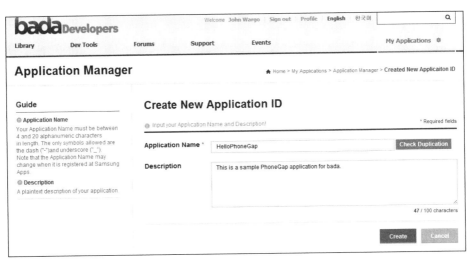

Figure 4-12   bada Application Manager: adding an application description

At this point, the application profile has been created, and the site will display the confirmation page shown in Figure 4-13. Before you continue, you must define at least one application version for the application. Click the Add a New Application Version link highlighted in Figure 4-13.

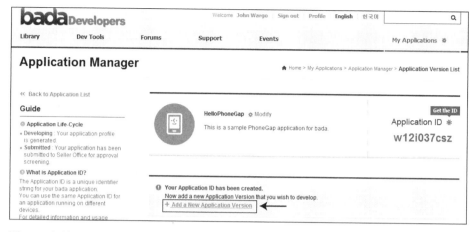

Figure 4-13   bada Application Manager: profile confirmation

On the next page that appears, enter a version number for the application, and then click the Save button, as shown in Figure 4-14. Notice how Samsung limits the major and minor version numbers to 35.

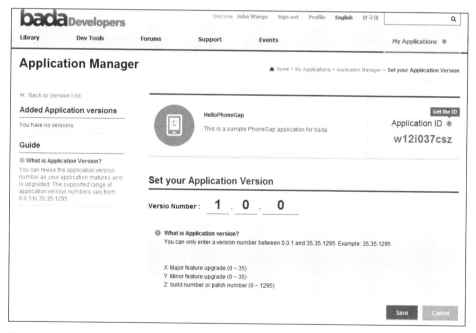

Figure 4-14   bada Application Manager: setting the application version

Next you will need to define the bada platform version you will be developing for. On the confirmation page shown in Figure 4-15, click the Select the bada API Version link highlighted in the figure.

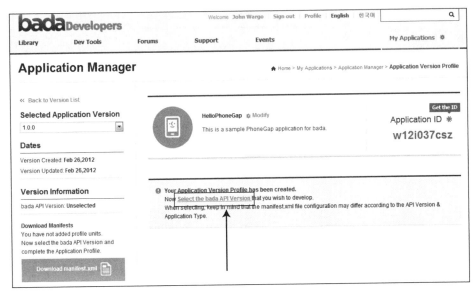

Figure 4-15   bada Application Manager: application version profile created

On the page that appears, the Application Manager will prompt you to select the version of the bada SDK the application will use (API version) plus the type of application that is being created, as shown in Figure 4-16. Select the appropriate options for the application, and then click the Save button. The form should default to SDK version 2.0, but since you're working with an older version of the SDK for PhoneGap development, you will want to change the selection to match the SDK version you're using.

At this point in the process, the Application Manager will display a page similar to the one shown in Figure 4-17. What you need to do next is configure application-specific security settings for the application. Click the Select your Privileged API Group link highlighted in Figure 4-17.

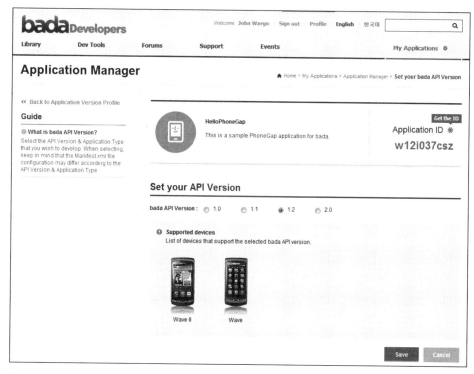

Figure 4-16   bada Application Manager: selecting API version and application type

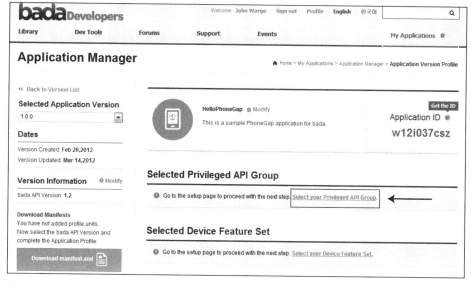

Figure 4-17   bada Application Manager: API version profile created

From the page that appears (shown in Figure 4-18), you can enable or disable as needed specific API permissions for the application profile. In this example, I've cropped the page to show only a few of the available options; when doing this for your own application profiles, you will see a much larger list of options. In Figure 4-18, the settings for access to the camera and image capture capabilities are expanded and enabled for this particular application as are settings related to working with web content. If the PhoneGap application you're building doesn't use either of those device features, you can disable access to those features within the application by deselecting the checkboxes shown. If you don't set these options correctly, any portion of your application that uses an API that is not enabled here will not work.

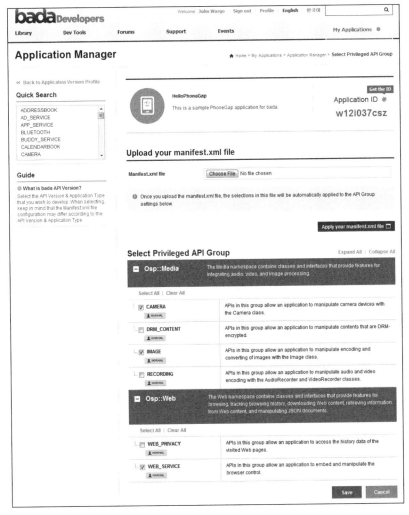

Figure 4-18   bada Application Manager: enabling API capabilities

You can also upload an existing manifest file to capture API settings already defined for a different application. To do this, click the Choose File button on the top of the page, and select the manifest file you want to use.

Click the Save button to complete the API profile. The Application Manager will display a page similar to the one shown in Figure 4-19. Next you need to select the device feature set for the application. To do this, click the Select your Device Feature Set link highlighted in Figure 4-19.

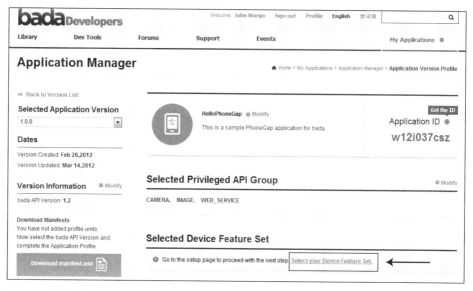

Figure 4-19   bada Application Manager: API capabilities created

The site will display a page similar to the one shown in Figure 4-20. Since there was only one device type supported with the bada 1.2 SDK, all you will need to do here is click the Save button shown on the bottom of the figure to continue.

Next you will see the page shown in Figure 4-21. From this page, click the Download manifest.xml button highlighted in the figure to download the application's manifest file to the local system. You will need this when you build your application in the bada IDE.

At any time, you can go back and update the settings for your application or create a profile for the next version of the application. When you return to the Application Manager, the list of defined profiles will display. Simply click the application's name to modify the settings or add a new application version.

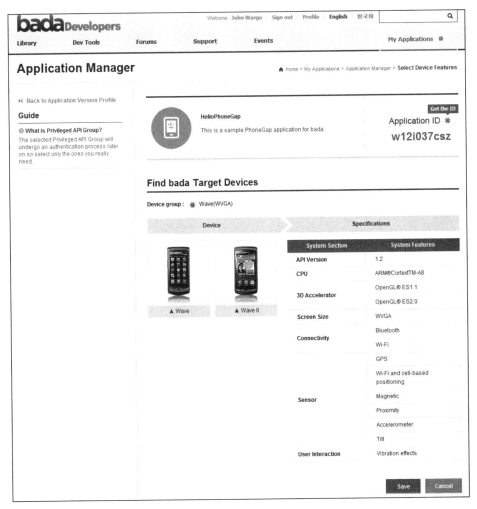

Figure 4-20   bada Application Manager: selecting target devices

Once you have a manifest file, you can add it to your PhoneGap project by right-clicking the project in the IDE's Project Explorer and selecting Properties. In the dialog that appears, expand the bada Build option, and then select Manifest Information, as shown in Figure 4-22.

Click the Import button at the bottom of the dialog, and then select the manifest file you just created. After you've selected the file, click the OK button to save the updated project properties. At this point, the application is ready to run with your application manifest instead of the one included with the PhoneGap project.

Figure 4-21   bada Application Manager: completed profile

Testing bada PhoneGap Applications

To launch an application in the bada emulator, right-click a project, open the Run As menu, and then select bada Emulator Web Application. The IDE will launch the bada device emulator and then load and execute the selected bada application. Figure 4-23 shows the HelloWorld3 application from Chapter 2 loaded in the emulator. The application source code had to be modified to accommodate the location of the phonegap.js file within the bada project's folder structure.

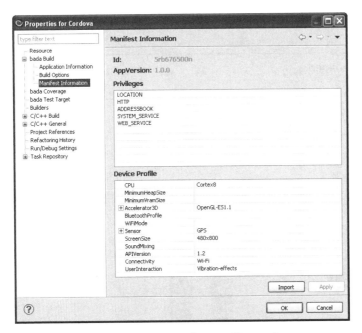

Figure 4-22 bada project properties manifest settings

Figure 4-23 bada device emulator

5

Configuring a BlackBerry Development Environment for PhoneGap

This chapter includes the instructions to follow to install and use the BlackBerry development tools to build PhoneGap applications for both BlackBerry smartphones and BlackBerry PlayBook tablet devices. To complete the steps outlined, you must first perform several installation steps using instructions provided elsewhere in the book:

1. Install the PhoneGap framework using the instructions provided in Appendix A.

2. (Windows only) Install the Oracle Java Developer Kit (JDK) using the instructions provided in Appendix B.

3. (Windows only) Install Apache Ant using instructions provided in Appendix C.

Once you've completed those steps, you're ready to start work on PhoneGap applications for BlackBerry.

Installing the BlackBerry WebWorks SDK

As mentioned in Chapter 1, BlackBerry PhoneGap applications are essentially BlackBerry WebWorks applications (a special kind of BlackBerry application) with some extra PhoneGap stuff baked in. To build PhoneGap applications for BlackBerry, you must leverage the BlackBerry WebWorks SDK. The tools consist of a series of command-line tools you use to create, build, and test WebWorks applications.

WebWorks Eclipse Plug-In

RIM used to distribute an Eclipse plug-in that could be used to build WebWorks applications but announced in 2011 that it would be ending support for the product at the end of the year. So, that's why you're stuck with command-line tools for PhoneGap development on BlackBerry.

To download the BlackBerry WebWorks SDK, point your browser of choice to www.blackberry.com/developers. On the WebWorks page, select the Tools & downloads option, and then download the latest version of the WebWorks SDK for the BlackBerry device for which you will be developing applications. The file is pretty large, so it may take a while to download; the toolkit includes the SDK as well as server components and device simulators needed to test applications for BlackBerry.

 Note: If you will be supporting both BlackBerry smartphones and the BlackBerry PlayBook tablet, you will have to download and install separate SDKs for each. Beginning with BlackBerry 10 devices, RIM is expected to use a single SDK for both device platforms.

The Macintosh and Windows installation steps are essentially the same: Once the download has completed, launch the downloaded file to start the installation process, and follow the prompts until the process completes.

On Windows systems, experience has proven that many Java applications have difficulty running from a location that contains spaces in the folder name. Other applications also seem to have difficulty running within the restricted security environment on Microsoft Windows Vista and Windows 7. For these reasons, it's recommended to install the WebWorks SDK off the root of the system's hard drive rather than in the Program Files folder.

For the WebWorks PlayBook SDK installation, you will also need to download and install the Adobe Air SDK from www.adobe.com/go/getairsdk and the VMware Player application (needed to run the PlayBook Simulator).

Signing Keys

You will need to register for a set of BlackBerry application-signing keys before you can deploy an application to a real device. RIM's security architecture for Black-Berry applications requires that any application that runs on a BlackBerry device must be signed by RIM. Part of this signing process involves acquiring a set of keys and installing them on the system requesting the signatures. The keys are free and easy to obtain, although it sometimes takes RIM three or more days to generate and distribute keys once requested.

You can find additional information about the signing process on the BlackBerry Developer's web site at http://us.blackberry.com/developers/javaappdev/codekeys.jsp. The process is also well documented in Chapter 12 of *BlackBerry® Development Fundamentals* (www.bbdevfundamentals.com).

Creating a BlackBerry PhoneGap Project

When you installed the PhoneGap project files, included with them is a sample project that demonstrates a wide range of PhoneGap project features. Figure 5-1 shows the sample project's folder. Unfortunately, there's currently no simple way to create a new blank BlackBerry project using the files provided, but I hope this will be changed in an upcoming release. You'll have to copy the existing sample project and then remove the code and any extra files included in the project.

 Note: The PhoneGap Getting Started guide for BlackBerry development (http://phonegap.com/start#blackberry) includes instructions that indicate that you can execute an `ant` command to create a new BlackBerry smartphone or tablet project. This was a feature of earlier versions of PhoneGap (prior to version 1.0) and is no longer a supported option. Ideally someday someone from the PhoneGap documentation team will remove that reference from the Getting Started guide.

To create a new BlackBerry PhoneGap project, simply copy the sample project folder shown in Figure 5-1 to a new folder, and then modify the contents of the `index.html` file (located in the www folder) to suit the needs of your application. For the web application code used throughout the remainder of this chapter, we'll use the HelloWorld3 application used in Chapter 2.

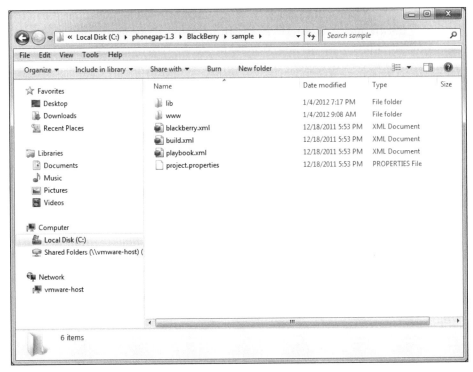

Figure 5-1 PhoneGap BlackBerry WebWorks project files

For BlackBerry WebWorks projects, RIM uses a W3C standard called the Widget Packaging and XML Configuration to define a file (`config.xml`) that contains settings that control part of the application build process. You can find the detailed information about the standard at www.w3.org/TR/widgets. By default, the `config.xml` file will be located in a PhoneGap project's www folder. For each PhoneGap application, you will need to modify the contents of this file with settings for your application. A sample `config.xml` file is shown here.

BlackBerry WebWorks `config.xml` File

```
<?xml version="1.0" encoding="UTF-8"?>

<!--
  Widget Configuration Reference:
    http://docs.blackberry.com/en/developers/deliverables/15274/
-->

<widget xmlns="http://www.w3.org/ns/widgets"
  xmlns:rim="http://www.blackberry.com/ns/widgets"
```

```
    version="1.0.0.0">

<name>Hello World</name>

<description>
  A sample PhoneGap application.
</description>

<license href="http://opensource.org/licenses/alphabetical">
</license>

<!-- PhoneGap API -->
<feature id="blackberry.system" required="true"
  version="1.0.0.0" />
<feature id="com.phonegap" required="true"
  version="1.0.0" />
<feature id="blackberry.find" required="true"
  version="1.0.0.0" />
<feature id="blackberry.identity" required="true"
  version="1.0.0.0" />
<feature id="blackberry.pim.Address" required="true"
  version="1.0.0.0" />
<feature id="blackberry.pim.Contact" required="true"
  version="1.0.0.0" />
<feature id="blackberry.io.file" required="true"
  version="1.0.0.0" />
<feature id="blackberry.utils" required="true"
  version="1.0.0.0" />
<feature id="blackberry.io.dir" required="true"
  version="1.0.0.0" />
<feature id="blackberry.app" required="true"
  version="1.0.0.0" />
<feature id="blackberry.app.event" required="true"
  version="1.0.0.0" />
<feature id="blackberry.system.event" required="true"
  version="1.0.0.0"/>
<feature id="blackberry.widgetcache" required="true"
  version="1.0.0.0"/>
<feature id="blackberry.media.camera" />
<feature id="blackberry.ui.dialog" />

<!-- PhoneGap API -->
<access subdomains="true" uri="file:///store/home" />
<access subdomains="true" uri="file:///SDCard" />

<!-- Expose access to all URIs, including the file and http
  protocols -->
<access subdomains="true" uri="*" />

<icon rim:hover="false" src="resources/icon.png" />
```

```
<icon rim:hover="true" src="resources/icon_hover.png" />

<rim:loadingScreen backgroundColor="#000000"
  foregroundImage="resources/loading_foreground.png"
  onFirstLaunch="true">
  <rim:transitionEffect type="fadeOut" />
</rim:loadingScreen>

<content src="index.html" />

<rim:permissions>
  <rim:permit>use_camera</rim:permit>
  <rim:permit>read_device_identifying_information
  </rim:permit>
  <rim:permit>access_shared</rim:permit>
  <rim:permit>read_geolocation</rim:permit>
</rim:permissions>


</widget>
```

Table 5-1 briefly describes each of the elements in the file. Additionally, an excellent reference for the settings in the `config.xml` file can be found at www.tinyurl.com/78q8sgr.

Table 5-1   Config.xml Elements

Element	Description
Name	The name of the application. The text provided here will appear on the Black-Berry home screen below the application's icon. Keep the application's name short and clear; it has only limited space assigned to it on the BlackBerry home screen and is not as valuable if the BlackBerry OS has to truncate it to make it fit on the screen.
Description	A description of the application. The text provided here will be displayed in the BlackBerry Application Manager application. It's used to help a user understand the purpose of a particular application installed on a BlackBerry device.
License	Represents the software license under which the application is released.
Feature	Identifies a particular API feature used by the application. A developer must list each API family the application uses. This is used by the BlackBerry Device Software to validate which APIs are used against what permissions the user has granted the application during installation or at a later time. This is part of RIM's standard application security infrastructure. The list of values provided in the default `config.xml` file should represent all of the possible options included in the PhoneGap application runtime container. It's best to leave the default list as shown; even though a particular PhoneGap application you create might not make use of one of the APIs listed, Java code for calling the APIs is still in the PhoneGap application container and therefore needs the feature enabled.

continues

Table 5-1   Config.xml Elements *(continued)*

Element	Description
Access	Defines the external resources the application can access (file, network). You can list each external resource individually, or you can use the asterisk to allow access to any resource. Examples of each are shown in the earlier sample file. If you don't define an entry for a particular resource, the application will not be able to access that resource and won't display an error message either.
Icon	Specifies the file resource URL for the application icons used by the application. Use the `rim:hover="true"` attribute to define that a particular icon is used when the application is selected on the BlackBerry home screen. Use `rim:hover="false"` for the alternate, unselected icon.
Loading Screen	Used to define settings for the application's load screen. As the PhoneGap application loads, the settings defined here will define what appears as the application initializes.
Content	Specifies the start page for the application. By default, most applications will use `index.html`, but if your PhoneGap application needs for whatever reason to use a different HTML file, then you would provide the file name here.
Permissions	Specifies the specific security permissions the application requires be enabled on the BlackBerry device. The required permissions listed here are used to prompt the user during installation to enable the settings required for the application. If the user disables one of the required permissions, the portion of the application that needs the permission will not function.

Using your text editor of choice, edit the application's `config.xml` file as needed with the appropriate settings for your application, and then save your changes. At this point, the application is ready to be built.

Building BlackBerry PhoneGap Applications

The default PhoneGap project includes an Ant script that manages the process of building the application plus some additional tasks that help with testing and deploying a PhoneGap application. The script is in a file called `build.xml`, and it is located in the root of the PhoneGap project folder. I'll cover the options for that particular file in a minute.

Beginning with PhoneGap 1.3, the PhoneGap development team added support for WebWorks tablet applications (applications built for the BlackBerry PlayBook tablet). With older versions of PhoneGap, all of the supported build processes were implemented in the `build.xml` file. Beginning with PhoneGap 1.3, the Ant script (described later) calls out to the `blackberry.xml` or `playbook.xml` file depending on the platform for which the application is being built.

Configuring the Build Process

The build process leverages configuration settings defined in a WebWorks project properties file called `project.properties`. This file is located in a WebWorks project's root folder and contains settings that tell the build script where to locate BlackBerry-specific applications that are used during the build, test, and packaging process. An example `project.properties` file is shown here.

BlackBerry `project.properties` File

```
# BlackBerry WebWorks Packager Directory
#
#  The BlackBerry WebWorks Packager (bbwp) is required for
#  compiling and packaging BlackBerry WebWorks applications for
#  deployment to a BlackBerry device or simulator.  The bbwp
#  utility is installed with the standalone BlackBerry WebWorks
#  SDK, and as part of the BlackBerry Web Plugin for Eclipse.
#
#  Please specify the location of the BlackBerry WebWorks
#  Packager in your environment.
#
#  Typical location of bbwp for standalone BlackBerry WebWorks
#  SDK installation:
#    C:\Program Files (x86)\Research In Motion\BlackBerry
#       Widget Packager
#
#  Typical location of bbwp for BlackBerry Web Plugin for
#  Eclipse installation:
#    C:\Eclipse-3.5.2\plugins\
#       net.rim.browser.tools.wcpc_1.0.0.201003191451-126\wcpc
#
#  The ANT script is brittle and requires you to escape the
#  backslashes. e.g. C:\some\path must be C:\\some\\path
#
#   Please remember to:
#     - Double escape your backslashes (i.e. \ must be \\)
#     - Do not add a trailing slash (e.g. C:\some\path)
#

blackberry.bbwp.dir=C:\\Program Files\\Research In Motion\\
  BlackBerry WebWorks Packager

playbook.bbwp.dir=C:\\Program Files\\Research In Motion\\
  BlackBerry WebWorks SDK for TabletOS 2.1.0.6\\bbwp

# (Optional) Simulator Directory
```

```
#  If sim.dir is not specified, the build script will use the
#  simulator directory within the Blackberry WebWorks Packager.
blackberry.sim.dir=C:\\Program Files\\Research In Motion\
  BlackBerry WebWorks Packager\\simpack\\6.0.0.227

# (Optional) Simulator Binary
#  If sim.bin is not specified, the build script will attempt
#  to use the default simulator in the simulator directory.
#blackberry.sim.bin=9800.bat

# (Optional) MDS Directory
#  If mds.dir is not specified, the build script will attempt
#  to use the MDS that is installed with the Blackberry
#  WebWorks Packager.
blackberry.mds.dir=C:\\Program Files\\Research In Motion\\
  BlackBerry WebWorks Packager\\mds

# BlackBerry Code Signing Password
#  If you leave this field blank, then the signing tool will
#  prompt you each time
blackberry.sigtool.password=

# Playbook Code Signing Password
#   If you leave these fields blank, then signing will fail
playbook.sigtool.csk.password=
playbook.sigtool.p12.password=

# BlackBerry Simulator Password
#  If you leave this field blank, then you cannot deploy to
#  simulator
blackberry.sim.password=

# Playbook Simulator IP
#  If you leave this field blank, then you cannot deploy to
#  simulator
playbook.sim.ip=

# Playbook Simulator Password
#  If you leave this field blank, then you cannot deploy to
#  simulator
playbook.sim.password=

# Playbook Device IP
#  If you leave this field blank, then you cannot deploy to
#  device
playbook.device.ip=
```

```
# Playbook Device Password
#  If you leave this field blank, then you cannot deploy to
#  device
playbook.device.password=
```

Table 5-2 lists a brief description of the relevant configuration options defined in the project.properties file. The BlackBerry and PlayBook development kits (at least for the moment) use different SDKs to build their applications. Since the `project.properties` file has to support configuration options for both SDKs, each of the properties defined within the file are predicated with a `blackberry.` or `playbook.` to indicate to which platform the property applies.

Table 5-2   Project.properties Configuration Options

Setting	Description
bbwp.dir	Specifies the location for the WebWorks SDK installed at the beginning of the chapter. If the WebWorks SDK was installed to its default location, the value for this setting should be correct. If installed in a different location, the value should be changed to point to the current location.
sim.dir	Specifies the folder location for the device simulator that will be used to test this application. This value is important only if you will be launching the simulator using the build script described later in this section. If you omit this value, the build process will use the default simulator included with the WebWorks SDK.
sim.bin	Specifies the name of the batch file for the device simulator that will be used to test this application. This value is important only if you will be launching the simulator using the build script described later in this section. If you omit this value, the build process will use the default simulator listed in the simulator folder.
mds.dir	Specifies the folder location for the MDS simulator that will be used when testing this application. If you omit this value, the build process will use the default MDS simulator included with the WebWorks SDK. Since the MDS simulator is included with the WebWorks SDK and the program is rarely updated, there is little likelihood that you will ever need to change this setting.
sigtool.password	Specifies the password you have assigned to secure the keys used by the BlackBerry signature tool to sign applications. By providing a value here, you bypass the need to type in the password every time the build process needs to sign an application being built.

Folder Tips: When specifying folder paths in the `project.properties` file, be sure to use double backslashes and to omit training backslashes as shown in the sample file.

The device simulators included with the WebWorks SDK can access local resources, but when they need to access data or applications residing on a network server, they leverage the BlackBerry Mobile Data System (MDS) server to provide that access. Included with the WebWorks SDK is a full-featured version of the BlackBerry MDS server component. The Ant scripts used to test PhoneGap applications (described later in the chapter) will automatically load the MDS simulator before loading the appropriate device simulator. When the MDS simulator launches, it will open a text-based window similar to the one shown in Figure 5-2. During testing of your application on a BlackBerry simulator, you'll want to leave this window open. It will display a series of entries every time the device simulator requests and receives data from a network resource such as a web server.

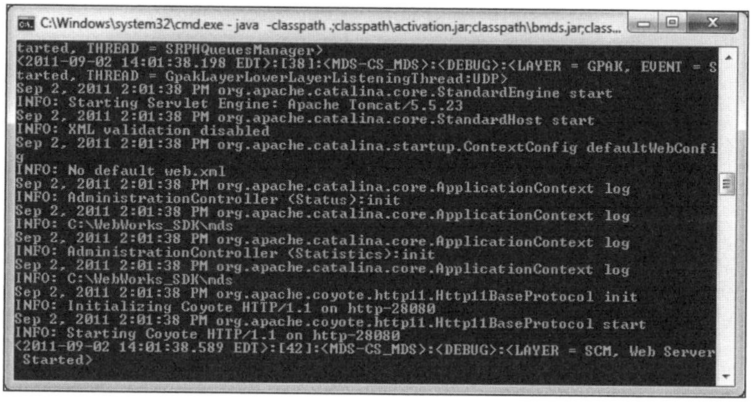

Figure 5-2   BlackBerry MDS simulator window

For additional information on the capabilities provided by MDS, refer to Chapter 4 of my other mobile development book, *BlackBerry® Development Fundamentals* (www.bbdevfundamentals.com).

Using your text editor of choice, modify the `project.properties` file as needed for your particular system's configuration and save your changes, and you're ready to build your application.

Executing a Build

To build a BlackBerry PhoneGap application, open a command prompt or terminal window, navigate to the project's root folder, and issue the following command:

```
ant blackberry build
```

Ant will read its instructions from the `build.xml` file included with the project and perform the steps needed to build the application.

To build a PlayBook PhoneGap application, issue the following command:

```
ant playbook build
```

A sample listing of the output from this process is shown here:

```
Buildfile: C:\Dev\PhoneGap\BlackBerry\sample\build.xml

blackberry:

build:

generate-cod-name:
     [echo] Generated name: PhoneGapSample.cod

clean:
    [delete] Deleting directory C:\Dev\PhoneGap\BlackBerry\
      sample\build

package-app:
    [mkdir] Created dir:
      C:\Dev\PhoneGap\BlackBerry\sample\build\widget
    [copy] Copying 9 files to
      C:\Dev\PhoneGap\BlackBerry\sample\build\widget
    [zip] Building zip:
      C:\Dev\PhoneGap\BlackBerry\sample\build\PhoneGapSample.zip

build:
    [exec] [INFO]     Parsing command line options
    [exec] [INFO]     Parsing bbwp.properties
    [exec] [INFO]     Validating application archive
    [exec] [INFO]     Parsing config.xml
    [exec] [WARNING]  Failed to find the <author> element
    [exec] [INFO]     Populating application source
    [exec] [INFO]     Compiling BlackBerry WebWorks application
    [exec] [INFO]     Generating output files
    [exec] [INFO]     BlackBerry WebWorks application packaging
      complete

BUILD SUCCESSFUL
Total time: 21 seconds

C:\Dev\PhoneGap\BlackBerry\sample>
```

If everything is configured correctly and the files are all in the right locations, at this point you'll have a compiled version of the application all ready to go.

During the build process, the script will create a new folder called `build` under the project's root folder. Within that folder are two folders that are important when it comes to deploying your application to BlackBerry smartphones: OTA Install and Standard Install. The OTA Install folder contains the files you will need to deploy the application over the air (OTA), pushed to devices by the BlackBerry Enterprise Server (BES). The files located in the Standard Install folder can be used to manually install an application (discussed later), be pulled down to a device from a web server, or be deployed through the BlackBerry App World. Each of these options is described in detail in Chapter 16 of *BlackBerry® Development Fundamentals* (www.bbdevfundamentals.com).

Besides the `build` command used in the previous example, the `build.xml` file also contains code supporting command-line options for the following processes:

- `load-device`
- `load-simulator`
- `package-app`
- `clean`
- `clean-device`
- `clean-simulator`
- `help`

To view information about each of these options, issue the command `ant help` in the same command prompt window used to build the application. The script will display usage instructions for each of the available options.

Testing BlackBerry PhoneGap Applications

To test the application, you have two options: You can test in the BlackBerry simulator, or you can test on a physical device. This section contains instructions for how to execute each option.

Testing on a BlackBerry Device Simulator

To test your PhoneGap application on a BlackBerry device simulator, open a command prompt, navigate to the project's root folder, and issue the following command:

```
ant blackberry load-simulator
```

The build script will load the BlackBerry MDS simulator and then load the appropriate device simulator (BlackBerry or PlayBook) using default options for the WebWorks SDK or using the specific settings you added to the project's `project.properties` file.

For BlackBerry devices, the location for the application's icon will vary depending on which version of BlackBerry Device Software the simulator is running. For newer BlackBerry Device Software versions, the application's icon can typically be found in the `Downloads` folder, but in some cases it's loaded directly on the Home Screen, as shown in Figure 5-3.

Figure 5-3 BlackBerry HelloWorld PhoneGap application icon

 Note: You can change the icon used for the application by copying the icon file to the project's resource folder and modifying the project's `config.xml` file to point to the new icon file name.

When you click the application's icon, the application will load and display a screen similar to the one shown in Figure 5-4.

Figure 5-4   BlackBerry HelloWorld PhoneGap application

To test your PhoneGap application on a BlackBerry Playbook device simulator, issue the following command to load the application onto the simulator:

```
ant playbook load-simulator
```

You will need to launch the simulator manually and configure the options in the `project.properties` file to load the application on the PlayBook simulator. Refer to the PlayBook developer resources web site at www.blackberry.com/developers for additional information on how to configure and use the PlayBook simulator.

For PlayBook tablets, the application will load onto the device's home screen. The PlayBook does not currently support the concept of folders for grouping application icons. To launch the application, simply touch the application icon on the device screen.

Testing on a Device

To test your PhoneGap application on a physical BlackBerry device, connect a device to the system using a USB cable, open a command prompt, navigate to the project's root folder, and issue the following command:

```
ant blackberry load-device
```

The build script will load the application on the physical device.

You can also use the BlackBerry JavaLoader program (`javaloader.exe`) to load the application onto a physical BlackBerry device. Navigate to the WebWorks SDK installation's `bin` folder, and then execute the following command:

```
JavaLoader.exe -u load codfilename.cod
```

In this example, `codfilename` refers to the relative path to the application's compiled executable (the `.cod` file), which for the current example is as follows:

```
JavaLoader.exe -u load c:\dev\phonegap\BlackBerry\HelloWorld\
Build\StandardInstall\HelloWorld.cod
```

JavaLoader will connect to the device over the USB cable and transfer the application's files to the device. Once the process has completed, you can navigate to the application's icon on the device's home screen and launch the application.

To test your PhoneGap application on a physical PlayBook device, connect a device to the system using a USB cable, open a command prompt window, navigate to the project's root folder, and issue the following command:

```
ant playbook load-device
```

Configuring an iOS Development Environment for PhoneGap

This chapter includes the instructions to follow to install and use the Apple development tools to build PhoneGap applications for iOS. You must have a Macintosh computer running Macintosh OS X in order to be able to build applications for iOS.

Registering as an Apple Developer

To access developer-related content on Apple's web site, you must first register as a developer in Apple's developer program. Apple keeps a very tight rein on its developer community; registration is free, but you will also need to join one of the developer programs before you can download the latest version of Xcode (Apple's proprietary IDE for Macintosh OS and iOS development) or deploy any iOS applications to individual devices or through Apple's App Store. The following developer programs are available:

- **Individual**: For individual developers creating free or commercial iOS applications for distribution through Apple's App Store

- **Company**: For commercial developer organizations creating free or commercial iOS applications for distribution through Apple's App Store

- **Enterprise**: For organizations building iOS applications for distribution through a private, enterprise App Store (for business applications)

- **University**: For higher educational institutions that include iOS development in their curriculum

There's a yearly membership fee for each of the listed programs except for the University program. You can find more information on the different program options at http://developer.apple.com.

Installing Xcode

Once you have registered for the appropriate Apple developer program, it's time to install Apple's development tools on your Macintosh computer. iOS development is performed using Xcode, which is available as a free download from the Apple App Store provided you have the appropriate Apple developer program membership. To install Xcode, launch the App Store application on your Macintosh and enter **Xcode** in the search box in the upper-right corner of the application window. The App Store will return a list of several options; click the Xcode option, and the application will display a screen similar to the one shown in Figure 6-1. Click the Free button, and then click the Install button that appears (in the same screen location) to begin the installation process.

Xcode is a very large download, so it will take some time to download and install the application. When you click the Install button in the App Store application, Xcode isn't actually installing; instead, the Xcode installer application is being downloaded and installed on the system. Once the Xcode installer's installation completes, there's still another installation that has to happen before you can start writing iOS applications using Xcode. Confused?

You'll be able to tell when the App Store download and installation completes, because the button on the Xcode page in the App Store says Installed rather than Free or Install. At this point, you can close the App Store application, and then open the Launcher application. Then switch to the Launcher's last page, as shown in Figure 6-2, and look for the Install Xcode application highlighted in the figure. Launch that application to begin the actual Xcode installation process, and navigate through the prompts until the installation completes.

Figure 6-1   Installing Xcode from the Apple App Store

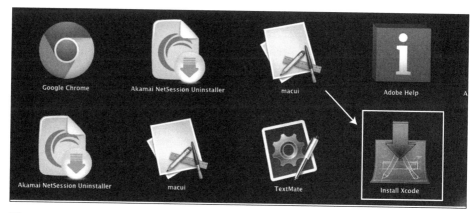

Figure 6-2   Xcode installation icon

Once you've completed the Xcode installation, you must now install the PhoneGap project files and the Xcode plug-in used to create PhoneGap applications for iOS. Refer to Appendix A for complete instructions.

Creating an iOS PhoneGap Project

With Xcode and the PhoneGap plug-in installed, you're ready to begin building PhoneGap applications for iOS. Note that the instructions and example screen shots in this section are for Xcode version 4.

When you launch Xcode for the first time, you will see a screen similar to the one shown in Figure 6-3. Select "Create a new Xcode project" to start the process. If you've used Xcode previously and have the checkbox for "Show this window when Xcode launches" disabled, then you will need to open the Xcode File menu and select New Project.

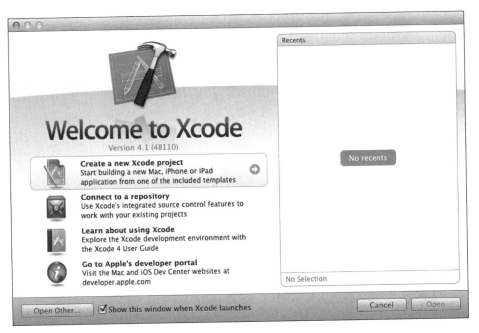

Figure 6-3   Xcode: welcome screen

Xcode will prompt you to select the type of project you will be creating. Select the option for iOS Applications on the left side of the window, as shown in Figure 6-4. Select the option for PhoneGap-based Application and click the Next button.

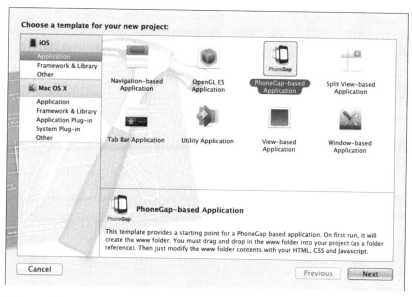

Figure 6-4   Xcode: new project window

Xcode will prompt you for a product name for your project and a company identifier, as shown in Figure 6-5. The product name and company identifier are concatenated together to form what should be a unique identifier for the particular project being created. When the appropriate options have been defined for your application, click the Next button to continue.

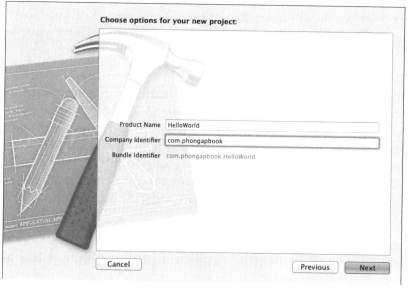

Figure 6-5   Xcode: defining project naming options

Xcode will then prompt you to select the destination folder for the new project, as shown in Figure 6-6. Select or create the appropriate folder location for the project, and click the Create button to continue. Note the option for creating a local Git repository for the project; as discussed later in the book, the IDE's integration with Git can make building applications using PhoneGap Build a simpler process.

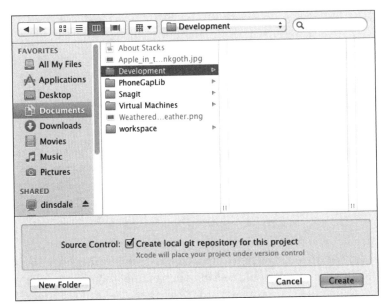

Figure 6-6   Xcode: defining the project location

At this point, Xcode will create the necessary iOS project folders and source files for the application. When completed, Xcode will display its workspace window similar to the one shown in Figure 6-7.

The left side of the window contains the navigator area that lets you browse the folder and file structure for the project. On the right is the editor area, which is currently displaying summary information for the application. You can switch between the tabs (Summary, Info, Build Settings, Build Phases, and Build Rules) to see the different possible options for the application's configuration. The available options won't be covered here; instead, we'll focus only on the PhoneGap-related topics. There are many great books on iOS development that should be referenced for a detailed discussion of Xcode and iOS development.

In the project summary, you will want to enter a version number for the application and then select the supported device orientations for the application. Many a PhoneGap developer has forgotten to enable the necessary options here and has been frustrated when the PhoneGap application will support only a single orientation (which is the default for iOS projects). There will be good reasons for some applications to support only one or two orientations, but in general you will probably want to enable all available options here for most applications. The PhoneGap application runtime container will fire an event that will allow your web application to execute code to deal with orientation changes as they happen, but only when you enable the correct options here.

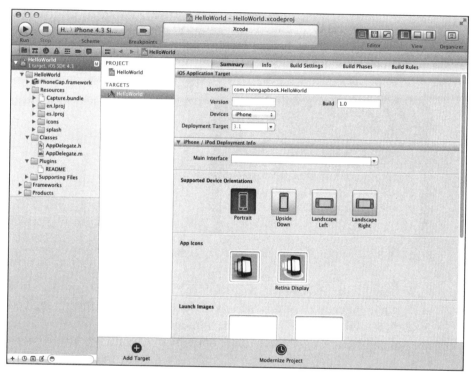

Figure 6-7   Xcode: new PhoneGap project

The Summary tab also displays the application icons and launch screens in use for the application. These images populate with default PhoneGap project images, but for any production application, you should provide your own custom images. To change the image for any of these options, right-click an image, and select an appropriate option from the menu that appears: Select File, Show in Finder, or Delete.

The PhoneGap Xcode project in its current state doesn't have access to the web content it needs to provide the application with its user interface or application logic. The last part of the process includes some counterintuitive steps that may not make much sense but are still required in order to make this work. These steps are not required for earlier versions of Xcode and may no longer be required for more recent versions of PhoneGap as they are released.

Launch the new PhoneGap project by clicking the Run icon in the upper-left corner of the Xcode window. Xcode will build the application, launch the default iPhone simulator, and then display the error message shown in Figure 6-8. Don't panic; this is expected behavior. For some reason, the PhoneGap new project wizard doesn't create the web content files when the project is first created; instead, it creates them the first time the application is launched, and even then it creates them in what appears to be the wrong location. At this point, close the iPhone simulator by opening the iOS Simulator menu and selecting Quit iOS Simulator.

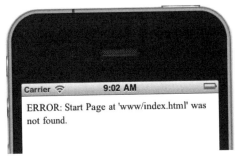

Figure 6-8   First launch of a new PhoneGap application in the iPhone simulator

Next, open Finder and navigate to the folder where you created the Xcode project, as shown in Figure 6-9. Notice the www folder highlighted in the figure; it contains the default web content files for the new PhoneGap project. What you're going to need to do here is drag the www folder onto the project in Xcode. Do not drag the www folder onto the project's folder in Finder, but instead drag it onto the PhoneGap project's entry in the Xcode navigator area, as shown in Figure 6-10.

	Name	Date Modified	Date Created	Size
FAVORITES	About Stacks	Aug 2, 2011 10:35 AM	Jun 10, 2011 6:33 PM	7.9 MI
All My Files	▼ Development	Today 9:04 AM	Today 8:49 AM	–
www	▼ HelloWorld	Today 9:04 AM	Today 8:50 AM	–
AirDrop	▶ HelloWorld	Today 8:50 AM	Today 8:50 AM	–
Applications	HelloWorld.xcodeproj	Today 8:50 AM	Today 8:50 AM	81 K
Desktop	▶ www	Today 9:01 AM	Today 9:01 AM	–
Documents	▶ PhoneGapLib	Today 7:00 AM	Today 7:00 AM	–
Downloads	▶ Snagit	Aug 4, 2011 10:01 AM	Aug 4, 2011 10:01 AM	–
Movies	▶ Virtual Machines	Aug 22, 2011 9:25 PM	May 21, 2011 8:14 PM	–
Music	▶ workspace	Yesterday 3:10 PM	Yesterday 3:10 PM	–
Pictures				
SHARED				

Figure 6-9   The PhoneGap project's web content folder in Finder

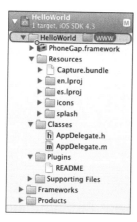

Figure 6-10   Dragging a PhoneGap project's web content into Xcode

To make this process easier, position Xcode and Finder so they take up only a portion of the screen and are positioned next to each other. Drag the folder over, and with the www folder contents positioned over the highest-level folder in the PhoneGap project (as shown in Figure 6-10), release the mouse button. Xcode will prompt you to select how copied the files are referenced in the Xcode project (Figure 6-11). Select the option "Create folder references for any added folders," and then click the Finish button to continue.

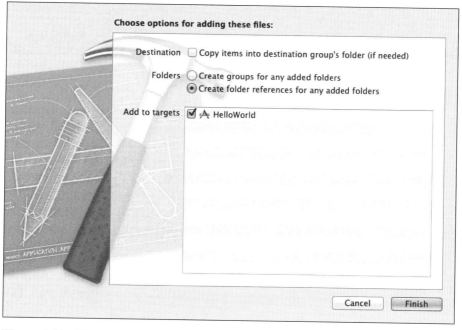

Figure 6-11   Xcode: options for adding files to a project

At this point, the new Xcode project will now have a reference to the web content files it needs, and you should be able to see the contents of the www folder in the Navigator area shown on the left side of Figure 6-12. Simply click the index.html file in the navigator to open the file in the Editor area, as shown in the figure.

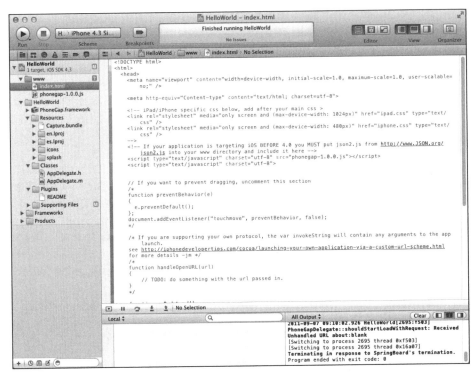

Figure 6-12 A new PhoneGap project in Xcode

As shown in the figure, the default iOS project for PhoneGap contains instructions and code designed to help a beginning PhoneGap developer build a better application. For your applications, you will simply augment the provided code with the appropriate HTML, CSS, and JavaScript for your application. For the example in this chapter, we'll use the code from the HelloWorld3 application from Chapter 2.

Testing iOS PhoneGap Applications

You've already seen how to launch a PhoneGap application in Xcode. Simply select the iPhone or iPad simulator version you want to test on, and then click the Run button in the upper-left corner of the Xcode UI. Xcode will build the application, launch the selected simulator, load the application into the simulator, and start the application. With the sample application code included in the default PhoneGap project, the application will display the screen shown in Figure 6-13.

Figure 6-13   Sample PhoneGap application running in the iPhone Simulator

7

Configuring a Symbian Development Environment for PhoneGap

On the Symbian platform, PhoneGap applications are implemented as Web Runtime (WRT) widgets, a standard application type for Symbian devices. With WRT, a web application's files are simply packaged into a compressed file before being deployed to mobile devices. There are some similarities here with the W3C widget specification described in Chapter 5, but since WRT widgets predate the specification, they are configured and packaged differently.

Symbian PhoneGap applications can be built on systems running Macintosh OS, Linux, or Microsoft Windows. Before getting started with Symbian development, you will need to install the PhoneGap framework using the instructions provided in Appendix A. In addition to the default PhoneGap files to build PhoneGap applications for Symbian, you will need to install the Nokia Web Tools as well as have access to the Make command-line utility.

Installing the Nokia Web Tools

Nokia offers a complete suite of tools for web development on the Symbian platform called Nokia Web Tools. Unfortunately, the most recent editions of the Nokia

SDK removed support for testing WRT applications with a simulator. To be able to work with PhoneGap applications on Symbian, you will need to download version 1.2 of Nokia Web Tools located at www.tinyurl.com/7b7nyng. Do not download the latest version of the SDK.

Download the appropriate file for the operating system your development system is running, launch the installer, and then follow the prompts to complete the installation.

 Note: The Nokia Web Tools SDK has an automatic update facility built in. Since we require version 1.2 of the SDK, you cannot allow the automatic update to happen.

Assuming you will want to use your favorite web content editor for PhoneGap development, most of the tools included in the download will likely go unused. The important tool for PhoneGap development is the web application simulator (called Web App Simulator on Windows and WebSDKSimulator on Macintosh OS), which will be described at the end of the chapter.

Installing the Make Utility

The default PhoneGap project for Symbian includes a makefile used by the Make utility to package the application for distribution to Symbian devices. Macintosh computers already include the appropriate files needed to process the makefile. For systems running Microsoft Windows, you will need to install additional software.

For Windows users, point your browser of choice to www.cygwin.com, and download the Cygwin installation file `setup.exe`. Launch the Cygwin installation program, and follow the prompts to install the software.

By default, Cygwin installs a minimal set of applications. At one point during the installation process, the installer will prompt you to select additional packages to install with Cygwin, as shown in Figure 7-1. For Symbian PhoneGap development, you will need to add the Make and Zip utilities to the list of programs installed during the installation.

You can either browse the categories listed in the dialog to locate the particular utility or type the utility's name in the search box on the dialog and press Enter. Once you have located the utility, click the refresh indicator on the line for the particular utility. This will change the option from Skip to the particular version of the utility being installed, as shown in Figure 7-1. Once both required utilities have been added to the installation, click the Next button to continue with the installation.

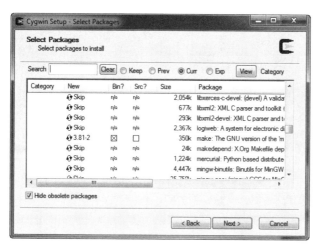

Figure 7-1   Cygwin installation: Select Packages dialog

At the conclusion of the installation, you should have a Cygwin icon on the desktop. When you double-click the icon, a Windows command window will open and display a dollar sign prompt indicating it is waiting for you to type in a command. At this time, we won't be using Cygwin, so type **exit** and press the Enter key to close the Cygwin window. We'll get back to that later.

By default, Cygwin configures its start-up folder to point to the Cygwin installation's home folder (c:\cygwin\home\ in the default installation location). It's likely your PhoneGap application projects will be in a different folder, so you will need to reconfigure Cygwin to use your source code folder as its root folder. This is accomplished by setting the HOME environment variable in Windows. To do this, open the Windows Control Panel, select System or right-click My Computer, and select Properties. In the System Properties application, click the Advanced System Settings tab, and then click the Environment Variables button on the bottom of the window.

Windows will display a dialog that lists the environment variables defined in the system. At the bottom of the dialog is the listing of system variables, the system-wide environment variables that affect all users. Click the New button in the System variables section of the dialog, and Windows will display a dialog similar to the one shown in Figure 7-2. Enter **HOME** in the Variable Name field, and for Variable Value enter the full path pointing to the folder you will be using for source code. Click the OK button to create the system variable, and then click OK again to close the Environment Variables dialog.

To test the changes you just made, open a Cygwin command prompt by double-clicking the Cygwin icon on the Windows desktop. At the command prompt, type ls, and then press the Enter key; if everything is configured correctly, you should see a directory listing of your source code folder.

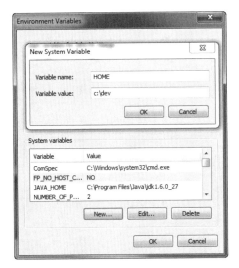

Figure 7-2 Adding a new Windows system variable

Creating a Symbian PhoneGap Project

The PhoneGap download package contains the skeleton of a simple Symbian PhoneGap application you can use to create new PhoneGap projects. Figure 7-3 shows the file structure for the project. To create a new Symbian PhoneGap application, simply copy the Symbian folder from the PhoneGap installation location to your project's source code folder, and then change the copied folder's name to the name of the new application project.

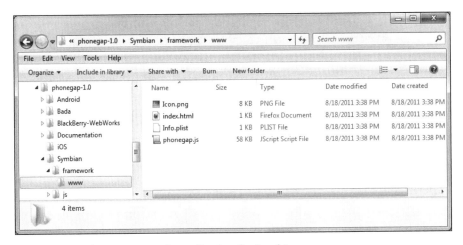

Figure 7-3 PhoneGap sample application for Symbian

As shown in Figure 7-3, the project's web content has been placed in the \framework\ www folder. Edit the index.html file and the other content in the folder to match the needs of your application.

Configuring Application Settings

Options for a Symbian WRT widget are defined in an XML-based configuration file called info.plist stored alongside the widget's web content, as shown in Figure 7-3. A sample info.plist file is shown here:

```
<?xml version="1.0" encoding="UTF-8"?>
<!DOCTYPE plist PUBLIC "-//Nokia//DTD PLIST 1.0//EN"
   "http://www.nokia.com/DTDs/plist-1.0.dtd">
<plist version="1.0">
<dict>
  <key>DisplayName</key>
  <string>HelloWorld</string>
  <key>Identifier</key>
  <string>com.phonegapbook.helloworld</string>
  <key>Version</key>
  <string>1.0</string>
  <key>AllowNetworkAccess</key>
  <true/>
  <key>MainHTML</key>
  <string>index.html</string>
  <key>MiniViewEnabled</key>
  <false/>
</dict>
</plist>
```

The widget's settings are defined as a dictionary of key/string pairs, as shown in the example. For each key defined within the file, there's a corresponding string value that defines the value associated with the key:

- DisplayName: Displays the string value displayed along with the widget's icon on the smartphone's home screen

- Identifier: Unique identifier identifying the widget

- Version: The version number for the widget

- AllowNetworkAccess: Controls whether the widget is allowed to access network resources (remote servers and so on)

- `MainHTML`: Identifies the file name for the application's start-up HTML page

- `MiniViewEnabled`: Controls whether the widget is designed to be a home page widget, an application that renders a content area on the device's home screen

To change settings for a widget, simply open the file using your text or XML editor of choice, make the appropriate changes for your widget, and save the file.

Modifying HelloWorld3 for Symbian

The HelloWorld3 application from Chapter 2 won't run on Symbian without modification. For a reason unknown to me, the `onLoad` event attribute for the HTML `<body>` tag doesn't work correctly, so you have to embed the code that adds the `deviceready` event listener directly within the HTML header, as shown in the following example:

```
<!DOCTYPE html>
<html>
  <head>
    <meta http-equiv="Content-type" content="text/html;
      charset=utf-8">
    <meta name="viewport" id="viewport"
      content="width=device-width, height=device-height,
      initial-scale=1.0, maximum-scale=1.0, user-scalable=no;"/>
    <script type="text/javascript" charset="utf-8"
      src="phonegap.js"></script>
    <script type="text/javascript" charset="utf-8">

document.addEventListener("deviceready", onDeviceReady,
  false);

function onDeviceReady() {
  //Get the appInfo DOM element
  var element = document.getElementById('appInfo');
  //replace it with specific information about the device
  //running the application
  element.innerHTML = 'PhoneGap (version ' +
    device.phonegap + ')<br />' + device.platform + ' ' +
    device.name + ' (version ' + device.version + ').';
}
```

```
    </script>
  </head>
  <body>
    <h1>HelloWorld3</h1>
    <p>This is a PhoneGap application that makes calls to the
      PhoneGap APIs.</p>
    <p id="appInfo">Waiting for PhoneGap Initialization to
      complete</p>
  </body>
</html>
```

Packaging Symbian PhoneGap Projects

When you're ready to test the application in a simulator or deploy the application to a device, you must first package the application. Packaging is essentially zipping the application's files into a zip archive and then changing the extension of the archive from `.zip` to `.wgz`. If you want, you can zip up the files manually and then change the file extension, but the Symbian PhoneGap project comes with a makefile that can be used to automate the packaging process.

 Note: When using a terminal window to navigate around in a file system, use the `cd` command to change directories and the `ls` command to list a folder's contents.

On Macintosh computers, open a terminal window; then navigate to the project's root folder. On Windows computers, launch Cygwin; then navigate to the project's root folder. Type `make` and press Enter to start the process; the terminal window will display a series of messages as the application is packaged, as shown in Figure 7-4. As you can see from the figure, the makefile first consolidates many of the PhoneGap JavaScript libraries into a single file called `phonegap.js`, creates a zip file containing the widget's web content, and then renames the file to the appropriate `.wgz` extension.

At this point, the PhoneGap application has been packaged into a file called `app.wgz` and can be loaded into the Symbian Web App Simulator or deployed to a real device. To change the file name for the packaged application, edit the makefile and change any references to `app.wgz` to the appropriate file name for your application.

Figure 7-4 Packaging a Symbian PhoneGap application using Make

Testing Symbian PhoneGap Applications

To test PhoneGap widgets for Symbian, launch the Symbian Web Application Simulator (the simulator application icon is labeled Web App Simulator on Windows and WebSDKSimulator on Macintosh OS). When the simulator launches, it will open two windows on the screen; the first is the toolbar (shown in Figure 7-5), a sort of simulator controller that allows you to poke and prod at the simulator while it's running, and the second is the device simulator window (shown in Figure 7-6). You will use the toolbar when loading widgets into the simulator and when debugging widgets.

Figure 7-5 Symbian Web App Simulator toolbar

 Note: If the option for the web simulator is missing, check to make sure you didn't inadvertently install a version of the Nokia Web Tools SDK newer than version 1.2.

To test a PhoneGap widget, launch the simulator, click the File button on the toolbar, navigate to the folder where the widget's `.wgz` file is located, and open the file. The widget will load in the simulator and then display a screen similar to the one shown in Figure 7-6.

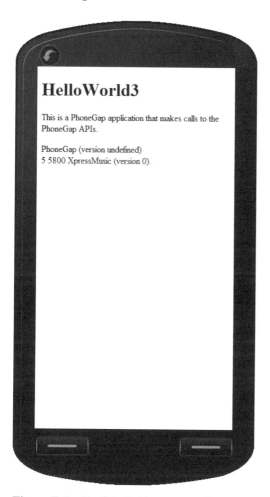

Figure 7-6 Symbian Web App Simulator

Notice that the HelloWorld3 application isn't displaying as much device information as with the same application on other platforms. It's clear that the PhoneGap development team has some work to do on Symbian.

The simulator represents a real device, and touch interactions with the device screen are performed using the mouse. Use the Location and Accelerator buttons on the toolbar to simulate a particular GPS location and control the perceived orientation of the device. Use the Events button to control events affecting the simulated device such as adding or removing power or a memory card, receiving SMS or MMS messages, and more.

The toolbar also provides capabilities that help with debugging widgets. Click the Web Inspector button to open the Web Inspector, as shown in Figure 7-7. The Web Inspector is essentially the Eclipse debug window with styling to match the other Nokia tools. You can click the different buttons across the top of the window to inspect and interact with different aspects of the widget currently running within the simulator including setting breakpoints, setting watches, evaluating variables, and more.

Figure 7-7　Symbian Web Inspector

8

Configuring a Windows Phone Development Environment for PhoneGap

Windows Phone is the most recent addition to the list of supported device platforms for PhoneGap; support for Windows Phone was added to the PhoneGap 1.1 release. Setting up a development environment for Windows Phone is similar to the iOS development setup; all you need to install is the standard development environment and the default PhoneGap installation files, and you're ready to go.

The Windows Phone development tools and device simulators are supported only on Microsoft Windows. You will need a Windows PC or a Macintosh computer running Windows or a Windows virtual machine in order to develop PhoneGap applications for Windows Phone.

Installing the Windows Phone Development Tools

The Microsoft Windows Phone SDK 7.1 provides the complete suite of tools you need to build mobile applications for the Windows Phone OS. Point Microsoft Internet Explorer to http://create.msdn.com and follow the prompts to download the SDK.

Note: The Windows Phone SDK has some hefty system requirements; be sure that the development system you have selected for Windows Phone development meets or exceeds the minimum requirements.

The Windows Phone Emulator will run only on current hardware with hardware graphics acceleration, so if you have an older machine, you should probably plan on a video card upgrade. When you try to test PhoneGap applications on a system that isn't supported by the emulator, the PhoneGap application won't even display any content on the emulator screen when it launches.

The SDK installer you downloaded won't take very long to download and consists of a simple application that pulls down the full SDK components as needed during installation. The SDK consists of Microsoft Visual Studio 2010 Express for Windows Phone, Windows Phone Emulator, and several other tools that aren't related to PhoneGap development. There's a lot of stuff included, so be sure to allocate a lot of time for the installation. Launch the downloaded file and follow the prompts to install the SDK. At the conclusion of the SDK installation, you will be prompted to launch the Visual Studio; go ahead and do that, if only to confirm that the installation completed successfully.

Once you've verified that Visual Studio installed correctly, close Visual Studio, and then install PhoneGap using the instructions provided in Appendix A. With the PhoneGap files installed into Visual Studio, your system is ready for PhoneGap development.

Creating a Windows Phone PhoneGap Project

To create a new PhoneGap project for Windows Phone, open Visual Studio; then open the File menu and select New Project. In the dialog that appears, select the Visual C# category in the navigator on the left side of the dialog. Select the GapAppStarter option, provide a name and destination for the application, and click the OK button, as shown in Figure 8-1.

Visual Studio will create a new PhoneGap project folder with a default index.html and style sheet and open the IDE window. In the Solution Explorer shown on the right side of Figure 8-2, expand the www folder, then double-click the index.html file to open the file in the editor.

Figure 8-1   Visual Studio New Project dialog

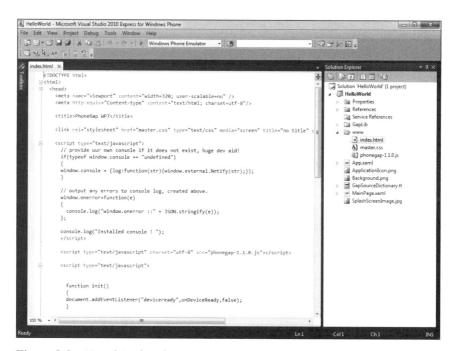

Figure 8-2   Visual Studio PhoneGap project window

To add new content to the application, simply add additional files to the Solution Explorer either directly from within the IDE or manually from the file system (by adding the files to the project's folder on the hard drive). When new content is added to the folder, you must refresh the project's file manifest included in the project. To do this, in the Visual Studio Solution Explorer for the project, right-click the GapSourceDictionary.tt item and select Run Custom Tool; then follow the prompts to execute the process. This will update the contents of the GapSourceDictionary.xml file included with the project, which instructs the packager on which content files to include with the packaged application.

One of the things the default sample application for Windows Phone does is add some additional code to the project to enable a console log function, as shown in bold in the following listing. As mentioned in Chapter 2, PhoneGap leverages the console functions enabled by the WebKit rendering engine. On Windows Phone, Microsoft is using its own rendering engine, so the WebKit features won't be available to the program. This code makes logging capabilities available within any PhoneGap application.

```
<!DOCTYPE html>
<html>
  <head>
    <title>HelloWorld3</title>
    <meta name="viewport" content="width=320;
      user-scalable=no" />
    <meta http-equiv="Content-type"
      content="text/html; charset=utf-8"/>
    <link rel="stylesheet" href="master.css" type="text/css"
      media="screen" title="no title" charset="utf-8"/>
    <script type="text/javascript">

      // provide our own console if it does not exist
      if(typeof window.console == "undefined") {
        window.console =
          {log:function(str){window.external.Notify(str);}};
      }

      // output any errors to console log, created above.
      window.onerror=function(e) {
        console.log("window.onerror ::" + JSON.stringify(e));
      };
      console.log("Installed console ! ");

    </script>
    <script type="text/javascript" charset="utf-8"
      src="phonegap-1.1.0.js"></script>
    <script type="text/javascript">
```

```
    function bodyLoad() {
      document.addEventListener("deviceready",
        onDeviceReady,false);
    }

    function onDeviceReady() {
      //Get the appInfo DOM element
      var element = document.getElementById('appInfo');
      //replace it with specific information about the device
      //running the application
      element.innerHTML = 'PhoneGap (version ' +
        device.phonegap + ')<br />' + device.platform + ' ' +
        device.name + ' (version ' + device.version + ').';
    }

  </script>

</head>
<body onLoad="bodyLoad();">
  <h1>HelloWorld3</h1>
  <p>This is a PhoneGap application that makes calls to the
    PhoneGap APIs.</p>
  <p id="appInfo">Waiting for PhoneGap Initialization to
    complete</p>
</body>
</html>
```

Testing Windows Phone PhoneGap Applications

Visual Studio supports testing applications on the Windows Phone emulator and on physical Windows Phone devices. When testing applications from within Visual Studio, the execution target for the application is controlled by the option selected in the toolbar drop-down highlighted on the right side of Figure 8-3.

Figure 8-3   Visual Studio toolbar

To test the application, open the Debug menu and select Start Debugging, press the F5 key, or click the green triangle to the left of the target device drop-down field shown in Figure 8-3. Visual Studio will do the following:

1. Build the application.

2. (Optionally) Launch the emulator if selected as the target and not already running.

3. Deploy the application to the selected target.

4. Launch the application on the emulator.

Using the modified version of the HelloWorld3 sample application from Chapter 2, the default emulator will display a screen similar to the one shown in Figure 8-4.

Figure 8-4   Windows Phone emulator

9

Using PhoneGap Build

As you can see from the previous chapters, building PhoneGap applications for multiple mobile platforms can be a challenging endeavor. You have to install each platform's SDK, as well as IDEs, build tools, simulators or emulators, and more. As you read through the chapters, you probably said to yourself, "There has got to be an easier way!" Fortunately, there is. The PhoneGap Build service provides the means to build PhoneGap applications in the cloud, without the need to install a bunch of software on a developer workstation. All you have to do is write your web applications using your web content editor of choice, upload the files to the cloud, and then let PhoneGap Build do the rest.

PhoneGap Build currently supports the following mobile platforms:

- Android
- BlackBerry
- iOS
- Symbian
- webOS

This chapter will describe how to use the PhoneGap Build service. It's important to note that the service is still in beta and the UI for the service changes dramatically on a regular basis. By the time you read this, it will look completely different, although the process should be about the same (or similar) to what is described here.

The Fit

You may be asking yourself if PhoneGap Build is so cool, why would you ever want to use the individual development SDKs to build your PhoneGap applications? With PhoneGap Build still in beta, there's no clear information regarding how widely adopted it will be by the PhoneGap community. The fact that it's going to be a for-fee service might also affect adoption of the service.

As you'll see later in the chapter, PhoneGap Build currently uses a single application icon and a single splash screen image for all versions of the application (except for iOS). If your application needs a different branding or look and feel on different platforms, then you will need to use the native SDK approach rather than PhoneGap Build.

In my testing of the service, I found that the build process could be quite slow, although this could have been caused by the service's beta status. With Build, the process of getting the built application onto a device, emulator, or simulator was more cumbersome than it would be on some platforms using native SDKs or even command-line tools. On platforms like Android or iOS, since there's an IDE to work with, saving your code and then building and deploying to a simulator or emulator takes a matter of seconds.

If you're like me, you'll write code and then save and test regularly; the delays caused by using Build could extend the length of time you spend working on the application.

On the other hand, as I worked on the chapters that followed, I found that building a single application and uploading it to the Build service in order to generate applications for multiple platforms made it very easy to put each sample application through its paces on multiple mobile platforms simultaneously. Without access to the Build service, it would have taken me much more time to accomplish what I needed for this book.

Getting Started

Before you can use PhoneGap Build for your PhoneGap projects, you must first create an account on the PhoneGap Build web site. Point your browser of choice to http://build.phonegap.com to begin the process. PhoneGap Build is free during the beta period but will switch to a for-fee service when it's released into production. Table 9-1 lists the planned pricing options for the service.

Table 9-1 PhoneGap Build Pricing Structure

	Developer	**Starter**	**Team**	**Corporate**
Pricing	Free	$12/month or $120/year	$30/month or $300/year	$90/month or $900/year
Public apps	Unlimited	Unlimited	Unlimited	Unlimited
Private apps	1	3	10	25
Private collaborators	1	1	3	10

Configuration

Several of the mobile platforms that PhoneGap Build supports require that applications are digitally signed before they can be loaded on devices or deployed to the appropriate application stores. For that reason, you must configure the PhoneGap Build service with the appropriate signing keys for each of the supported platforms.

For Android and BlackBerry devices, the PhoneGap Build process will work without any signing keys, but you will want to configure your specific keys for those platforms before releasing an application for distribution through an application store. Android applications require only a signature before deployment to the Android Market. BlackBerry applications will not run on a device without being signed. By default, PhoneGap Build signs BlackBerry applications using Nitobi's signing keys, with the expectation that you will provide your own signing keys before releasing the application to distribution.

For iOS development, Apple tightly controls the signing process and severely limits what a developer can do with an application. For this reason, PhoneGap Build will not even build an iOS application without the appropriate developer credentials first being configured in PhoneGap Build.

To configure signing keys in PhoneGap Build, open your browser of choice, and then log into the PhoneGap Build web site using the credentials you supplied when creating an account. Click the "Edit account" link currently located on the bottom of the page. PhoneGap Build will open a page similar to the one shown in Figure 9-1.

For each of the platforms you will be supporting that require application signing, click the "Add a key" link. PhoneGap Build will open a dialog similar to the one shown in Figure 9-2. Depending on the mobile platform, you may need to upload multiple files as shown in the figure (Android uses only a single file; BlackBerry and iOS require two). Provide a title for the set of keys, select the appropriate files as needed, and click the Create button. Repeat this process as many times as needed for each set of keys you will be using and each platform you will be supporting.

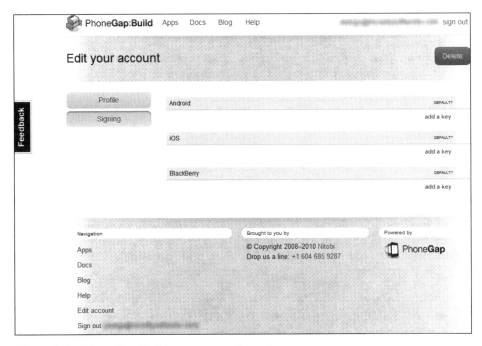

Figure 9-1   PhoneGap Build: account configuration

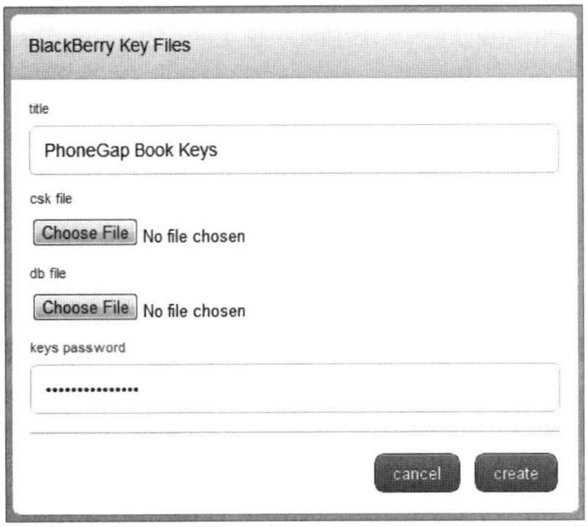

Figure 9-2   PhoneGap Build: key file upload dialog

While a particular developer might need only a single set of keys for Android and BlackBerry applications, the title field shown in the dialog allows you to give a unique name to each set of keys being defined within PhoneGap Build. Since a developer may be building applications for multiple customers and each customer will have a specific set of keys, this allows a developer to define settings for each set of signing keys they work with and then pick the appropriate keys to use on an application-by-application basis. Since Apple's provisioning profiles are associated with one or more iOS devices, a developer might define different sets of keys depending on which devices will be working with a particular build of an application (during testing for example), switching to a publically distributable profile before releasing through Apple's App Store.

Once you've defined a set of keys for a particular platform, you can configure PhoneGap Build to use that key as the default key for the platform. To enable this feature, in the list of keys shown in Figure 9-1, simply enable the Default radio button (not shown in the current figure) next to the key you want to use as the default for the selected platform.

Creating an Application for PhoneGap Build

When working with PhoneGap Build, a PhoneGap application can be nothing more than a simple `index.html` file or as complicated as a folder containing the `index.html` file plus additional JavaScript, CSS, media files, and any additional content the application needs. The application in this case is simply the web content files, nothing else. Unlike what you saw with configuring an application for any of the supported mobile platforms individually, with PhoneGap Build there don't have to be any special files or special folder structures for the application. All you have to do is get the web content up to the PhoneGap Build server, and it takes care of everything else for you.

Chapter 2 explained that the PhoneGap JavaScript file was named differently depending on which mobile platform you were working with, but with PhoneGap Build your application simply has to make a reference to a generic `phonegap.js` file, as shown next. You don't even need to include the `phonegap.js` file in the package uploaded to the server; PhoneGap Build will make sure the latest version of PhoneGap is copied over and used by the project.

```
<script type="text/javascript" charset="utf-8"
  src="phonegap.js"></script>
```

PhoneGap Build will use default settings such as application icon, splash screen, security settings, and more unless you tell it differently. To configure application-specific settings for your PhoneGap application, PhoneGap Build uses the `config.xml` file defined as part of the W3C Widget Packaging and XML Configuration specification described in Chapter 5.

The specification includes the means to define a single set of application icons (a home screen and optionally, for BlackBerry, a hover image) and a loading screen (splash) image. Unfortunately, application icon resolution (and sometimes graphics file format) varies across mobile device platforms and even across mobile devices. To fix this particular problem (and others), the PhoneGap Build developers have implemented some PhoneGap and PhoneGap Build–specific settings to the options available in the `config.xml` file.

As of this writing, the PhoneGap Build development team is still making enhancements to the features, options, and configuration settings for the service. Because of this, it's best to refer to their up-to-date documentation for specifics on the supported `config.xml` file options. Anything I wrote here about those settings could be nullified at any time by the PhoneGap Build development team. Detailed information about the PhoneGap Build–supported settings can be found at http://build.phonegap.com/docs/config-xml.

One of the things I learned when working with the service is that when building applications for iOS, PhoneGap Build requires that the `config.xml` file's `widget` element contains an `id` attribute that contains a unique in reverse domain format, as shown in the following example:

```
<widget xmlns=http://www.w3.org/ns/widgets
  xmlns:rim=http://www.blackberry.com/ns/widgets
  version="1.0.0.0" id="com.phonegapbook.kitchensink">
```

If you don't have that setting defined, the application will not build.

Creating a PhoneGap Build Project

When the PhoneGap web application is ready, it's time to upload the files and start the build process.

Upload Options

PhoneGap Build supports several mechanisms for delivering the application's files to the build server:

- **Index.html Upload**: For applications that don't use any external Java-Script, CSS, or media files, simply upload the `index.html` file to the PhoneGap Build server. PhoneGap Build will build the application using default settings for all options.

- **Zip Upload**: For applications that consist of more than one content file (optionally including the `config.xml` file), compress the application's files into a zip file and upload to the PhoneGap Build server.

- **Pull from Repository**: PhoneGap Build retrieves the application's files from a public Git or Subversion repository. You can even create a new Git repository, hosted by PhoneGap Build, while creating a new PhoneGap Build project.

New Project

When you log into PhoneGap Build and there are no applications defined, PhoneGap Build will prompt you to create a new application project, as shown in Figure 9-3. If adding an additional application project to your account, click the Apps menu item at the top of the page, and then click the New App button.

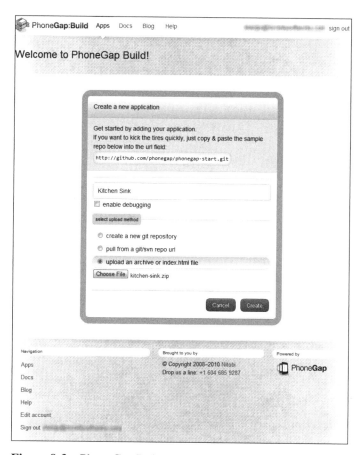

Figure 9-3   PhoneGap Build: new project dialog

In the dialog, specify a name for the application and the method you'll use to provide Build with the application's web content files. The "enable debugging" option will be described later. Depending on which option is chosen for "select upload method," you will be prompted either to provide the files for upload or for information related to the repository where the application's files are or will be stored. When everything is set correctly, click the Create button to start the build process. PhoneGap Build will update the page to indicate build status as the process runs, as shown in Figure 9-4.

Figure 9-4   PhoneGap Build: waiting for the build to complete

The Build Process

Unless you have a default key configured for iOS, PhoneGap Build will immediately register an error (the exclamation point icon shown in Figure 9-4) for the iOS application because PhoneGap Build doesn't have any provisioning profile for the application. You'll see how to fix that error later. In a few seconds, or a few minutes, depending on how busy the PhoneGap Build servers are, the screen will update to show that the build process has completed for each platform, as shown in Figure 9-5.

Project Configuration

Click on the application's name to view details for the application project. PhoneGap Build will display a page similar to the one shown in Figure 9-6.

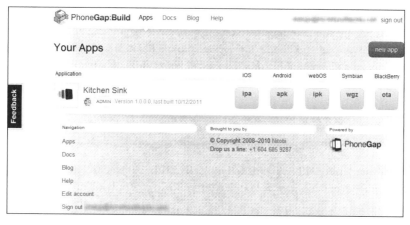

Figure 9-5   PhoneGap Build: build complete

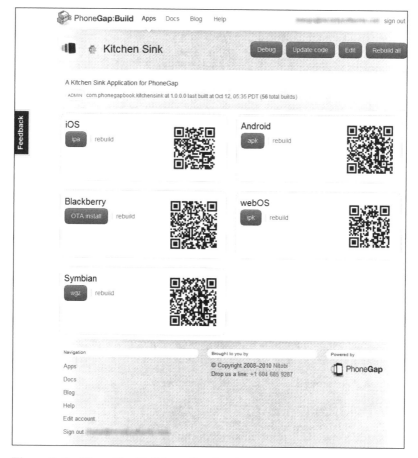

Figure 9-6   PhoneGap Build: application details

If you included a `config.xml` file with your application's content files, PhoneGap Build will ignore the project title you supplied when you created the project and instead use the value specified for the config file's `Name` element. The application's description, displayed in Figure 9-6, will be populated from the config file's `Description` element.

From this page you can download or install the application executables for each supported mobile platform; this will be described later in the chapter. For now, let's fix the issue with the iOS application.

The warning symbol shown for the iOS application is indicating that the appropriate signing information has not been defined for the application. To fix this problem, click the Edit button at the top of the page; then on the page that opens, click the Signing button. PhoneGap Build will display a page similar to the one shown in Figure 9-7.

For each of the operating systems, select a key from the drop-down list shown in Figure 9-7, and click the Update Code button to save your changes and build the application with the selected signing keys.

Figure 9-7 Setting the signing options for the application

Dealing with Build Issues

When the build service encounters an error building an application for a particular platform, it will display a frowny face for the particular application's build status, as shown in Figure 9-8. In this case, it's indicating that the BlackBerry build process failed.

Figure 9-8   PhoneGap Build: build errors

If you hover your mouse over the frowny icon, the page will display information about the error, as shown in Figure 9-9. If you click the icon, a page will open that lists possible error conditions and recommended solutions for each.

Figure 9-9   PhoneGap Build: build error information

At this point, you will need to dig into the error condition and resolve the problem before continuing. With the service still in beta and the Nitobi folks still working out the kinks, sometimes simply rebuilding the application solves the problem.

As indicated in Figure 9-9, the BlackBerry build process found that there were invalid characters in file names within the application. This particular error has popped up inconsistently with the applications I've built using the service. If you looked at the application's content, you would see that the file names for jQuery Mobile have dashes in them. If you remove the dashes from the file names, update `index.html` to reflect the file name changes, and upload the updated content to the Build service, you should see that the application builds correctly.

The problem, though, is that this particular issue doesn't occur with every application; it's hit-or-miss whether this will occur with any particular build. Additionally, the BlackBerry WebWorks Packager utility (described in Chapter 5), the utility actually doing the build for BlackBerry, doesn't have any issues with dashes in a file name. This is a clearly a bug with PhoneGap Build that has been in place for a very long time, and I hope it will be addressed before the service goes live or soon thereafter.

Testing Applications

You can load applications created by PhoneGap Build onto a device, simulator, or emulator in several ways.

OTA Download

When the PhoneGap Build process completes, the application's entry on the service's web site contains links to the individual application executables for each supported platform, as shown in Figure 9-10. On platforms that support application downloads, on a physical device, or from a device simulator or emulator, you can open a web browser, navigate to the PhoneGap Build web site, log in, and then download the application directly.

Figure 9-10   PhoneGap Build: application download buttons

For Android, Symbian, and webOS, the download link points directly to the application executable, so if you want to download the file first from a desktop browser and then transfer the file to a device for testing, that's not a problem. For BlackBerry, it points you to the application's .jad file, which is essentially a text file pointing to the installation executable. If you configure signing keys for the BlackBerry application, a link will be provided that allows you to download the installation files separately.

You will also find similar links on the application details page shown in Figure 9-6.

Via Camera

You can also load an application using a code-scanner application on a compatible smartphone. Many smartphone models ship with some sort of code-scanning application preinstalled. If one is not preinstalled, several free code scanner applications are available in the smartphone app stores; AT&T even offers a free one for many common mobile platforms at www.wireless.att.com/businesscenter/solutions/mobile-marketing/mobile-barcode-download.jsp.

To view an application's code, open the application's details page shown in Figure 9-6. For each platform, PhoneGap Build displays a two-dimensional code, as shown in Figure 9-11. To load the application on a physical device, launch a code-scanning application on the device, and point it at the appropriate code for the operating system the device is running. When the scanner application recognizes the code, it will launch the browser and open the downloadable version of the application.

Figure 9-11 PhoneGap Build: application scan code

Debug Mode

When you enable debug mode for an application, PhoneGap Build leverages the Weinre debug server (described in Chapter 2) to allow you to debug the built application directly on a device. With this feature enabled, PhoneGap Build modifies your PhoneGap application so it includes the Weinre JavaScript library `Target-script-min.js` and then exposes a debug server within the PhoneGap Build console, which allows you to interactively debug the application. Refer to Chapter 2 for more detailed information on how this process works.

When you look at the details page for an application that has been built with debug mode enabled, a Debug button will appear at the top of the page, as shown in Figure 9-12.

Figure 9-12 PhoneGap Build: debug-enabled application

Click the Debug button to begin a debug session on the server. The browser will open a new window and display the Weinre debug server console. At this point, the debug console is waiting for a debug-enabled version of the application to connect to the debug server. On a compatible, network-connected smartphone, open the browser, navigate to the PhoneGap Build web site, and install the application using the instructions provided in this section; then launch the application once the download has completed. After the application has launched and completed its initialization procedures, the application will automatically connect to the debug server. When the debug server receives a connection from the device, it will update the console with information about the device, as shown in Figure 9-13.

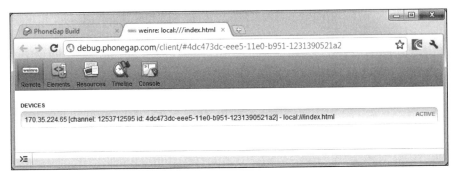

Figure 9-13 PhoneGap Build: Weinre debug console, device connected

At this point, you perform the standard debug functions supported by Weinre. As you interact with the application on the device, you can use the console to view console messages, inspect page elements (shown in Figure 9-14), and more. Refer to Chapter 2 or the Weinre documentation for information on the capabilities of Weinre.

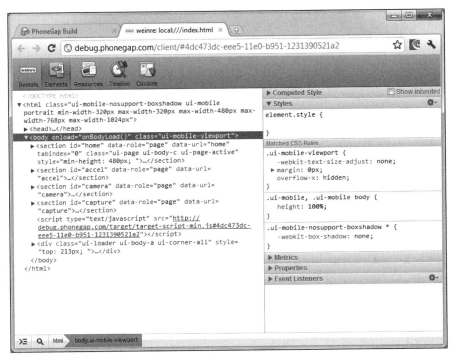

Figure 9-14 PhoneGap Build: Weinre debug console

Part III

PhoneGap APIs

This part of the book describes in detail each of the PhoneGap APIs and provides example code demonstrating how to use the functionality provided by each API.

10

Accelerometer

The Accelerometer API allows a PhoneGap application to determine a device's orientation in a three-dimensional space (using X, Y, and Z coordinates). The current PhoneGap API documentation claims that the values returned by the accelerometer indicate the changes in a device's motion through space, but in testing what the accelerometer returns are values that define the device's actual orientation in a three-dimensional space. If the accelerometer were actually measuring motion through space, then the accelerometer API would return no information when the device is stationary, which is not the case.

For example, on an Android device, with the device lying flat on a tabletop, the accelerometer will return approximately the following values: X:0, Y:0, Z:10. As the device is flipped so it's standing on its left edge, the values will adjust to approximately X:10, Y:0, Z:0. If you instead move the device so it's standing on its bottom edge, the values will adjust to approximately X:0, Y:10, Z:0. Standing the device on its top edge will result in approximate accelerometer values of X:0, Y:-10, Z:0. An application uses these values to determine how a user is holding the device and is most useful for games and interactive applications.

PhoneGap developers can query an API to determine a device's orientation at a particular time or can watch the accelerometer to monitor the device's acceleration repeatedly over a periodic time interval. Determining motion through space is simply a matter of comparing subsequent orientation measurements and calculating the difference between them.

The API returns accelerometer values that vary depending on the device OS. For example, devices running BlackBerry Device Software 7 return values from about –1000 to 1000, while Android devices as shown return values from about –10 to 10. Your applications will need to provide for this variance and adjust their accelerometer scaling depending on which mobile platform the application is running on. This is yet another reason why testing on physical devices and on all supported platforms is important for any developer.

Holding the device in position will result in some variance in values; the device is "moving" the tiniest bit after all, so your applications will have to adjust for minor movement of the device and respond to what are clearly true movements of the device through space. Most likely your application will simply ignore the last few decimal places in the measurement or convert to the nearest integer.

In most cases, you will need to test applications that use the Accelerometer API on physical devices. The iPhone simulator and the Android emulators, for example, don't include an option for setting device orientation except in the iPhone's case where you can simulate shaking the device. Only a physical device will give you the ability to put this API through its paces.

Unfortunately, there's no way with PhoneGap to determine programmatically whether a device has an accelerometer except to query the accelerometer and then deal with any errors that are returned. If your application relies upon the ability to determine a device's orientation, say for a driving game or a bubble level application, then you will likely need to abort the application when the accelerometer API returns an error.

Note: Not all smartphones have an accelerometer. The iPhone series of devices have always had one, but RIM didn't add one until the BlackBerry Storm running BlackBerry Device Software 4.7.

Querying Device Orientation

The Accelerometer API allows an application to query the current orientation of the device using the following code:

```
navigator.accelerometer.getCurrentAcceleration(onAccelSuccess,
   onAccelFailure);
```

The function takes as parameters the names of two functions: the onAccelSuccess function is executed when accelerometer data is available; the onAccelFailure function is executed when there is an error retrieving accelerometer data.

Accelerometer data is passed to the onAccelSuccess function through an acceleration object, namely, the accel object shown in the following example. The object encapsulates four values reflecting the current orientation (X, Y, and Z values plus a timestamp indicating when the measurement was taken) of the device, as shown here:

```
function onAccelSuccess(accel) {
  xPos = accel.x;
  yPos = accel.y;
  zPos = accel.z;
  tStamp = accel.timestamp;
}
```

If you think about it, there are probably not a lot of use cases for just determining the device's orientation a single time. In any game or application that truly uses orientation, determining the way the application user is orienting the device over time is much more useful than just checking it once. You could write the application so it periodically checks the device orientation manually (through repeated calls to getCurrentAcceleration), but defining an accelerometer watch (described in the next section) is a more efficient way to do this. If your application needs to perform a lot of calculation or do some work using network resources between checking orientation, then checking orientation when you want using this API would work, but you run the risk of the application not appearing responsive to the end user.

The iPhone doesn't support the concept of determining orientation through a direct API call; instead, you must use an accelerometer watch to obtain orientation information. In this case, a call to getCurrentAcceleration simply causes the successFunction to be called and passed the accelerometer value from the last firing of an accelerometer watch.

Let's take a look at a sample application that uses the getCurrentAcceleration API (see Example 10-1). The application creates a simple page with a button the user can click to refresh the device's orientation data within the page.

Example 10-1

```
<!DOCTYPE html>
<html>
  <head>
    <meta http-equiv="Content-type" content="text/html;
      charset=utf-8">
    <meta name="viewport" id="viewport"
      content="width=device-width, height=device-height,
      initial-scale=1.0, maximum-scale=1.0,
      user-scalable=no;" />
    <script type="text/javascript" charset="utf-8"
      src="phonegap.js"></script>
    <script type="text/javascript" charset="utf-8">
```

```
//Accelerometer content
var ac;
//PhoneGap Ready variable
var pgr = false;

function onBodyLoad() {
  document.addEventListener("deviceready", onDeviceReady,
    false);
}

function onDeviceReady() {
  //Get a handle we'll use to adjust the accelerometer
  //content
  ac = document.getElementById('accelInfo');

  //Set the variable that lets other parts of the program
  //know that PhoneGap is initialized
  pgr = true;
}

function getAcceleration() {
  if (pgr == true) {
    //Clear the current orientation
    ac.innerHTML = "";
    //get the current orientation
    navigator.accelerometer.getCurrentAcceleration(
      onAccelSuccess, onAccelFailure);
  } else {
    alert("Please wait,\nPhoneGap is not ready.");
  }
}

function onAccelSuccess(accel) {
  //We received something from the API, so...
  //first get the timestamp in a date object
  //so we can work with it
  var d = new Date(accel.timestamp);
  //Then replace the page's content with the
  //current acceleration retrieved from the API
  ac.innerHTML = "<b>Current acceleration</b><hr />X: " +
    accel.x + "<br />Y: " + accel.y + "<br />Z: " +
    accel.z + "<br />Timestamp: " + d.toLocaleString() +
    "<hr />Click the button to refresh.";
}

function onAccelFailure() {
  alert("Accelerometer error!");
}

</script>
```

```
    </head>
    <body onload="onBodyLoad()">
      <h1>Example 10-1</h1>
      <p>This is a PhoneGap application that measures
        Device acceleration using the Accelerometer API.</p>
      <p><input type="button"
        value="Refresh Orientation" onclick="getAcceleration();">
      </p>
      <p id="accelInfo">Nothing to see here (yet),
        click the button.</p>
      </body>
    </html>
```

The JavaScript code within the application starts by defining a couple of variables. The application uses the ac variable to give it an easy way to update the acceleration content every time the button is clicked. Since the application user can click the button before PhoneGap has finished initializing, the pgr variable is used as a flag to allow the application to determine whether the onDeviceReady function has been executed yet. When pgr is false, the application will not attempt to query the accelerometer.

When the user clicks the button, the application executes the getOrientation function, which calls the getCurrentAcceleration API and passes in the names of the functions that are executed on success (onAccelSuccess) and failure (onAccelFailure). After accelerometer values are retrieved, the API calls the onAccelSuccess function passing in the current accelerometer values. At this point, the application updates the current page with the accelerometer data.

When you run the application on an Android device, you will see a screen similar to the one shown in Figure 10-1.

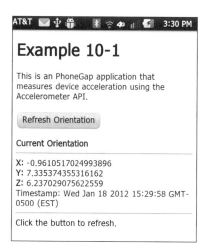

Figure 10-1   Example 10-1 running on an Android device

Watching a Device's Orientation

Instead of querying a device's orientation through repeated calls to `getCurrentAcceleration`, a PhoneGap application can set up an accelerometer watch that automatically measures accelerometer data at specific intervals. To define an accelerometer watch, use the following code:

```
watchID = navigator.accelerometer.watchAcceleration(
  onAccelSuccess, onAccelFailure, accelOptions);
```

This will enable the watch and, through the `accelOptions` object, define options that control how the watch operates.

As with `getCurrentAcceleration` (described in the previous section), the names of two functions are passed to the API when the watch is created. In the example shown, the `onAccelSuccess` function is executed when accelerometer data is available, and the `onAccelFailure` function is executed when there is an error retrieving accelerometer data.

The third parameter to `watchAcceleration` is an optional value that defines how often the watch fires. This watch frequency is passed to the function as an object, as shown in the following example:

```
var accelOptions = { frequency: 1000 };
```

The frequency value is represented in milliseconds (1 second = 1,000 milliseconds). If the `accelOptions` value is omitted, the watch defaults to measuring accelerometer data every 10 seconds.

In the example call to `watchAcceleration` shown earlier, you'll notice that the result of the call to `watchAcceleration` is assigned to the `watchID` variable. An application will use the `watchID` value later when canceling a watch when it is no longer needed, as shown in the following example:

```
navigator.accelerometer.clearWatch(watchID);
```

Let's take a look at Example 10-2, an application that uses the `watchAcceleration` API. This application is an extension of Example 10-1; it removes the Refresh button and instead automatically updates accelerometer data every half second (500 milliseconds).

Example 10-2

```
<!DOCTYPE html>
<html>
  <head>
    <meta http-equiv="Content-type" content="text/html;
      charset=utf-8">
```

```
    <meta name="viewport" id="viewport"
      content="width=device-width, height=device-height,
      initial-scale=1.0, maximum-scale=1.0, user-scalable=no;"
     />
    <script type="text/javascript" charset="utf-8"
      src="phonegap.js"></script>
    <script type="text/javascript" charset="utf-8">

      // Accelerometer watcher ID
      var awID;
      //Orientation content
      var ac;

      function onBodyLoad() {
        document.addEventListener("deviceready", onDeviceReady,
          false);
      }

      function onDeviceReady() {
        //Get a handle we'll use to adjust the
        //acceleration content
        ac = document.getElementById('accelInfo');

        //Accelerometer Options, read the accelerometer
        //every half second (500 milliseconds)
        var accelOptions = { frequency: 500 };

        //Add the accelerometer watcher
        awID = navigator.accelerometer.watchAcceleration(
          onAccelSuccess, onAccelFailure, accelOptions);
      }

      function onAccelSuccess(accel) {
        //Then replace the page's content with the
        //current orientation retrieved from the API
        ac.innerHTML = "<b>X:</b> " + accel.x +
          "<br /><b>Y:</b> " + accel.y +
          "<br /><b>Z:</b> " + accel.z;
      }

      function onAccelFailure() {
        alert("Accelerometer error! Clearing Watch ID");
        //Cancel the watch
        navigator.accelerometer.clearWatch(awID);
      }

    </script>
  </head>
```

```
<body onload="onBodyLoad()">
  <h1>Example 10-2</h1>
  <p>Apache PhoneGap Accelerometer Watcher</p>
  <p><b>Current Orientation</b><hr /></p>
  <p id="accelInfo">Waiting for PhoneGap to initialize.
    </p>
  <hr />
</body>
</html>
```

In the application's onDeviceReady function, the application first creates the accelOptions variable that defines the watch frequency. Then, the application creates the watch using a call to watchAccelerometer. Every half second, the application calls onAccelSuccess to update the page with the latest values from the accelerometer. When you run the application on an Android device, you will see a screen similar to the one shown in Figure 10-2.

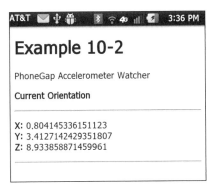

Figure 10-2   Example 10-2 running on an Android device

Be sure to check the PhoneGap API documentation at http://docs.phonegap.com/en/1.1.0/phonegap_accelerometer_accelerometer.md.html for information about platform-specific oddities with this particular API.

11

Camera

The PhoneGap Camera API provides an application with the ability to work with images, either captured directly from the camera or retrieved from the device's photo repository. When retrieving an image, the API can return either a URI pointing to the image file on the device's file system or the base64-encoded string representing the content from the image.

The API provides a single method, `navigator.camera.getPicture`, which is used to retrieve an image, and a `cameraOptions` object that's used to define parameters around how the image is obtained, how it's formatted, and more.

Applications can also use the PhoneGap Capture API to capture images using the camera. Refer to Chapter 12 for more information about this API. The Camera and Capture APIs are different enough that you will want to evaluate both before selecting an option for your application.

Accessing a Picture

To obtain a picture from the device, an application should execute the following function:

```
navigator.camera.getPicture( onCameraSuccess, onCameraError,
  cameraOptions );
```

Like other PhoneGap APIs, the call to `getPicture` requires that you pass in two functions that are executed on success and failure of the call. In this case, they're the `onCameraSuccess` and `onCameraError` functions. The `onCameraSuccess` function is executed when an image is obtained (I'll explain more about where the images come from and how you configure the API in the "Configuring Camera

Options" section later in this chapter). The onCameraError function is executed when the user cancels the process of retrieving an image once started or when an error occurs with the process.

Example 11-1 shows the Camera API being used with its default options. According to the PhoneGap API documentation, the cameraOptions parameter is optional, but that turns out to be true for some platforms and false on others. Let's take a look at the example application and then discuss the exceptions afterward.

Example 11-1

```html
<!DOCTYPE html>
<html>
  <head>
    <title>Example 11-1</title>
    <meta http-equiv="Content-type" content="text/html;
      charset=utf-8">
    <meta name="viewport" id="viewport"
      content="width=device-width, height=device-height,
      initial-scale=1.0, maximum-scale=1.0, user-scalable=no;"
    />
    <script type="text/javascript" charset="utf-8"
      src="phonegap.js"></script>
    <script type="text/javascript" charset="utf-8">

      function onBodyLoad() {
        document.addEventListener("deviceready", onDeviceReady,
          false);
      }

      function onDeviceReady() {
        navigator.notification.alert("onDeviceReady");
      }

      function takePhoto() {
        navigator.camera.getPicture(onCameraSuccess,
          onCameraError);
      }

      function onCameraSuccess(imageURL) {
        navigator.notification.alert("onCameraSuccess: " +
          imageURL);
      }

      function onCameraError(e) {
        navigator.notification.alert("onCameraError: " + e);
      }
    </script>
  </head>
```

```
<body onload="onBodyLoad()">
  <h1>Example 11-1</h1>
  <p>Using the PhoneGap Camera API<br />
    <input type="button" value="Take a Picture"
      onclick="takePhoto();">
  </p>
</body>
</html>
```

In this application, there's a simple page with a button that the user clicks to take a picture using the camera. When the button is clicked, the takePhoto function is executed, which simply calls the getPicture method, passing in the onCameraSuccess and onCameraError functions.

In this example, we're not passing in a cameraOptions object, so getPicture will just use the default options of getting the image from the camera and returning a file URI pointing to where the image was stored after it was taken. Once an image has been obtained from the camera, the onCameraSuccess function is called and passed to the URI pointing to the image file that was just created. In your applications, you'll probably do something with the image URI, but in this case all the application does is display an alert and show the file URI passed to the function.

Figure 11-1 shows the Example 11-1 application running on an Apple iPhone.

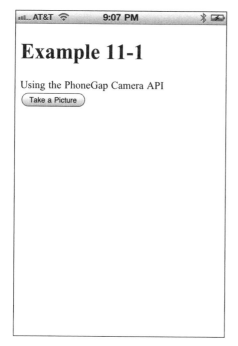

Figure 11-1 Example 11-1 running on an Apple iPhone

When you click the Take a Picture button, there's a slight delay, and then the standard camera application will open and allow you to take a picture. The delay can be quite long, so your application may want to display a "please wait" screen before calling the API. Once a picture has been taken, iOS will display the preview window shown in Figure 11-2. At this point, you can either retake the picture or click the Use button to return to the PhoneGap application.

Figure 11-2   Camera preview on iPhone

Notice from the figure that there's no way to cancel the process at this point. If the user initiates the taking of a picture in a PhoneGap application running on iOS, there's no way to cancel the process and not take a picture.

Counterintuitive Process

In my testing, the picture capture process was not very user friendly; only BlackBerry provided an intuitive interface for this part of the process. On BlackBerry, after you take the picture, you're immediately returned to the PhoneGap application.

For iOS and Android, you're presented with a preview window you can use to validate that the picture is the one you want. While this is a good thing from the user's standpoint, the way you transition from the preview screen back to the PhoneGap application can be a counterintuitive part of the process.

On iOS, you have to click the Use button shown in Figure 11-2, which makes some sense but may not be completely clear to the user what "use" means. On some flavors of the Android OS, there's no label on the button; you have to know to click the paper clip icon highlighted in Figure 11-6. Fortunately, some Android devices display OK, Retake, and Cancel buttons on the preview window.

Be aware of these inconsistencies and take them it into account when creating applications that leverage the camera.

On iOS, when control returns to the calling program, the application displays an alert and shows the file URI for the image file just created, as shown in Figure 11-3.

Figure 11-3   Example 11-1 displaying an image file URI

One of the things to note about the iOS version of the application is that the file URI returned to the program references a temporary location that is available only to the application. If you take a look at Figure 11-3, you'll see that the file URL refers to the following:

```
file://localhost/var/mobile/Applications/
169DF9CB-25D0-4EC8-85B2-380A6342E08D/tmp/photo_001.jpg
```

In this file URI, the `file://localhost/var/mobile/Applications/` location refers to a file system area allocated to application data. The `169DF9CB-25D0-4EC8-85B2-380A6342E08D` part refers to a unique identifier associated with each iOS application. The `tmp` folder refers to a temporary storage location allocated to the application; when the application closes, there's a high likelihood that the temporary storage allocated to the application will be cleared, and you will lose access to the image file. If your application needs access to the image file at a later time, it will need to make a copy of the image file (using the File API described in Chapter 18) in a less volatile location before the application closes.

Absent Camera Simulators

One of the frustrating things about the iOS simulator and older Android emulators is that Google and Apple omitted camera simulators in their simulation products. When testing an application that uses the PhoneGap Camera API on one of these products, it will fail, even though the real devices support the capability. Newer Android emulators have apparently been outfitted with a camera simulator.

Fortunately, on iOS, the PhoneGap `device.name` property (described in Chapter 16) will accurately report whether the application is running on a physical device or a simulator. An application could detect when it's running on a simulator and retrieve an image from the photo library instead of the camera.

For Android, there's no direct way to determine whether the application is running on an emulator or a physical device. When testing camera functionality, the emulators won't work; you'll have to resort to on-device testing exclusively.

When you run Example 11-1 on an Android or BlackBerry device, you'll have problems. In my testing, on Android it takes a picture but then crashes the PhoneGap application as it returns picture information to the application. On BlackBerry, it won't even take the picture; you click the button, and nothing happens. Apparently the default value for `Camera.DestinationType` in `cameraOptions` for those two platforms is DATA_URL, which, because of memory limitations described elsewhere in this chapter, will cause an application to crash when a picture is taken at full resolution. This bug has been identified and should be fixed in PhoneGap 1.4.

To make the application work on Android and BlackBerry, you must modify the call to getPicture to include a simple cameraOptions object, as shown in the following example:

```
function takePhoto() {
  navigator.camera.getPicture(onCameraSuccess, onCameraError,
    {quality: 50,
    destinationType: Camera.DestinationType.FILE_URI }
  );
}
```

With that in place, you can run the application on BlackBerry and then click the Take a Picture button to see a screen similar to the one shown in Figure 11-4.

Figure 11-4   Example 11-1 taking a picture on a BlackBerry device

When you click the camera button at the bottom middle of the screen, the captured image will be returned to the PhoneGap application, as shown in Figure 11-5. Notice from the figure that the image file is stored in the default BlackBerry photo storage location, so unlike iOS, any pictures taken by the application will be available after the application terminates.

Figure 11-5   Example 11-1 camera image file location on BlackBerry

If you do not want your application's photos to be left lying around after your application closes, you will need to manually delete the image file(s) once your application is through processing them. The application can use the PhoneGap File API (described in Chapter 18) to delete the file after the application is done with it.

Figure 11-6 shows Example 11-1 running on an Android device. In this case, the picture has already been taken, and what's shown is the picture preview window that the Android OS provides users. The frustrating part of what's shown in the figure is that from the user's standpoint, it's hard to know what to do next here. It's likely clear to the user that he is previewing a picture he just took (he did just take the picture after all), and it's possible that he will figure out that he can take another picture by clicking the camera image and can delete the image by clicking the trash can icon. The purpose of the paper clip icon, highlighted in Figure 11-6, is unclear, but when you click it, information about the selected image is returned to the PhoneGap application.

Figure 11-6   Example 11-1 image preview on Android

You might be asking yourself, what do I do with this image file URI once I get it back from the camera? Well, it's a file pointer pointing to an image file, so once the application knows where the file is, it can read from the file, copy it somewhere else (using the PhoneGap File API, described in Chapter 18), or even pass the file URI to the PhoneGap application's UI to display the image within the application.

Example 11-2 is a slightly modified version of Example 11-1. In this version, when the image URI is returned to the application, an HTML image tag is written to the index.html page so the captured image will appear on the screen.

Example 11-2

```
<!DOCTYPE html>
<html>
  <head>
    <title>Example 11-2</title>
    <meta http-equiv="Content-type"
      content="text/html; charset=utf-8">
    <meta name="viewport" id="viewport"
```

```
      content="width=device-width, height=device-height,
        initial-scale=1.0, maximum-scale=1.0, user-scalable=no;"
    />
    <script type="text/javascript" charset="utf-8"
      src="phonegap.js"></script>
    <script type="text/javascript" charset="utf-8">

      function onBodyLoad() {
        document.addEventListener("deviceready", onDeviceReady,
          false);
      }

      function onDeviceReady() {
        navigator.notification.alert("onDeviceReady");
      }

      function takePhoto() {
        navigator.camera.getPicture(onCameraSuccess,
          onCameraError,
          {quality : 50,
          destinationType : Camera.DestinationType.FILE_URI});
      }

      function onCameraSuccess(imageURL) {
        //Get a handle to the image container div
        ic = document.getElementById('imageContainer');
        //Then write an image tag out to the div using the
        //URL we received from the camera application.
        ic.innerHTML = '<img src="' + imageURL +
          '" width="50%" />';
      }

      function onCameraError(e) {
        console.log(e);
        navigator.notification.alert("onCameraError: " + e +
          " (" + e.code + ")");
      }
    </script>
  </head>
  <body onload="onBodyLoad()">
    <h1>Example 11-2</h1>
    <p>
      Using the PhoneGap Camera API
      <br />
      <input type="button" value="Take a Picture"
        onclick="takePhoto();">
      <div id="imageContainer"></div>
    </p>
  </body>
</html>
```

The major change is in the onCameraSuccess function shown here. It's been rewritten so it grabs the content of the imageContainer <div> and then replaces it with an <img> tag that references the file URI returned by the getPicture function.

```
function onCameraSuccess(imageURL) {
  //Get a handle to the image container div
  ic = document.getElementById('imageContainer');
  //Then write an image tag out to the div using the
  //URL we received from the camera application.
  ic.innerHTML = '<img src="' + imageURL + '" width="50%" />';
}
```

Figure 11-7 shows the application running on an Android device.

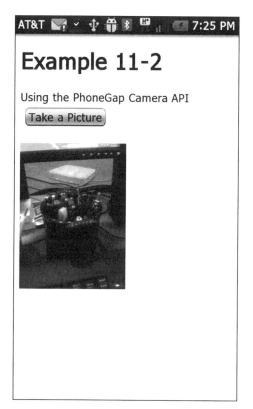

Figure 11-7   Example 11-2 running on an Android device

Configuring Camera Options

Now that you know how to take pictures using the camera, let's talk about options you can use to configure how the process works. As you may remember from the previous section, when calling getPicture, a developer can pass in a cameraOptions object that defines parameters controlling how the picture is obtained. The cameraOptions object supports the following properties:

- quality
- destinationType
- sourceType
- allowEdit
- encodingType
- targetWidth
- targetHeight
- mediaType

Each of these options will be described in greater detail in the following sections. Like with many other features of PhoneGap APIs, certain API options (such as allowEdit in the Camera API) apply on only a limited number of mobile platforms.

Here's an example of a fully configured cameraOptions object you could use in one of your PhoneGap applications:

```
var cameraOptions = { quality : 75,
  sourceType : Camera.PictureSourceType.CAMERA,
  destinationType : Camera.DestinationType.FILE_URI,
  allowEdit : true,
  encodingType: Camera.EncodingType.JPEG,
  targetWidth: 1024,
  targetHeight: 768 };
```

When passed to the getPicture function, this cameraOptions object tells getPicture to get the picture from the camera (sourceType), return a file URI that points to the image file captured (destinationType), allow the user to edit the picture before returning it to the program (allowEdit), return the picture as a .jpeg file (encodingType), configure the encoded image file to use 75% image quality (quality), and set the image dimensions to 1024 by 768 pixels (targetWidth and targetHeight).

Now let's describe each of the cameraOptions properties in greater detail.

quality

When working with smartphone cameras, higher-resolution optics in the camera lens plus limited memory storage and network bandwidth available to devices drove the need to be able to compress images so they took up less storage space and transmission bandwidth. As part of this compression process, standards such as the JPEG specification included support for using image quality to control compression rates when an image file is being saved. By using different image quality settings, defined as percentages, you can dramatically affect the physical size of an image file.

An image quality of 100% shows the image at its full capacity, with no reduction in image quality, and gives you the best possible picture. As you reduce the image quality, you will see some degradation in clarity in the image, but for most purposes it will be acceptable—only smaller in file size.

The `quality` parameter allows a developer to specify the percentage image quality for a picture captured using the Camera API. In most cases, you will use values from 50% to 100% for your images. This is not so much because you care about image quality, but more because you need to reduce image quality in order to reduce image file size.

As you'll see in the following section, developers can have an image file URI returned from a call to `getPicture` or the actual raw, base64-encoded image file data. Using the image file URI is easy; it's just a file pointer, and you've already seen examples here of how to use it in your applications. When obtaining raw image data from `getPicture`, you have to deal with the fact that the device and the JavaScript interpreter on the device have limits on how much data they can process. As newer smartphones get higher and higher resolution cameras, you must reduce image quality so that a PhoneGap application can successfully process the returned image data. When processing raw data from a high-resolution picture at 100% quality, you'd be processing a huge string, and the application might just crash without telling you why (like we saw when using default options for `cameraOptions` in Example 11-1). When you reduce image quality, you reduce the amount of data the application must process and increase the likelihood it will actually work.

Unfortunately, there is no guideline I can give you for how much you have to reduce your image quality to guarantee success. You'll just have to guess and test and know that the value may differ on different platforms and even on different devices on the same platform. The folks working on PhoneGap recommend using 50% image quality (or lower) when working with raw image data.

To configure a `cameraOptions` object to use a picture quality of 50%, use the following code:

```
quality : 50
```

According to the PhoneGap documentation, this option is ignored on the Black-Berry platform.

destinationType

When capturing an image using `getPicture`, applications will use `destinationType` to control whether the image information is returned as a file URI pointing to the image file stored in device memory:

```
destinationType: Camera.DestinationType.FILE_URI
```

To receive the picture's image data as a base64-encoded string value, use the following:

```
destinationType: Camera.DestinationType.DATA_URL
```

Working with file URIs is easy, as shown in Example 11-2. The application has a file pointer than can be manipulated within the application either by populating an HTML `img` tag or when using the File API to copy the file to another location. Once you know where the file is, accessing the image file is a simple process.

Figure 11-8 shows the output from Example 11-1 when a `destinationType` of `Camera.DestinationType.DATA_URL` is used. As you can see from the figure, what you have to work with is just a huge string, which, as mentioned in the previous section, may cause memory overflow and crash your program if the string is too big.

Figure 11-8 Raw image data rendered in an Android alert dialog

Using this raw image data, you can still render the picture in the UI, but you're more likely going to want to either store the data in a database or upload the data to a file server. There's just too much risk in trying to manipulate the image on the mobile device.

sourceType

The `sourceType` parameter is used to define where `getPicture` gets its picture from. When `sourceType` is omitted, `getPicture` will simply use the camera (`Camera.SourceType.CAMERA`) to grab the picture. Applications can specify to use the device's photo library using the following:

```
sourceType : Camera.SourceType.PHOTOLIBRARY
```

To retrieve photos from a saved photo album, use the following:

```
sourceType : Camera.SourceType.SAVEDPHOTOALBUM
```

On most platforms, specifying a `sourceType` of SAVEDPHOTOALBUM or PHOTOLIBRARY does essentially the same thing. As shown in Figure 11-9, when the application makes a call to `getPicture`, the device will open the photo library application and allow the user to first select a photo album and then select a single picture before returning the selected picture to the PhoneGap application.

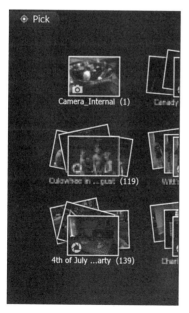

Figure 11-9   Photo gallery application on Android

On iOS devices, the two operate differently. When a sourceType of PHOTOLIBRARY is specified, the application behaves similarly to what is highlighted in Figure 11-9. When specifying a sourceType of SAVEDPHOTOALBUM, the application will open the standard iOS Camera Roll photo library and allow the user to select a picture from there.

According to the PhoneGap documentation, this option is ignored on the Black-Berry platform.

allowEdit

An iOS application can use the allowEdit option to instruct getPicture to allow the user to edit the selected image before returning it to the PhoneGap application. To configure a cameraOptions object for this option, use the following:

```
allowEdit : true
```

Once enabled in an application, after the camera takes a picture, the device will display a screen similar to the one shown in Figure 11-10. At this point, the user can pinch, prod, and slide the picture around to fit the portion of the image they want to capture into the reticle shown in the figure. When the user clicks the Choose button, the edited picture is returned to the calling PhoneGap application.

Figure 11-10   Picture editing on the iPhone

encodingType

A PhoneGap application uses the `encodingType` `cameraOption` to tell `getPicture` what kind of picture to take. Supported options are JPEG and PNG, with JPEG being the default on most, if not all, platforms. To configure `getPicture` to return a JPEG file, use the following:

```
encodingType: Camera.EncodingType.JPEG
```

To use PNG files, use the following:

```
encodingType: Camera.EncodingType.PNG
```

This option is not supported on all platforms; refer to the PhoneGap documentation for specifics.

targetHeight and targetWidth

The `targetHeight` and `targetWidth` parameters control the height and width of the image obtained using `getPicture`. You can set either `targetHeight` or `targetWidth`, and the image will be scaled accordingly. If you specify both, the image will be scaled to the one that results in the smallest aspect ratio. Either way, the aspect ratio will be maintained.

Since there's no way to programmatically determine the camera resolution or the supported aspect ratio before taking a picture, there is therefore no way to accurately set these values within an application without guessing or direct testing on each supported device.

To define a `cameraOptions` object that specifies `targetHeight` and `targetWidth` for the image, use the following code:

```
targetHeight: 100, targetWidth: 100
```

mediaType

Since many modern smartphones can typically store multiple media types in a photo library or photo library, the PhoneGap Camera API supports the addition of a `mediaType` value in the `cameraOptions` object in cases where the `sourceType` is set to PHOTOLIBRARY or SAVEDPHOTOALBUM. The parameter supports the following options:

- DEFAULT: Returns image information using the format specified in the `destinationType` value

- ALLMEDIA: Allows selection from all media types

- PICTURE: Allows the selection of photographs only
- VIDEO: Allows selection of video files only

When the option for VIDEO is selected, only a file URI will be returned to the calling program. Returning the raw video image data in a JavaScript String variable would certainly overload the JavaScript interpreter included in the browser and would most likely crash the application.

Dealing with Camera Problems

As with any computer or smartphone development, there are lots of places where things can go wrong. The purpose of this section is to highlight some of the ways you can tell what's going on when the Camera API fails.

When the onCameraError function fires, the Camera API passes in an error object that can be queried to determine the cause of the error. As shown in Figure 11-11, the error is a simple text message that tells what happened. In this case, the user clicked the Cancel button in Figure 11-10, so there's no image information to return to the PhoneGap application.

Figure 11-11   An example of the onCameraError function firing in a PhoneGap application

When the application runs on a device that doesn't have a camera, you will see an error similar to the one shown in Figure 11-12.

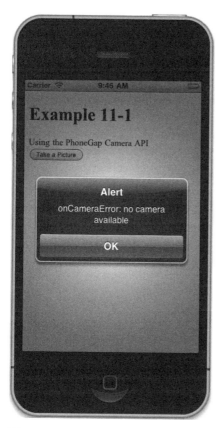

Figure 11-12   An example of the onCameraError function firing on an iOS simulator

If your application is running on a device that doesn't have a camera, it's likely, but not guaranteed, that the onCameraError function will be executed by the Camera API. If an application fails and you're not sure why, don't forget that the console log may contain information that can help. Figure 11-13 shows a portion of the iOS console with Example 11-1 running. Notice that when the I click the Take a Picture button, the console logs an error indicating that source type 1 (the camera) is not available.

```
2012-03-13 12:42:55.835 CameraTest[34224:fb03] Device initialization: DeviceInfo = { name":"iPhone
Simulator","uuid":"001ECDDE-CB30-5633-BAEE-181F6CAC1786","platform":"iPhone
Simulator","gap":"1.2.0","version":"4.3.2","connection":{"type":"wifi"}};
2012-03-13 12:43:00.286 CameraTest[34224:fb03] Camera.getPicture: source type 1 not available.
2012-03-13 12:43:00.289 CameraTest[34224:fb03] [INFO] no camera available
[Switching to process 34224 thread 0x16407]
```

Figure 11-13   Using the console to debug camera issues

This is one of those weird examples where even though the device supports a camera, Apple hasn't decided it's important enough to include that functionality in the device simulator. In this case, to be able to test on the iOS simulators, your application will need to check to see which device it's running on and use a photo library rather than the camera in cases where the camera is not available.

If your application seems to be running properly but when you take a picture nothing happens or the application crashes, it's likely caused by the application returning raw camera data (rather than a file URI) and the device isn't capable of processing a string of that size. When this happens, try cranking down image quality (using the `cameraOption quality` setting) to 50% or less to see whether this fixes the problem. If it does, then you're going to have to do some work to determine the optimal image quality setting for your application and the devices it's running on.

12

Capture

The PhoneGap Capture API allows an application to capture audio, video, and image files using the appropriate built-in application on a mobile device. The device's default camera application is used to capture pictures and videos, while the device's default voice recorder application is used for capturing audio clips.

PhoneGap's implementation of the Capture API is based on the W3C Media Capture API (www.w3.org/TR/media-capture-api). For whatever reason, though, the PhoneGap team has omitted support for many of the options supported by the W3C API. So, as you'll see later, while the API is based upon a standard, with PhoneGap many of the API options just don't work or haven't even been implemented.

Camera vs. Capture

You may be asking yourself why PhoneGap implemented both Camera and Capture APIs considering that there's some overlap between the two in that they can both capture images. Essentially, the Camera API was implemented before PhoneGap adopted the W3C Capture API. It is likely PhoneGap just kept the Camera API for backward compatibility with existing applications.

While both APIs capture images, the APIs operate in different ways. The Camera API can capture only images but supports alternate sources for the image files, while the Capture API will only allow you to interact directly with the capture application and allow multiple captures with a single API call.

Using the Capture API

As with most PhoneGap APIs, the Capture API is accessed through a call to one of the capture methods while passing in both success and failure functions plus an options object that controls aspects of the capture event. Each of the parameters passed to the capture functions will be explained later in the chapter.

To capture one or more audio files, an application would make a call similar to the following:

```
navigator.device.capture.captureAudio(onCaptureSuccess,
   onCaptureError, captureOptions);
```

To capture one or more image files, an application would use the following:

```
navigator.device.capture.captureImage(onCaptureSuccess,
   onCaptureError, captureOptions);
```

To capture one or more video files, an application would use the following:

```
navigator.device.capture.captureVideo(onCaptureSuccess,
   onCaptureError, captureOptions);
```

In these examples, the onCaptureSuccess function is called after the capture application (either the device's camera application or audio recorder) has finished capturing the appropriate media type. When the function is called, the API passes in an array containing information about the media files that were captured by the call to the Capture API. The function should then loop through the array and process each of the media files generated during the capture, as shown in the following example:

```
function onCaptureSuccess(fileList) {
   var len, i;
   //See how many files are listed in the array
   len = fileList.length;
   //Make sure we had a result; it should always be
   //greater than 0, but you never know!
   if(len > 0) {
      //Media files were captured, so let's process them
      for( i = 0, len; i < len; i += 1) {
         //========================================
         //Do something with the returned file list
         //========================================

      }
   } else {
      //This will probably never execute
      alert("Error: No files returned.");
   }
}
```

The file list array passed to the function supports the following properties:

- name: The short name for the file (a file name plus extension)
- fullPath: The full file path for the file (a file path, file name, and extension)
- type: The file's Multipurpose Internet Mail Extensions (MIME) type
- lastModifiedDate: The date and time the file was last modified
- size: The file's size in bytes

An application can use these properties to locate and manipulate each file returned from the capture event, typically rendering the file within the application's UI or uploading them to a server for processing or storage.

In the following example, the file list is parsed, and the application's UI is updated to include an ordered list of file short names that can be clicked to open the file.

```
function onCaptureSuccess(fileList) {
  var i, len, htmlStr;
  len = fileList.length;
  if(len > 0) {
    //Get a handle to the results area of the screen/page
    res = document.getElementById("captureResults");
    htmlStr = '<p>Results:</p><ol>';
    for( i = 0, len; i < len; i += 1) {
      htmlStr += '<li><a href="file:/' +
      fileList[i].fullPath + '">' + fileList[i].name +
      '</a></li>';
    }
    htmlStr += '</ol>';
    //Set the results content
    res.innerHTML = htmlStr;
  }
}
```

There's a function an application can call to obtain information about a media file:

```
mediaFile.getFormatData(successCallback, errorCallback);
```

Information about the media file is obtained in the successCallback function through the MediaFileData object passed to the function. Unfortunately, as you look at the PhoneGap API documentation, there is very limited support for this capability today.

Calls to the Capture API will create media files for each capture event. These files will be left wherever the capture application places them before passing the file list back to the PhoneGap application that called the Capture API. When your application is done processing the captured files, you may want to delete the files to save space and keep the user from seeing media files that are no longer useful.

The onCaptureError callback function is executed whenever there is an error with a particular capture event. The function is passed an error object that can be queried to determine the cause of the error. The Capture API includes several constants that can be evaluated against to determine the specifics of the error:

- CaptureError.CAPTURE_INTERNAL_ERR: The camera or microphone failed to capture an image or sound.

- CaptureError.CAPTURE_APPLICATION_BUSY: The camera or audio capture application is busy serving another capture request.

- CaptureError.CAPTURE_INVALID_ARGUMENT: The application made an invalid use of the API (an invalid or missing parameter, for example).

- CaptureError.CAPTURE_NO_MEDIA_FILES: The application user exited the camera or audio capture application before completing a capture.

- CaptureError.CAPTURE_NOT_SUPPORTED: The specified capture operation is not supported.

The following is an example of an onCaptureError callback function that uses these properties:

```
function onCaptureError(e) {
  var msgText;
  //Build a message string based on the
  //error code returned by the API
  switch(e.code) {
    case CaptureError.CAPTURE_INTERNAL_ERR:
      msgText = "Internal error, the camera or microphone
        failed to capture image or sound.";
      break;
    case CaptureError.CAPTURE_APPLICATION_BUSY:
      msgText = "The camera application or audio capture
        application is currently serving other capture
        request.";
      break;
    case CaptureError.CAPTURE_INVALID_ARGUMENT:
      msgText = "Invalid parameter passed to the API.";
      break;
    case CaptureError.CAPTURE_NO_MEDIA_FILES:
      msgText = "User likely canceled the capture process.";
      break;
    case CaptureError.CAPTURE_NOT_SUPPORTED:
      msgText = "The requested operation is not supported
        on this device.";
      break;
```

```
  default:
    //Create a generic response, just in case the
    //following switch fails
    msgText = "Unknown Error (" + e.code + ")";
  }
  //Now tell the user what happened
  console.log(msgText);
  alert(msgText);
}
```

In my work with the Capture API, I discovered that iOS applications returned the correct error object when the user canceled a capture, but Android devices I tested on did not. The Android devices regularly returned an unknown error and triggered the default portion of the switch statement shown in the example. For that reason, an application might not really be able to tell what happened when a capture failed.

Configuring Capture Options

Each of the supported capture methods accepts an optional captureOptions object that controls aspects of how the capture is performed. The available properties supported by captureOptions are as follows:

- duration
- limit
- mode

All options are not supported across all capture types. Table 12-1 illustrates where each option applies to the different capture types.

Table 12-1 Capture Options

Capture Type	Capture Option		
	Duration	**Limit**	**Mode**
Audio	X	X	X
Image		X	X
Video	X	X	X

A valid captureOptions object would be defined using the following code:

```
var captureOptions = {duration: 5, limit: 3};
```

This example creates a captureOptions object that configures a maximum capture recording duration of five seconds and a maximum of three captures during the capture event.

duration

The duration property applies to only audio and video capture and is designed to control the length (in seconds) of a particular media capture. It allows an application to specify the maximum number of seconds an audio or video clip can be. When used in an application, the user can record media clips shorter than, but no longer than, the number of seconds set for this property.

Looking at the current PhoneGap API documentation, the duration captureOption is not supported on Android and BlackBerry, and it is supported only on iOS for audio capture. Because of this limitation, it's probably best not to use this option in your PhoneGap applications.

limit

The inappropriately named limit captureOption defines the number of captures performed with the call to the particular capture method. It would make more sense if they called this quantity, but since it's part of the W3C specification, they had to support the options as defined.

According to the documentation, the limit value is supposed to define a maximum number of captures performed, indicating that the application user could perform less than the maximum. In my testing, it doesn't work that way; if a user takes less than limit captures, the onCaptureError function is called indicating that the capture process has been aborted.

If this option is used in an application, a value of 1 or greater must be defined.

mode

The mode property is supposed to define the recording mode for each of the supported capture types. When a device supports multiple file formats for a particular capture type (such as JPEG and PNG for image captures, for example), the mode property is supposed to allow you to specify which is used for a capture event. Unfortunately, this particular feature has issues on PhoneGap.

For an application to use this feature, it would need to be able to determine programmatically what modes are supported on the device before making the call to the Capture API. To make things easier for the developer, PhoneGap even includes the following properties, which are supposed to return the list of supported modes:

- supportedAudioModes
- supportedImageModes
- supportedVideoModes

Unfortunately, none of the properties is populated by recent versions of the PhoneGap framework because the information is not exposed through an API on most mobile device platforms.

Capture at Work

Now that we've worked through all of the options for the Capture API, it's time to show a complete example of how to use the API plus illustrate how the capture function actually works on mobile devices. To highlight the capabilities of the Capture API, I created Example 12-1, the application shown in Figure 12-1. It essentially provides a single interface that can be used to demonstrate most of the options supported by the Capture API. Because of the limitations of the mode capture option described previously, the application provides an interface only for the duration and limit options for the Capture API.

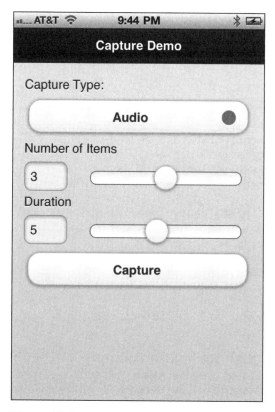

Figure 12-1   Capture API demo running on an iPhone

The application uses jQuery Mobile (www.jquerymobile.com) to provide a simple but elegant interface for the application. It uses the default theme to create a simple header bar, the standard iOS buttons, and a cleaner interface for the slider controls used in the application.

An application user selects a capture type using the picker control at the top of the form and then makes selections for `limit` and `duration`; then the user clicks the Capture button to begin capturing media files. At this point, the button's `onClick` event calls the `doCapture` function to start the capture process.

The `doCapture` function retrieves the current settings from the capture type picker and the number of items and duration fields, and it then makes a call to the appropriate capture method, passing in a `captureOptions` object to tell the method what to do.

The application uses the `onCaptureSuccess` and `onCaptureError` functions highlighted earlier in the chapter to update the UI with capture results and to let the user know when problems occur. Example 12-1 shows the complete listing.

Example 12-1

```
<!DOCTYPE html>
<html>
  <head>
    <title>Example 12-1</title>
    <meta name="viewport" content="width=device-width,
      height=device-height initial-scale=1.0,
      maximum-scale=1.0, user-scalable=no;" />
    <meta http-equiv="Content-type" content="text/html;
      charset=utf-8">
    <link rel="stylesheet" href="jquery.mobile1.0b3.min.css" />
    <script type="text/javascript" charset="utf-8"
      src="jquery1.6.4.min.js"></script>
    <script type="text/javascript" charset="utf-8"
      src="jquery.mobile1.0b3.min.js"></script>
    <script type="text/javascript" charset="utf-8"
      src="phonegap.js"></script>
    <script type="text/javascript" charset="utf-8">
      var results;

      function onBodyLoad() {
        //Add the PhoneGap deviceready event listener
        document.addEventListener("deviceready", onDeviceReady,
          false);
      }
```

```
function onDeviceReady() {
  //Get a handle to the results area of the page
  //we'll need it later
  res = document.getElementById("captureResults");
}

function doCapture() {
  //Clear out any previous results
  res.innerHTML = "Initiating capture...";
  //Get some values from the page
  var numItems =
    document.getElementById("numItems").value;
  var capDur =
    document.getElementById("duration").value;
  //Figure out which option is selected
  var captureType =
    document.getElementById("captureType").selectedIndex;
  switch(captureType) {
    case 0:
      //Capture Audio
      navigator.device.capture.captureAudio(
        onCaptureSuccess, onCaptureError,
        {duration: capDur, limit: numItems});
      break;
    case 1:
      //Capture Image
      navigator.device.capture.captureImage(
        onCaptureSuccess, onCaptureError,
        {limit: numItems});
      break;
    case 2:
      //Capture Video
      navigator.device.capture.captureVideo(
        onCaptureSuccess, onCaptureError,
        {duration: capDur, limit: numItems});
      break;
  }
}
```

```
function onCaptureSuccess(fileList) {
  var i, len, htmlStr;
  len = fileList.length;
  //Make sure we had a result; it should always be
  //greater than 0, but you never know.
  if(len > 0) {
    htmlStr = "<p>Results:</p><ol>";
    for( i = 0, len; i < len; i += 1) {
      //alert(fileList[i].fullPath);
      htmlStr += '<li><a href="file:/' +
        fileList[i].fullPath + '">' + fileList[i].name +
        '</a></li>';
    }
    htmlStr += "</ol>";
    //Set the results content
    res.innerHTML = htmlStr;
  }
}

function onCaptureError(e) {
  var msgText;
  //Clear the results text, nothing to show
  res.innerHTML = "";
  //Now build a message string based upon the
  //error returned by the API
  switch(e.code) {
    case CaptureError.CAPTURE_INTERNAL_ERR:
      msgText = "Internal error, the camera or microphone
        failed to capture image or sound.";
      break;
    case CaptureError.CAPTURE_APPLICATION_BUSY:
      msgText = "The camera application or audio capture
        application is currently serving other capture
        request.";
      break;
    case CaptureError.CAPTURE_INVALID_ARGUMENT:
      msgText = "Invalid parameter passed to the API.";
      break;
    case CaptureError.CAPTURE_NO_MEDIA_FILES:
      msgText = "User likely cancelled the capture
        process.";
      break;
    case CaptureError.CAPTURE_NOT_SUPPORTED:
      msgText = "The requested operation is not supported
        on this device.";
      break;
```

```
            default:
              //Create a generic response, just in case the
              //following switch fails
              msgText = "Unknown Error (" + e.code + ")";
          }
          //Now tell the user what happened
          navigator.notification.alert(msgText, null,
            "Capture Error");
        }
    </script>
  </head>
  <body onload="onBodyLoad()">
    <div data-role="header">
      <h1>Capture Demo</h1>
    </div>
    <div data-role="content">
      <label for="captureType">Capture Type:</label>
      <select id="captureType" name="captureType">
        <option value="0">Audio</option>
        <option value="1">Image</option>
        <option value="2">Video</option>
      </select>
      <label for="numItems">Number of Items</label>
      <input type="range" name="numItems" id="numItems"
        value="1" min="1" max="5" />
      <label for="duration">Duration</label>
      <input type="range" name="duration" id="duration"
        value="5" min="1" max="10" />
      <input type="button" id="captureButton" value="Capture"
        onclick="doCapture();">
      <div id="captureResults"></div>
    </div>
  </body>
</html>
```

The first thing you'll notice when you use the API in your applications is that on some devices there's a fairly long delay after calling the capture method before the device's default capture application launches to perform the capture. Because of this delay, your application may need to include a Loading Capture Application window or something to let the user know what's going on during this delay.

You will also notice inconsistencies in the implementation of capture functionality across different Android devices; some examples of this will be provided later in the chapter. Additionally, even though the API documentation doesn't indicate this, on the BlackBerry platform, the limit option is ignored, so no matter what setting you use, the BlackBerry will perform only one capture per call to the Capture API.

Let's look at some examples of Example 12-1 in action.

In Figure 12-2, the application is running on an iPhone device and is configured to capture an image in addition to grabbing three images when the user clicks the Capture button. Since image capture is being performed, the duration option has no effect on the capture process.

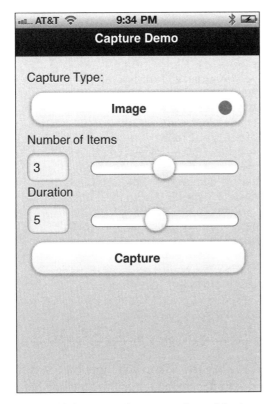

Figure 12-2   Example 12-1 configured for image capture

When the user clicks the Capture button, the iOS camera application will load and prompt the user to take three pictures, one at a time. As each image is captured, iOS will prompt the user to use the current image or discard it and take a different picture, as shown in Figure 12-3. The user must click the Use button to accept the current picture and either take another picture or return to the calling program.

Figure 12-3   Example 12-1 image preview on iOS

When the images are returned to the calling program, it will update the UI to show the list of image files, as shown in Figure 12-4. In this example, it's showing links to the image files that can be clicked to open the images for viewing. For audio and video captures, the links may open but won't display properly because of some limitations in the device OS.

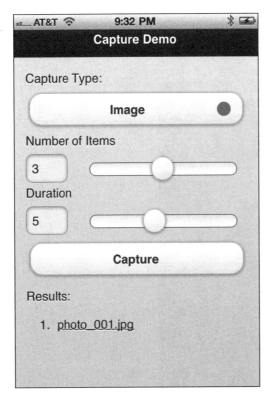

Figure 12-4   Example 12-1 image capture results

With the application configured for audio clip capture, the sound recorder application will load, as shown in Figure 12-5. When finishing the recording of the audio clip, the user must click the Done button to return information about the captured audio files to the calling program.

With the application configured for video capture, the video recorder application will load, as shown in Figure 12-6. When finishing recording of the clip, the user must click the Use button to return information about the captured video files to the calling program.

As you can see from these iOS examples, the process is pretty straightforward, but even on iOS there are inconsistencies. In some cases, the user clicks a Use button to return to the calling program, but in other cases it's a Done button. Additionally, if you're doing multiple captures, there's no visual indication of how many captures are being performed and how many have been completed. For this reason, I recommend that you do only a single capture at a time (use the default for limit, which is a single capture) to make it clearer to your application user what's going on.

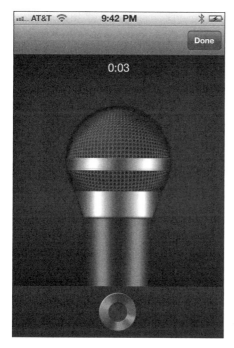

Figure 12-5   Example 12-1 audio capture

Figure 12-6   Example 12-1 video capture

Figure 12-7 shows the same application running on an Android device. As you can see from the figure, the application looks (almost) the same as it does on iOS; this is made possible by jQuery Mobile, which takes care of the UI so you don't have to. In this example, the application is configured for image capture and will grab two images when the user clicks the Capture button.

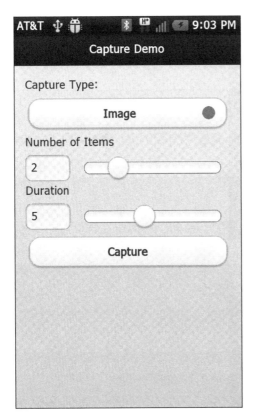

Figure 12-7   Example 12-1 running on an Android device

When the user clicks the Capture button, the camera application for the specific device will load and prompt the user to take two pictures, one at a time. As each image is captured, Android will prompt the user to use the current image or discard it and take a different picture, as shown in Figure 12-8. For the device I used for testing, the user must click the highlighted paperclip button to accept the current picture and either take another picture or return to the calling program. Other Android devices may have a different UI for the camera application that could include different buttons or different button labels.

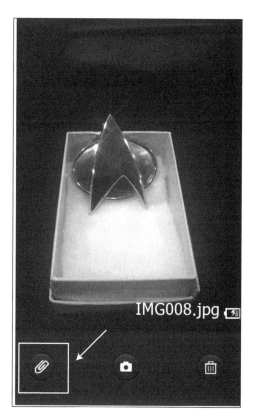

Figure 12-8   Example 12-1 Android image preview

Where this gets interesting is when you attempt to capture an audio file on an Android device. When the user clicks the Capture button, the default Android Voice Recorder application will launch, as shown in Figure 12-9. When the user clicks the Record button in the bottom middle of the voice recorder application screen, the application will record an audio clip using the device microphone (or a headset microphone if one is plugged into the device).

When the user clicks the Stop button (the button with the square on it in the bottom-right corner of Figure 12-9) to end the recording, the voice recorder application will display a screen similar to the one shown in Figure 12-10 (the screen will vary depending on the Android OS version and possibly the device manufacturer). The problem here is that for the particular devices I used for testing, there is no way to indicate to the voice recorder application that you're done recording and want to return to the calling program. On other devices such as the Motorola Droid smartphone, it will show a "Use this recording" button and pass the recorded file back to the PhoneGap application.

Figure 12-9   Example 12-1 Android audio capture

The PhoneGap application can use the Capture API to launch the voice recorder application, but there's no way within the voice recorder application to pass information about the captured media files back to the PhoneGap application. On the device I used for testing, shown in Figure 12-10, you can play the audio clip, re-record the clip, share or delete the clip, and even access a listing of captured audio files, but there's no way to get the captured audio clip back to the PhoneGap application. Other manufacturers' devices may show more appropriate options to the user.

When capturing video on an Android device, the application will launch the video recorder application to capture the video. When the recording process is complete, the video recorder application will display the preview screen, as shown in Figure 12-11. In this case, the application is running on a LG Thrill device. When satisfied with the video clip, the user must click the paperclip icon highlighted in the figure to return information about the video clip(s) to the calling program.

Figure 12-10   Android voice recorder audio clip options

Figure 12-11   Video preview on an Android LG Thrill device

On Samsung Infuse 4G Android devices, the preview window is different, showing only the save and discard options shown in Figure 12-12.

Figure 12-12   Video preview on an Android Samsung Infuse 4G device

The application will run unmodified on newer BlackBerry devices. The only issue affecting developers is that the BlackBerry platform ignores the limit option, so no matter what your application expects, on a BlackBerry only one capture event will occur for every call to the Capture API.

13

Compass

The Compass API allows a PhoneGap program to determine the device's heading along a two-dimensional plane roughly corresponding to the surface of the earth. Many modern smartphones have a physical compass (on a chip), and the API simply queries the chip and returns an angle between 0 and 360 indicating the direction the device is pointing. A value of 0 indicates the device is pointing north, 90 indicates it is pointing east, 180 refers to south, and 270 refers to west.

 Note: Not all smartphones have a compass. The iPhone series of devices have always had one, but RIM didn't add one until BlackBerry 7 OS devices.

The Compass API works in a very similar manner to the Accelerometer API described in Chapter 10. Using the API, developers can manually query the device's orientation or can set up a watch to have the API periodically report orientation to the application on a specific frequency or when the device's orientation changes by a minimum threshold.

Getting Device Heading

To query the device's orientation, simply call the following method:

```
navigator.compass.getCurrentHeading(successFunction,
    errorFunction);
```

Passed to the API are the names of two functions that are called depending on whether the API is returning a result. The successFunction is called when a reading has been successfully made, and the errorFunction is called when there is an error reading the compass.

When called, the `successFunction` is passed the `compassHeading` object, which consists of the following components:

- `magneticHeading`: The device's current heading in degrees ranging from 0 to 359.99.

- `trueHeading`: The device's current heading relative to the geographic North Pole in degrees ranging from 0 to 359.99. A negative value indicates that a value could not be determined.

- `headingAccuracy`: A value indicating the deviation, in degrees, between the `magneticHeading` and `trueHeading` values.

- `timestamp`: The time when the heading values were measured (in milliseconds since the Unix Epoch, January 1, 1970).

The earth has two North Poles: the geographic North Pole (which is the exact, geographic top of the earth) and the magnetic North Pole (which regularly moves around because of magnetic changes in the earth's core). You'll have to determine which matters for your particular application. On the Android platform, the associated APIs return values only for `magneticHeading`, so `headingAccuracy` will always be zero.

Unlike the Accelerometer API, when the Compass API calls the `errorFunction`, it passes in a `CompassError` object that allows a program to understand a little bit about why the error occurred. The most useful aspect of this is that you can tell whether the compass is supported on the device.

Let's take a look at an application that implements this API. Example 13-1 is an application that queries the compass and updates the screen with the current heading every time a button is clicked. This is not necessarily the most robust example, but it illustrates how the API works.

Example 13-1

```
<!DOCTYPE html>
<html>
  <head>
    <title>Example 13-1</title>
    <meta http-equiv="Content-type" content="text/html;
      charset=utf-8">
    <meta name="viewport" id="viewport"
      content="width=device-width, height=device-height,
      initial-scale=1.0, maximum-scale=1.0, user-scalable=no;"
    />
    <script type="text/javascript" charset="utf-8"
```

```
    src="phonegap.js"></script>
<script type="text/javascript" charset="utf-8">

  // Heading content
  var hc;
  //PhoneGap Ready variable
  var pgr = false;
  //Has compass, assume true
  var hasCompass = true;

  function onBodyLoad() {
    //alert("onBodyLoad");
    document.addEventListener("deviceready", onDeviceReady,
      false);
  }

  function onDeviceReady() {
    //Get a handle we'll use to adjust the heading
    //content
    hc = document.getElementById('headingInfo');
    //Set the variable that lets other parts of the program
    //know that PhoneGap is initialized
    pgr = true;
  }

  function getHeading() {
    if (pgr == true) {
      if  (hasCompass == true) {
        //Clear the current heading content,
        //just in case it takes some time to get the reading
        hc.innerHTML =
          "Getting heading information from compass.";
        //get the current heading
        navigator.compass.getCurrentHeading(
          onHeadingSuccess, onHeadingError);
      } else {
        alert("No compass, please stop clicking
          the button.");
      }
    } else {
      alert("Please wait. PhoneGap is not ready.");
    }
  }

  function onHeadingSuccess(heading) {
    //We received something from the API, so...
    //first get the timestamp in a date object
    //so we can work with it
    var d = new Date(heading.timestamp);
```

```
        //Then replace the page's content with the
        //current acceleration retrieved from the API
        hc.innerHTML = "<b>Magnetic Heading:</b> " +
          heading.magneticHeading +
          "<br /><b>True Heading:</b> " + heading.trueHeading +
          "<br /><b>Heading Accuracy:</b> " +
          heading.headingAccuracy + "<br /><b>Timestamp:</b> " +
          d.toLocaleString();
    }

    function onHeadingError(compassError) {
        if (compassError.code ==
          CompassError.COMPASS_NOT_SUPPORTED) {
          hc.innerHTML = "Compass not available."
          alert("Compass not supported.");
          hasCompass == false;
        } else if (compassError.code ==
          CompassError.COMPASS_INTERNAL_ERR) {
          alert("Compass Internal Error");
        } else {
          alert("Unknown heading error!");
        }
    }

  </script>
</head>
<body onload="onBodyLoad()">
  <h1>Example 13-1</h1>
  <p>This is an Apache PhoneGap application that measures
      device heading using the Compass API.<br />
  <input type="button" value="Measure Heading"
    onclick="getHeading();"></p>
  <p id="headingInfo">Nothing to see here (yet), click the
    button.</p>
</body>
</html>
```

The application starts by defining several variables that are used to control the application. Since the application relies upon the user clicking a button to measure the heading, the application will need to know whether PhoneGap has initialized yet, so the pgr variable is used to track status. The hasCompass variable is used to track whether the Compass API returns an error indicating that the compass is not available. These variables prevent the application from trying to do things that are not supported.

In getHeading, the application checks to make sure PhoneGap has initialized and that a previous call to getCurentHeading didn't return an error indicating that the compass wasn't available. When all is clear, it makes a call to `getCurrentHeading` to measure the device's heading. If this is successful, the `onHeadingSuccess` function is called, and the application's UI is updated with heading information. If there's a problem, `onHeadingError` is called, the user is told what happens, and `hasCompass` is updated if needed.

The value for `timestamp` is converted to human readable format using the following code:

```
var d = new Date(heading.timestamp);
hc.innerHTML = "Timestamp: " + d.toLocaleString();
```

Figure 13-1 shows the application running on an Android device.

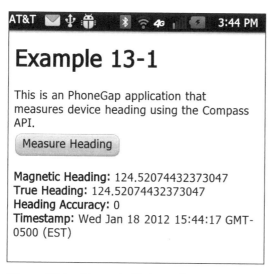

Figure 13-1   Example 13-1 running on a Android device

Notice that heading accuracy is zero and the magnetic and true heading values are the same; that's because the Android OS supports only the magnetic heading.

Watching Device Heading

For an application that relies upon heading information, manually querying the compass is inefficient. Fortunately, PhoneGap provides simple watch mechanisms that allow an application to query the compass repeatedly over a specific time interval or whenever the heading changes by more than a configurable number of degrees. The following sections describe each of these options in detail.

watchHeading

The watchHeading function allows an application to define a compass watch that fires repeatedly on a specific time interval. An application defines the watch using the following code:

```
var watchOptions = { frequency: 250 };
watchID = navigator.compass.watchHeading(onHeadingSuccess,
  onHeadingError, watchOptions);
```

When creating the watch, a program must pass in the names of two functions that are called depending on whether the heading measurement is successful. The successFunction is called when a reading has been successfully made, and the errorFunction is called when there is an error reading the compass. When called, the successFunction is passed the compassHeading object that contains information obtained from the compass. The previous section describes the compassHeading object in detail.

In this example, the code first creates a watchOptions object that defines a watch frequency of 250 milliseconds (0.25 seconds). A frequency value of 1000 would configure a watch that fired every second. Next, the code creates the watch and assigns the result of that operation in the watchID variable. The watchID is important since it allows you to later cancel the watch using the following code:

```
navigator.compass.clearWatch(watchID);
```

Let's take a look at an application that implements this API. Example 13-2 is an application that displays a simple compass graphic and periodically (four times a second) queries the compass and rotates the compass image to show the device's current heading.

Example 13-2

```html
<!DOCTYPE html>
<html>
  <head>
    <title>Example 13-2</title>
    <meta http-equiv="Content-type"
      content="text/html; charset=utf-8">
    <meta name="viewport" id="viewport"
      content="width=device-width, height=device-height,
      initial-scale=1.0, maximum-scale=1.0, user-scalable=no;"
    />
    <script type="text/javascript" charset="utf-8"
      src="jquery.js"></script>
    <script type="text/javascript" charset="utf-8"
      src="jQueryRotate.2.1.js"></script>
    <script type="text/javascript" charset="utf-8"
      src="phonegap.js"></script>
```

```
<script type="text/javascript" charset="utf-8">

  var hi, watchID;

  function onBodyLoad() {
    document.addEventListener("deviceready", onDeviceReady,
      false);
    //Get a handle to the headingInfo element of the page
    hi = document.getElementById('headingInfo');
  }

  function onDeviceReady() {
    //Set up the watch
    //Read the compass 4 times a second
    var watchOptions = { frequency: 250 };
    watchID = navigator.compass.watchHeading(
      onHeadingSuccess, onHeadingError, watchOptions);
  }

  function onHeadingSuccess(heading) {
    var hv = Math.round(heading.magneticHeading);
    hi.innerHTML = "<b>Heading:</b>" + hv + " degrees";
    $("#compass").rotate(-hv);
  }

  function onHeadingError(compassError) {
    //Remove the watch since we're having a problem
    navigator.compass.clearWatch(watchID);
    //clear the Heading value from the page
    hi.innerHTML = "";
    //Then tell the user what happened.
    if (compassError.code ==
      CompassError.COMPASS_NOT_SUPPORTED) {
      alert("Compass not supported.");
    } else if (compassError.code ==
      CompassError.COMPASS_INTERNAL_ERR) {
      alert("Compass Internal Error");
    } else {
      alert("Unknown heading error!");
    }
  }

</script>
</head>
<body onload="onBodyLoad()">
  <h1>Example 13-2</h1>
  <img src="compass.png" id="compass" align="middle" /><br />
  <p id="headingInfo"></p>
</body>
</html>
```

Instead of muddying the example by filling these pages with the code needed to rotate the graphic, I decided to use a jQuery (www.jquery.com) plug-in called jQueryRotate (http://code.google.com/p/jqueryrotate) to take care of that aspect of the program for me. This approach dramatically simplifies the example and allows me to get right to the PhoneGapness of the application.

Looking at the code, you'll see two `<script>` tags at the start of the application that load the jQuery module and the jQueryRotate plug-in.

```
<script type="text/javascript" charset="utf-8"
  src="jquery.js"></script>
<script type="text/javascript" charset="utf-8"
  src="jQueryRotate.2.1.js"></script>
```

Once those are in place, the application can rotate the graphic using the following single line of code:

```
$("#compass").rotate(angle);
```

The `$()` is a jQuery function that gives an application programmatic access to a particular page element, in this case an image with an ID of compass. Once it has a handle on the element, it calls the `rotate` function to rotate the graphic by the angle passed to the function.

With that out of the way, let's take a look at the application.

The watch is created in the `onDeviceReady` function, so the application starts updating the compass as soon as PhoneGap is done initializing. As defined, it queries the compass four times a second and then updates the compass orientation accordingly. The `watchID` variable is defined at a global level, so it's available to multiple parts of the application.

When the watch fires, it calls the `onHeadingSuccess` function and passes in the `heading` object defined in the previous section. There the application rounds the heading value to the nearest whole number and stores it in a variable for use later. It does that to minimize flicker as the compass adjusts itself, forcing the value to a whole number minimizes the number of changes made to the screen. Next the application updates the screen to show the numeric value for the heading and then calls the `rotate` function to rotate the graphic.

```
function onHeadingSuccess(heading) {
  var hv = Math.round(heading.magneticHeading);
  hi.innerHTML = "<b>Heading:</b>" + hv + " degrees";
  $("#compass").rotate(-hv);
}
```

When you look at the code, you may notice that the application converts the heading value (through the hv variable in the code) to a negative number when calling rotate. This is because while the device might be pointing in a certain direction, for the compass graphic to illustrate this accurately, it must rotate the north heading away from the horizontal axis of the device. So, as the device turns 10° to the right, the compass graphic must then rotate 10° to the left in order to still be pointing north.

If there's an error querying the compass, the onHeadingError function is called so the application can alert the user. Passed to the function is a compassError object that includes information about the source of the error. Since we've had an error, the first thing the application does is cancel the watch; there's no reason to continue to query the compass when you know it's not working. After the watch has been canceled, the application provides some feedback to the user so they know why the application is no longer updating the compass.

Figure 13-2 shows the application running on an Android device.

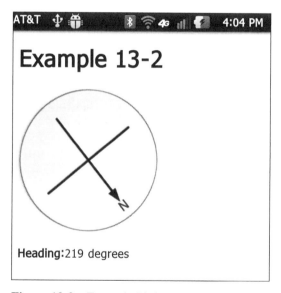

Figure 13-2   Example 13-2 running on an Android device

watchHeadingFilter

As useful as it is to query the compass on a time interval, sometimes an application might want to know only when the device orientation changes. To support this, the PhoneGap Compass API includes a function that can be called to define a watch that's fired only when the heading changes by more than a configurable number of degrees. This option works in a very similar way to the previous example; the only differences are the names of the functions used to set and clear the watch and the watch options passed to the function that creates the watch.

In this case, the watch is created using the following code:

```
var watchOptions = { filter : 5 };
watchID = navigator.compass.watchHeadingFilter(
  onHeadingSuccess, onHeadingError, watchOptions);
```

The watch is created using watchHeadingFilter instead of the watchHeading function used in the previous example. The application still needs to create a watchOptions object, but instead of specifying a frequency variable, a filter is used instead. The filter variable defines the number of degrees used to filter the watch. In this case, the onHeadingSuccess function will fire whenever the heading changes by at least the value specified by the filter.

To remove the watch, call the following function and pass in the watchID being canceled:

```
navigator.compass.clearWatchFilter(watchID);
```

Unfortunately, as useful as this option is, it doesn't work on all platforms. Today only iOS provides support for this function.

Example 13-3 shows the relevant portions of Example 13-2 updated to leverage the watchHeadingFilter function. The majority of the changes are to the onDeviceReady function where you'll see a different watchOptions variable definition and the call to watchHeadingFilter instead of watchHeading. In the onHeadingError function, the call to clearWatch has been replaced with a call to clearWatchFilter instead. Beyond those minor changes, the application is otherwise the same as Example 13-2.

Example 13-3

```
function onDeviceReady() {
  //Set up the watch to fire whenever the compass moves 5 degrees
  var watchOptions = { filter : 5 };
  watchID = navigator.compass.watchHeadingFilter(
    onHeadingSuccess, onHeadingError, watchOptions);
}

function onHeadingSuccess(heading) {
  var hv = Math.round(heading.magneticHeading);
  hi.innerHTML = "<b>Heading:</b>" + hv + " degrees";
  $("#compass").rotate(-hv);
}

function onHeadingError(compassError) {
```

```
        //Remove the watch since we're having a problem
        navigator.compass.clearWatchFilter(watchID);
        //clear the Heading value from the page
        hi.innerHTML = "";

        //Then tell the user what happened.
        if(compassError.code == CompassError.COMPASS_NOT_SUPPORTED) {
          alert("Compass not supported.");
        } else if (compassError.code ==
          CompassError.COMPASS_INTERNAL_ERR) {
          alert("Compass Internal Error");
        } else {
          alert("Unknown heading error!");
        }
    }
}
```

14

Connection

The PhoneGap Connection object provides an application with information about the current network connection available to the application. The object exposes a single property, connection.type, as well as the following constants:

- Connection.CELL_2G
- Connection.CELL_3G
- Connection.CELL_4G
- Connection.ETHERNET
- Connection.NONE
- Connection.UNKNOWN
- Connection.WIFI

An application will query the connection.type property and compare the results against these constants to determine the specific type of connection available. You'll see an example of this shortly.

Modern smartphones include multiple radios, so the device can connect to several types of networks throughout the day. The device typically maintains a constant connection to the cellular network whenever possible, which it uses for both voice and data communication. Devices typically connect to Wi-Fi networks as well, primarily for data communication but sometimes for voice communication.

When it comes to data communication, the type of connection a mobile application would use to communicate with server-based resources, the device typically prioritizes its connections and uses the fastest (and least expensive) connection whenever possible. For example, a device will typically place a higher priority on Wi-Fi connections and use cellular connections only when a Wi-Fi connection is not available.

Because of this prioritization, PhoneGap's `connection.type` property will return the primary connection type, which is the connection type currently being used for data communication. As the device moves in and out of cellular and Wi-Fi coverage throughout the day, it typically doesn't lose its network connectivity; the device instead seamlessly transitions between available network types doing its best to keep the connection available.

An application would use the online and offline events (described in Chapter 17) to determine whether connectivity is available but would use `connection.type` (possibly in conjunction with those events) to determine how robust the connection is. When transferring a small to medium amount of data (ranging from bytes to kilobytes, for example), the network speed is important but not critical. When an application prepares to transmit or receive a large amount of data across the network, though, knowledge of the type of network is critical, and that's the primary reason `connection.type` exists.

Before starting a large download or upload, an application might want to check to see whether the device has a high-speed (Wi-Fi or 4G) connection and defer the transmission unless a high-speed connection is available.

```
var networkState = navigator.network.connection.type;
if (networkState == Connection.NONE) {
  //No network available, so tell the user
  //and defer the update

}
```

The PhoneGap API documentation provides a simple example of how you can use the connection object to detect the current network type and display an alert to the user. Unfortunately, that's not an example that can really be used in a production application. I thought I'd tweak it a bit to make it more useful. Take a look at the following code:

```
var states = {};
states[Connection.UNKNOWN]  = 'Unknown';
states[Connection.ETHERNET] = 'Ethernet';
states[Connection.WIFI]     = 'Wi-Fi';
states[Connection.CELL_2G]  = 'Cell 2G';
states[Connection.CELL_3G]  = 'Cell 3G';
states[Connection.CELL_4G]  = 'Cell 4G';
```

```
states[Connection.NONE] = 'No network';

function getConnectionTypeStr() {
  //get the network state
  var networkState = navigator.network.connection.type;
  //return a string representing the current network state
  return states[networkState];
}
```

In this example, I pulled the population of the `states` object out of the function and instead execute that code within the script directly so it executes only once. Next I updated the function so it returns a string representing the network type, so an application could, for example, update its UI with the current network type if appropriate for the application.

Example 14-1 shows the function put to use in an application. It's the same application used to demonstrate the use of the Event API's `online` and `offline` events (described in Chapter 17). In this example, the application's main page gets updated with the network connection type every time the device goes online.

Example 14-1

```
<!DOCTYPE html>
<html>
  <head>
    <title>Example 14-1</title>
    <meta http-equiv="Content-type" content="text/html;
      charset=utf-8">
    <meta name="viewport" id="viewport"
      content="width=device-width, height=device-height,
      initial-scale=1.0, maximum-scale=1.0, user-scalable=no;"
    />
    <script type="text/javascript" charset="utf-8"
      src="jquery.js"></script>
    <script type="text/javascript" charset="utf-8"
      src="phonegap.js"></script>
    <script type="text/javascript" charset="utf-8">

      //build an accessible representation of the different
      //network state values
      var states = {};
      states[Connection.UNKNOWN] = 'Unknown';
      states[Connection.ETHERNET] = 'Ethernet';
      states[Connection.WIFI] = 'Wi-Fi';
      states[Connection.CELL_2G] = 'Cell 2G';
      states[Connection.CELL_3G] = 'Cell 3G';
```

```
    states[Connection.CELL_4G] = 'Cell 4G';
    states[Connection.NONE] = 'No network';

    function onBodyLoad() {
      document.addEventListener("deviceready", onDeviceReady,
        false);
    }

    function onDeviceReady() {
      navigator.notification.alert("PhoneGap is ready!");
      //Add the online event listener
      document.addEventListener("online", isOnline, false);
      //Add the offline event listener
      document.addEventListener("offline", isOffline, false);
    }

    function isOnline() {
      var d = new Date();
      $('#networkInfo').prepend("Online (" +
        getConnectionTypeStr() + ")<br />");
    }

    function isOffline() {
      var d = new Date();
      $('#networkInfo').prepend("Offline<br />");
    }

    function getConnectionTypeStr() {
      //get the network state
      var networkState = navigator.network.connection.type;
      //return a string representing the current network state
      return states[networkState];
    }
    </script>
  </head>
  <body onload="onBodyLoad()">
    <h1>Example 14-1</h1>
    <p id="networkInfo"></p>
  </body>
  </body>
</html>
```

Figure 14-1 shows the application running on an Android device.

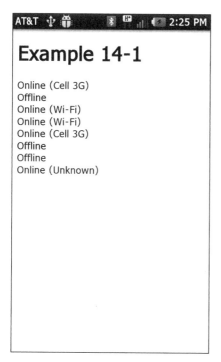

Figure 14-1   Example 14-1 running on an Android device

The application appends the current network status to the top of the list, so what you see in the figure is activity over time with the most recent event at the top. The application uses the jQuery $().prepend method to accomplish this. As you can see from the example, with the cellular and Wi-Fi radios on, the connection defaults to the Wi-Fi network. When I turned the radio off (third line from the top), the device fired the offline event first (even though the cellular connection was still available); then it fired the online event when it transferred to the cellular connection (the top line).

15

Contacts

The PhoneGap Contacts API provides applications with an interface that can be used to create, locate, edit, copy, and delete contact records from the device's native Contacts application. The API is not proprietary; instead, it's an implementation of the W3C's Contacts API (www.w3.org/TR/2011/WD-contacts-api-20110616/). This API interfaces with the native Contacts APIs provided by the mobile platform, and because of the way the internal API views contact information, there are quite a few quirks that manifest themselves across mobile device platforms.

Example Applications

Two sample applications have been created to help illustrate the features of the Contacts API. Example 15-1 illustrates how to create a new contact within a PhoneGap application, and Example 15-2 shows how to use the Contacts API's search capabilities to locate a contact in an application.

Because of the length of the applications, it was not possible to include the application source code in this chapter. Relevant portions of the application code and screen shots of the application in action are shown within the chapter, but to see the completed application code, you will need to point your browser of choice to the book's web site at www.phonegapessentials.com and look for the example project files in the Code section of the site.

Creating a Contact

Creating a contact from within a PhoneGap application is pretty straightforward; simply execute the following code:

```
var contact = navigator.contacts.create();
```

When the call to `navigator.contacts.create` completes, the `contact` object exists that contains nothing more than a representation of the different fields that define a contact as would be rendered within the device's native Contacts application. At this point, the `contact` object doesn't contain any information about the contact; all you have is an object that can be populated with contact information and saved to the Contacts application's database. You must manually save any changes to the contact using the `navigator.contacts.save` method described later in the chapter.

> **Note:** One of the most common problems people encounter with the PhoneGap Contacts API stems from their failure to save their changes to a contact once they've made them. Many a developer has created a contact, set the appropriate properties for the contact, and then scratched their head when the changes are found to have not been written to the device's contacts database. Be sure to call `navigator.contacts.save` when you've completed making changes to a contact's properties.

The call to `navigator.contacts.create` is one of the few synchronous API calls implemented by PhoneGap. Instead of using callback functions to register success or failure of an API call as illustrated in other chapters, the call simply creates a `contact` object in memory and returns; there's no need for callback functions here. Once an application has a `contact` object to work with, the application must populate the contact fields defined within the object and then save the contact to complete the process.

Defined within the contact object are a group of strings and objects that specify different aspects of the contact, as shown in the following list:

- `id`: A unique identifier for the contact; this variable is assigned a unique value during the call to `navigator.contacts.create`.

- `displayName`: The name of the contact; on most devices, this is the name that is displayed in contact lists and address picker dialogs. Unfortunately, this field is not supported on all platforms (such as iOS).

- `name`: An object defining the different components of a contact's name, such as given name, family name, middle name, and so on.

- `nickname`: A casual name for the contact.

- phoneNumbers: An array containing the contact's phone numbers.

- emails: An array containing the contact's email addresses.

- addresses: An array containing the contact's physical addresses (home, business, and so on).

- ims: An array containing the contact's instant messaging (IM) addresses.

- organizations: An array containing the organizations the contact is associated with.

- birthday: The contact's birthday.

- note: A variable used to contain text-based notes related to the contact.

- photos: An array containing photos of the contact.

- categories: An array containing user-defined categories associated with the contact.

- urls: An array containing the web addresses associated with the contact.

The name object includes the string values shown in the following list:

- formatted: The contact's complete name.

- familyName: The contact's family name.

- givenName: The contact's given name.

- middleName: The contact's middle name.

- honorificPrefix: The prefix associated with the contact (examples: Dr., Mr., or Mrs.).

- honorificSuffix: The suffix associated with the contact (example: Ph.D.).

When you look at these lists, you may notice that the contact's name components are represented in different places in the object. The displayName and nickname values are associated with the contact, while everything else is associated with the contact.name object. I expected that all name components would be associated with the name object, but for some reason they're not.

Many of the other components of the contact object are simple arrays representing multiple values of the same type. The addresses array is a two-dimensional array of ContactAddress objects consisting of the following values:

- pref: Boolean value that defines whether the entry is the default address for the contact

- `type`: A string value defining the type of address being defined such as home or work

- `formatted`: The full address formatted for display

- `streetAddress`: The full street address

- `locality`: The city or locality associated with this address

- `region`: The state or region associated with this address

- `postalCode`: The ZIP or postal code associated with this address

- `country`: The country associated with this address

The `organizations` array is a two-dimensional array of `ContactOrganization` objects consisting of the following values:

- `pref`: Boolean value that defines whether the entry is the preferred or default organization for the contact

- `type`: A string value defining the type of organization being defined such as home or work

- `name`: The name of the organization

- `department`: The department where the contact works

- `title`: The contact's title within the organization

The contact's `phoneNumbers`, `emails`, and `ims` values are all populated the same way, using an array of values shown in the following list:

- `type`: A string value defining the type of value being defined such as home or work

- `value`: The contact value such as phone number or email address

- `pref`: Boolean value that defines whether the entry is the default entry for this type of contact method

Some smartphone platforms are picky about the values assigned to the `type` property. Even though PhoneGap will accept anything for this value, your target mobile device might not display the values unless the right values are assigned here. My testing has shown that it's best to use standard values like home, work, and mobile for `type`.

Now that you have a good understanding of the contact properties, let's take a look at an example of how all of this is implemented in code. In the Example 15-1 sample application (available from the www.phonegapessentials.com web site), the application retrieves contact information from an external source (in this case external .js files) and allows the application user to add information about a selected user to the local contacts database. The following is an example of the contact object for one of the contacts used in the application:

```
{
  "FullName": "Michael Palin",
  "LastName": "Palin",
  "FirstName": "Michael",
  "EmailAddress": "michael@montypython.com",
  "OfficePhone": "330.123.4567",
  "MobilePhone": "330.987.6543"
}
```

 Note: I made up that email address for Michael Palin; he may have an email address, but I definitely don't know what it is. It's probably best not to send any email messages to that address; there's no telling where it would go or what would happen.

In the application, the contact information shown is assigned to the `contactInfo` object and passed to the following function so the contact's information can be added to the local contacts database:

```
function addContact(contactInfo) {
  //Create a new contact object
  var contact = navigator.contacts.create();

  //Populate the contact object with values
  contact.displayName = contactInfo.FullName;
  contact.nickname = contactInfo.FullName;

  //Populate the Contact's Name entries
  var tmpName = new ContactName();
  tmpName.givenName = contactInfo.FirstName;
  tmpName.familyName = contactInfo.LastName;
  tmpName.formatted = contactInfo.FullName;
  //Then add the name object to the contact object
  contact.name = tmpName;

  //Populate Phone Number Entries by creating and populating
  //an array of phone number information
  var phoneNums = [2];
  phoneNums[0] = new ContactField('work',
    contactInfo.OfficePhone, false);
  phoneNums[1] = new ContactField('mobile',
    contactInfo.MobilePhone, true);
  contact.phoneNumbers = phoneNums;
```

```
//Populate Email Address the same way that you did the
//phone numbers
var emailAddresses = [1];
emailAddresses[0] = new ContactField('home',
  contactInfo.EmailAddress, true);
contact.emails = emailAddresses;

// save the contact object to the device's contact database
contact.save(onContactSaveSuccess, onContactSaveError);
}
```

You can also create a contact object and populate it at the same time by passing in a properly formatted contact object to the `create` method, as shown here:

```
var contact = navigator.contacts.create({displayName:
  'Michael Palin', nickname: 'Mike', name: {givenName:
  'Michael', familyName: 'Palin'}});
contact.save(onContactSaveSuccess, onContactSaveError);
```

There are some quirks in the way each individual mobile device platform stores the contact information passed to the `contact` object. You will need to refer to the PhoneGap documentation for specifics about these quirks since they're likely to change over time. For some examples, though, the BlackBerry platform doesn't support the `displayName` field directly, so the value is stored in the `user1` field and the `nickname` field returns null. On iOS, the `displayName` field isn't directly supported, but different values may be returned depending on what values are defined for the contact.

As mentioned previously, the changes you make to a contact's properties will not be written to the device's contacts database until you execute the following code:

```
contact.save(onContactSaveSuccess, onContactSaveError);
```

In this example, I'm passing in two functions: an `onContactSaveSuccess` function that is executed after the `contact` has been successfully saved to the contacts database and an `onContactSaveError` function that is executed if there's an error writing to the database.

The `onContactSaveSuccess` function is quite simple; it just lets the user know that the save completed successfully, as shown in the following example:

```
function onContactSaveSuccess() {
  alert(contactInfo.FullName + " was successfully saved to the
    device contacts database");
}
```

If there's an error saving the contact, the `onContactSaveError` function is called, and an error object is passed to the function that allows an application to understand the nature of the error and react according to the needs of the application. In the following example, the code displays a different error message for the user depending on the nature of the nature of the error encountered by the application.

```
function onContactSaveError(e) {
  var msgText;
  //Now build a message string based upon the error
  //returned by the API
  switch(e.code) {
    case ContactError.UNKNOWN_ERROR:
      msgText = "An Unknown Error was reported while saving
        the contact.";
      break;
    case ContactError.INVALID_ARGUMENT_ERROR:
      msgText = "An invalid argument was used with the Contact
        API.";
      break;
    case ContactError.TIMEOUT_ERROR:
      msgText = "Timeout Error.";
      break;
    case ContactError.PENDING_OPERATION_ERROR:
      msgText = "Pending Operation Error.";
      break;
    case ContactError.IO_ERROR:
      msgText = "IO Error.";
      break;
    case ContactError.NOT_SUPPORTED_ERROR:
      msgText = "Not Supported Error.";
      break;
    case ContactError.PERMISSION_DENIED_ERROR:
      msgText = "Permission Denied Error.";
      break;
    default:
      //Create a generic response, just in case the
      // switch fails
      msgText = "Unknown Error (" + e.code + ")";
  }
  //Now tell the user what happened
  navigator.notification.alert(msgText, null,
  "Contact Save Error");
}
```

In your applications, you will likely want to do something more substantive when an error occurs. For some of the errors, there's not much the application can do except to perhaps try again later. The INVALID_ARGUMENT_ERROR is most likely caused by a coding error and would likely not appear in a properly tested application (unless PhoneGap changed the Contacts API options behind the scenes).

The PERMISSION_DENIED_ERROR is important and would affect users depending on how they answer the security prompt they receive on BlackBerry and Android devices when they install new applications. On each platform, you must configure the application project with a list of the APIs used by the application. If your application doesn't properly identify that it uses the Contacts API, the device may block access to the API. On BlackBerry and Android, the user is prompted to allow access to the different APIs used by the application; if the user doesn't allow access to the Contacts API when installing the application, the application will not function properly and will likely return the permission denied error. To configure your projects with the appropriate permissions, refer to the documentation that accompanies the mobile platform development tools you are using.

When working with PhoneGap Build (described in Chapter 9), the build service takes care of configuring each development environment for you. To enable access to the Contacts API on Android, add the following line to the project's `config.xml` file, and be sure to include it with the project files uploaded to the PhoneGap Build service:

```
<feature name="http://api.phonegap.com/1.0/contacts" />
```

This enables the `READ_CONTACTS`, `WRITE_CONTACTS`, and `GET_ACCOUNTS` permissions on Android.

For a BlackBerry WebWorks application, you must include the following line in the `config.xml` file:

```
<feature id="blackberry.pim.Contact" />
```

The following listing shows a completed PhoneGap Build `config.xml` for this application:

```
<?xml version="1.0" encoding="UTF-8"?>
<widget xmlns = "http://www.w3.org/ns/widgets"
  xmlns:gap = "http://phonegap.com/ns/1.0"
  id = "com.phonegapessentials.ex151"
  version = "1.0.0">

  <name>Example 15-1</name>
  <description>An example application that uses the PhoneGap
    Contacts API</description>
  <author href="http://johnwargo.com"
  email="developer@somecompany.com">John M. Wargo</author>
  <gap:platforms>
    <gap:platform name="android" minVersion="2.1" />
    <gap:platform name="webos" />
    <gap:platform name="symbian.wrt" />
    <gap:platform name="blackberry" project="widgets"/>
  </gap:platforms>
  <feature name="http://api.phonegap.com/1.0/contacts" />
  <feature id="blackberry.pim.Contact" />

</widget>
```

One of the quirks of the Android platform is that an application must have a Google account configured on the device in order to access contact information from a PhoneGap application. I discovered this issue when I was testing on a device that I'd done a complete security wipe on before testing the application. Without a Google account defined in the Android Accounts and Sync area of Settings, the application returned an Unknown Error whenever it tried to write a contact to the contacts database. As soon as I configured the device for my Gmail account, the error went away. If you are using the Android emulator, you will need to use an emulator based upon the Google APIs, not the default SDK.

Let's take a look at the application in action. Figure 15-1 shows the Example 15-1 application running on a BlackBerry Torch simulator. It starts by showing a list of contacts from an external data source.

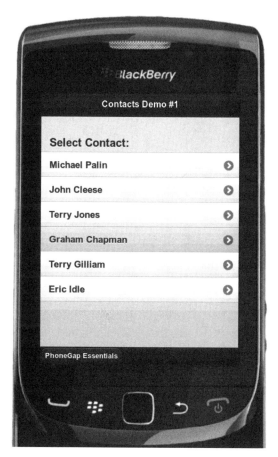

Figure 15-1   Example 15-1 running on a BlackBerry Torch simulator

When the user selects a contact, the application opens a page that displays detailed information about the contact, as shown in Figure 15-2.

Figure 15-2   Example 15-1: contact details

When the user clicks the Add Contact button, the application adds the selected contact to the contacts database and displays the confirmation dialog shown in Figure 15-3.

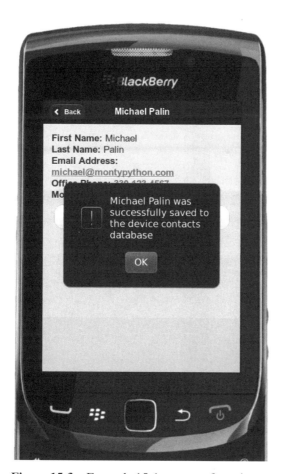

Figure 15-3   Example 15-1: save confirmation

Opening the BlackBerry Contacts application and searching for and then opening the new contact will show a screen similar to the one shown in Figure 15-4.

Figure 15-4   New contact information in the BlackBerry Contacts application

Figure 15-5 shows the results of the same activity on an Android smartphone.

Figure 15-6 shows the results of the same activity on an Apple iPhone.

With each of these examples, the native contacts application makes the phone number, email address, and other electronic contact fields clickable so the user can click an item and initiate contact through the selected option.

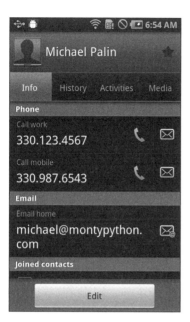

Figure 15-5   New contact information in the Android Contacts application

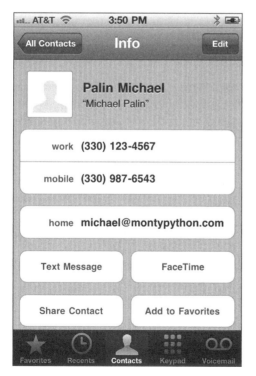

Figure 15-6   New contact information in the iOS Contacts application

Searching for Contacts

Another useful feature of the Contacts API is the ability to search the device's local contacts database for contacts. To initiate a search, an application should execute the following code:

```
navigator.contacts.find(contactFields, onContactSearchSuccess,
  onContactSearchError, searchOptions);
```

The `contactFields` parameter passed to the `find` method defines the list of contact field names whose values will be included in the search results. In some cases, you may want the search function to return all fields, in which case you would use the following:

```
contactFields = ['*'];
```

In other cases, you might want to limit your search results to a limited number of contact fields, as shown in the following example:

```
contactFields = ['displayName', 'name', 'nickname'];
```

The `name` entry refers to the `name` object described in the previous section and includes `familyName`, `givenName`, `middleName`, and more.

As you build your applications, you may think you can just use the `displayName` field and catch most contact names. The problem with this approach is that `displayName` is not supported on iOS, so if you rely upon that field name for searches targeted at iOS devices, the search will likely not return any values.

The `onContactSearchSuccess` and `onContactSearchError` functions passed as parameters to `find` are standard callback functions you've seen in other examples in this book. The `onContactSearchSuccess` function is executed when the search succeeds, and the `onContactSearchError` function is executed if an error is encountered performing the search. You'll learn more about these functions later.

The `searchOptions` parameter is an object defining options used to control how the search is performed. It consists of two values, `filter` and `multiple`, as shown in the following example:

```
var searchOptions = { filter : searchStr, multiple : true };
```

The `filter` value defines the search string used when searching the device's contacts database, and the `multiple` value is a Boolean value that defines whether the application should return multiple results or return a value as soon as a single item that matches the search criteria is found.

Let's take a look at an example application that puts all of this to use. In the Example 15-2 application (available for download from www.phonegapessentials.com), the application displays the simple form shown in Figure 15-7. In the application, I used the jQuery (www.jquery.com) and jQuery Mobile (www.jquerymobile.com) frameworks to provide the application with a more professional-looking interface without having to write a bunch of interface code myself.

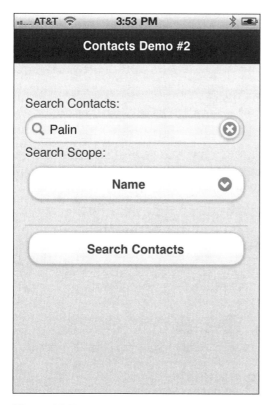

Figure 15-7   Example 15-2 running on an Apple iPhone

On the form, the search field is defined using the following HTML markup:

```
<input type="search" id="editSearch" />
```

The search scope picker is defined using the following markup:

```
<select id="searchScope" name="searchScope">
  <option>All</option>
  <option>Name</option>
  <option>Address</option>
  <option>Notes</option>
</select>
```

The code behind the Search Contacts button is defined in the following function:

```
function searchContacts() {
  //Get the search string from the page
  var searchStr =
    document.getElementById("editSearch").value;
  //Figure out which search option is selected
  var searchScope =
    document.getElementById("searchScope").selectedIndex;
  //Then populate searchOptions with the list of fields being
  //searched
  var contactFields = [];
  switch(searchScope) {
    case 1:
      //Return just name fields
      contactFields = ['displayName', 'name', 'nickname'];
      break;
    case 2:
      //Return address fields
      contactFields = ['name', 'streetAddress', 'locality',
        'region', 'postalCode', 'country'];
      break;
    case 3:
      //Return name and contents of the Notes field
      contactFields = ['name', 'note'];
      break;
    default:
      //return all contact fields
      contactFields = ['*'];
  }
  //Populate the search options object
  var searchOptions = { filter : searchStr, multiple : true };
  //Execute the search
  navigator.contacts.find(contactFields,
    onContactSearchSuccess, onContactSearchError, searchOptions);
}
```

In the function, the code grabs the value from the search field and the selected value from the search scope picker. Using those values, it defines the values for the contactFields variable based upon which picker option was selected and passes the search string in the filter value in the searchOptions object.

That's it—that's all an application has to do to search the local contacts database. The onContactSearchError function is the same as the onContactSaveError function described in the previous section. When the search completes, the find method calls the onContactSearchSuccess function, which is shown next. The function essentially builds an on-screen list of the search results (displaying the name of the contact if it can be determined).

```
function onContactSearchSuccess(contacts) {
  // alert("onContactSearchSuccess");
  //Populate the contact list element of the contact list page
  var i, len, theList;
  //Store the contact data in our global variable so the
  //other functions have something to work with
  contactList = contacts;
  //Did we get any results from the search?
  len = contacts.length;
  if(len > 0) {
    theList = '<ul  data-role="listview">';
    for( i = 0, len; i < len; i += 1) {
      //on iOS displayName isn't supported, so we can't
      //use it
      if(contacts[i].displayName == null) {
        theList += '<li><a onclick="showContact(' + i +
          ');">' + contacts[i].name.familyName + ", " +
          contacts[i].name.givenName + '</a></li>';
      } else {
        theList += '<li><a onclick="showContact(' + i +
          ');">' + contacts[i].displayName + '</a></li>';
      }
    }
    theList += '</ul>';
    $('#contacts').html(theList);
    //Then switch to the Contact Details page
    $.mobile.changePage("#contactList", "slide", false, true);
  } else {
    navigator.notification.alert('Search returned 0 results',
      null, 'Contact Search');
  }
}
```

In onContactSearchSuccess, the function is passed an array containing contact entries for each of the contact records containing the search string. The code first checks to see whether the array has any values; if not, a message is displayed to the user letting them know that there are no search results. If there are results, the function loops through the results array and creates an unordered list containing the name of each contact included in the search results. In the application, the unordered list is assigned a data-role attribute of listview, which is used by jQuery Mobile to render the interactive list shown in Figure 15-8. In this case, there's only one result, but if there had been more, the list would scroll down the length of the screen as needed.

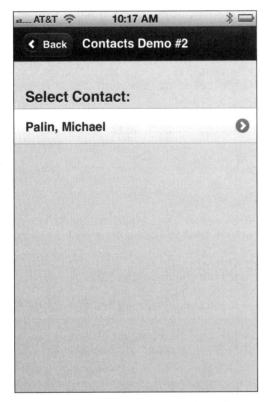

Figure 15-8   Example 15-2: search results

Looking at the function, you may have noticed that when creating the list view, the code first checks to see whether `displayName` is `null` and uses the contact's `givenName` and `familyName` to create the list entry. This is because `displayName` is not supported on iOS, so I had to find another way to ensure that something would display in the list.

```
if(contacts[i].displayName == null) {
  theList += '<li><a onclick="showContact(' + i + ');">' +
    contacts[i].name.familyName + ", " +
    contacts[i].name.givenName + '</a></li>';
} else {
  theList += '<li><a onclick="showContact(' + i + ');">' +
    contacts[i].displayName + '</a></li>';
}
```

Each entry in the list view has an `onclick` event defined that causes the `showContact` function to be executed when the user selects a contact; passed to `showContact` is the index for the selected contact. The function retrieves information about the selected contact and displays a page similar to the one shown in Figure 15-9.

Figure 15-9   Example 15-2: contact detail

As you can see from the figure, the application displays some common field values at the top of the page and lists all of the contact field values below the horizontal rule. I built the application this way to help me validate what was returned by the search function. When using the application, as you select different search scopes, you can easily see what contact fields are (and aren't) returned to the application when performing a search. Here's the code that generates the field/value list:

```
//Show all of the contact fields
dt = "<hr />";
for(myKey in contact) {
  dt += "Contact[" + myKey + "] = " + contact[myKey] + "<br />";
}
$('#detailContent').html(dt);
```

Cloning Contacts

To make a clone of an existing contact, an application simply calls the `clone` method, as shown in the following example:

```
var contact2 = contact1.clone();
```

The `contact` object points to an existing contact obtained by creating a new contact via a call to `navigator.contacts.create`, as described in the beginning of the chapter, or retrieved by searching the local device contacts database using the `find` method, as described in the previous section.

Once the application has the cloned copy of the original contact, it can manipulate the properties of the clone, changing whatever properties are appropriate for the application and then calling `navigator.contacts.save` to write the updates to the contacts database. When the clone is created, the cloned contact object exists solely in memory and must be written to disk for any changes to be maintained.

Removing Contacts

To remove an existing contact, an application simply calls the `remove` method, as shown in the following example:

```
contact.remove(onContactRemoveSuccess, onContactRemoveError);
```

The `contact` object points to an existing contact obtained by creating a new contact via a call to `navigator.contacts.create`, as described in the beginning of the chapter, or retrieved by searching the local device contacts database using the `find` method, as described in an earlier section.

The `onContactRemoveSuccess` and `onContactRemoveError` parameters passed to the call to `remove` are callback functions that are executed by the `remove` method. The `onContactRemoveSuccess` function is executed after the contact has been successfully removed, while the `onContactRemoveError` function is the same as the `onContactSaveError` function described in the first section of this chapter.

16

Device

The PhoneGap Device object allows an application to access a limited amount of information about the application and device running a PhoneGap application. The device object represents the following properties:

- `device.name`: Returns the name assigned to the device; this could be something assigned by the device manufacturer or assigned by the smartphone user depending on the mobile device platform.

- `device.phonegap`: Returns the version of the PhoneGap framework used to build the application.

- `device.platform`: On most platforms, returns the name of the mobile device platform the application is running on. Exceptions will be discussed later in the chapter.

- `device.uuid`: Returns the universally unique identifier (UUID) associated with the device (http://en.wikipedia.org/wiki/Universally_Unique_Identifier).

- `device.version`: Returns the OS version running on the device.

The device object has scope at the window level, so you can access any of the device properties using the following:

```
var deviceName = window.device.name;
```

or this:

```
var deviceName = device.name;
```

An example application using device properties was shown in Chapter 2. Example 16-1 highlights each of the supported device properties.

Example 16-1

```
<!DOCTYPE html>
<html>
  <head>
    <title>Example 16-1</title>
    <meta http-equiv="Content-type" content="text/html;
      charset=utf-8">
    <meta name="viewport" id="viewport"
      content="width=device-width, height=device-height,
      initial-scale=1.0, maximum-scale=1.0, user-scalable=no;"
    />
    <script type="text/javascript" charset="utf-8"
      src="phonegap.js"></script>
    <script type="text/javascript" charset="utf-8">

      function onBodyLoad() {
        document.addEventListener("deviceready", onDeviceReady,
          false);
      }

      function onDeviceReady() {
        //HTML Break string
        var br = "<br />";

        //Get the appInfo DOM element
        var element = document.getElementById("deviceInfo");
        //replace it with specific information about the
        //device running the application
        element.innerHTML =
          "<b>device.name: " + device.name + br +
          "<b>device.phonegap:</b> " + device.phonegap + br +
          "<b>device.platform:</b> " + device.platform + br +
          "<b>device.uuid:</b> " + device.uuid + br +
          "<b>device.version:</b> " + device.version + br;
      }

    </script>
  </head>
  <body onload="onBodyLoad()">
    <h1>Example 16-1</h1>
    <p id="deviceInfo">Waiting for PhoneGap Initialization to
      complete</p>
  </body>
</html>
```

In this example, once PhoneGap has initialized, the `onDeviceReady` function is executed, and the application replaces the `deviceInfo` content on the page with values from each of the properties of the device object.

Let's take a look at the output of this application on different devices.

Figure 16-1 shows Example 16-1 running on a LG Thrill smartphone. As you can see from the example, the `device.name` property reports the name the manufacturer has assigned to the device. I built this application using PhoneGap Build, so they're using the latest (at the time) version of PhoneGap, version 1.1.0. The device is running Android version 2.2.2.

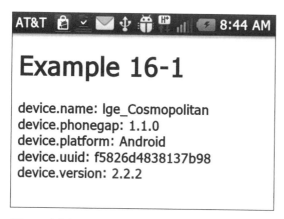

Figure 16-1   Example 16-1 running on an Android device

Figure 16-2 shows the same application running on the BlackBerry simulator. As you can see, PhoneGap on BlackBerry has an issue displaying the platform name, reporting 3.0.0.100 instead of the word BlackBerry.

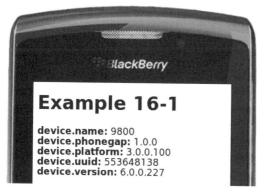

Figure 16-2   Example 16-1 running on a BlackBerry simulator

When you take a look at the source code in the phonegap.js file for the Black-Berry platform, you see the following:

```
function Device() {
  this.platform = phonegap.device.platform;
  this.version  = blackberry.system.softwareVersion;
  this.name     = blackberry.system.model;
  this.uuid     = phonegap.device.uuid;
  this.phonegap = phonegap.device.phonegap;
};
```

PhoneGap is simply calling JavaScript methods provided by the BlackBerry Web-Works platform, and for some bizarre reason, the developer has chosen to implement the device.name property using a system call that returns the version number of the BlackBerry platform running on the device rather than the word BlackBerry. In reality, the code should really look like this:

```
this.name = "BlackBerry";
```

RIM provides a Java API that allows an application to know whether the application is running on a physical device or a simulator, which is useful information to have when testing an application. Unfortunately, the developer of PhoneGap for BlackBerry has not chosen to expose that distinction, which as you'll see next has been implemented on iOS.

Figure 16-3 shows Example 16-1 running on an iPhone device. For this OS, the device.name property returns the name the user has assigned to the device in iTunes.

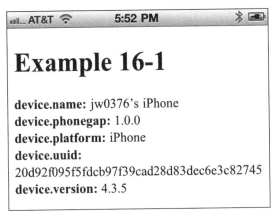

Figure 16-3   Example 16-1 running on an iPhone device

Figure 16-4 shows Example 16-1 running on the iPad simulator, but the PhoneGap application is configured in Xcode as an iPhone application. This particular configuration puts the application in compatibility mode, running as an iPhone application in a little iPhone window on the iPad. Users can click the 2X button in the bottom-right corner of the screen to expand the window so the application runs full-screen.

Figure 16-4   Example 16-1 running on the iPad simulator as an iPhone application

The application reports that it's running on an iPhone, but in reality `device.platform` should return iOS since that's the OS platform the application is running on. Expect that this will change someday, and any code you have that looks for iPhone will have to be updated to check for iOS as well.

Notice too that on iOS PhoneGap reports correctly when the application is running on a simulator. This particular feature makes it easier to perform testing in situations where a particular feature (like the camera) is available only on a physical device; your code can test to see whether the application is running on a simulator and run substitute code in those cases.

Figure 16-5 shows Example 16-1 running on the iPad simulator. Happily, the application is now running in full-screen mode and reports correctly that it's running on an iPad rather than an iPhone, as shown in Figure 16-4.

Figure 16-5   Example 16-1 running on the iPad simulator

17

Events

The PhoneGap Events API provides an application with the ability to register event listeners for different events that occur on a supported smartphone device. The following is a list of the types of events supported by PhoneGap:

- `deviceready` event
- Application status events
- Network events
- Button events

The subsequent sections in this chapter will describe each of these event types in detail.

Creating an Event Listener

To create an event listener in a PhoneGap application, execute the following code:

```
document.addEventListener("eventName", functionName,
  useCapture);
```

The parameters passed to `addEventListener` are as follows:

- `eventName`: String value specifying the name of the event the listener will be listening for
- `functionName`: The function that will be executed when the event fires
- `useCapture`: Boolean value that specifies the scope of the event; since with PhoneGap we're capturing system events rather than object events, you will most likely just use `false` for this parameter

The following sections will cover the different categories of events supported by PhoneGap.

To remove an event listener, simply call the JavaScript removeEventListener method.

deviceready Event

The deviceready event is a fundamental part of any PhoneGap application. The event is fired by PhoneGap to indicate that PhoneGap has completed initialization and that PhoneGap APIs are available to be used by the application. An application does not have to listen for this event; it can try to use a PhoneGap API any time it wants, but a well-behaved application will perform actions using PhoneGap APIs only after the deviceready API has fired.

Example 17-1 shows the typical implementation of an event listener that listens for the deviceready event.

Example 17-1

```
<!DOCTYPE html>
<html>
  <head>
    <meta http-equiv="Content-type" content="text/html;
      charset=utf-8">
    <meta name="viewport" id="viewport"
      content="width=device-width, height=device-height,
      initial-scale=1.0, maximum-scale=1.0, user-scalable=no;"
    />
    <script type="text/javascript" charset="utf-8"
      src="phonegap.js"></script>
    <script type="text/javascript" charset="utf-8">

      function onBodyLoad() {
        document.addEventListener("deviceready",
          onDeviceReady, false);
      }

      function onDeviceReady() {
        //PhoneGap is ready, so go ahead and call PhoneGap APIs

      }

    </script>
  </head>
  <body onload="onBodyLoad()">
```

```
    <h1>Example 17-1</h1>
    <p>This is a sample PhoneGap application.</p>
    </body>        .
</html>
```

Application Status Events

Most modern smartphones allow a user to switch between applications. As a running application transitions from the foreground to paused or to running in the background (depending on the smartphone platform), PhoneGap will fire the pause event. As a suspended application becomes active or an application running in the background transitions to the foreground, PhoneGap will fire the resume event.

Most smartphone platforms automatically switch an application into the background whenever another application is launched or when the user switches to another application. This allows the application to continue to process in the background, retrieving data from a server, for example. On iOS, Apple has decided that only certain applications have the right to run in the background, so your PhoneGap application will automatically be suspended whenever the user switches to another application.

The purpose of each event is to allow an application to perform whatever cleanup tasks are needed before an application makes the transition. As an example, a running application might want to close data or database connections and turn off any media files being played before suspending or transitioning to the background. A suspended or background application transitioning to the foreground may want to reestablish those network or database connections and restart any media files once the application is restarted.

Example 17-2 shows a sample application that implements pause and resume event listeners. It is a simple application that updates the screen every time one of the events fire. When the resume event fires, the application indicates how long the application was suspended or running in the background.

Example 17-2

```
<!DOCTYPE html>
<html>
  <head>
    <meta name="viewport" content="width=device-width,
      height=device-height initial-scale=1.0, maximum-
      scale=1.0, user-scalable=no;" />
```

```
<meta http-equiv="Content-type" content="text/html;
  charset=utf-8">
<script type="text/javascript" charset="utf-8"
  src="phonegap.js"></script>
<script type="text/javascript" charset="utf-8">

  //Start time variable
  var startTime, endTime;
  //pauseInfo page content variable
  var pi;
  //FirstTime variable
  var firstTime;

  function onBodyLoad() {
    document.addEventListener("deviceready",onDeviceReady,
      false);
  }

  function onDeviceReady() {
    pName = device.platform;
    if ((pName == "Android") || (pName == "3.0.0.100")) {
      firstTime = true;
    } else {
      firstTime = false;
    }
    //Add our Pause event listener
    document.addEventListener("pause", processPause, false);
    //Add our Resume event listener
    document.addEventListener("resume", processResume,
      false);
    //Get a handle to the pauseInfo page element
    pi = document.getElementById("pauseInfo");
  }

  function processPause() {
    //Clear the previous counter
    pi.innerHTML = "Application paused.";
    //Set startTime to the current date/time
    startTime = new Date();
  }

  function processResume() {
    //We want to skip the first time this fires
    if(firstTime == true) {
      //Clear our firstTime variable
      firstTime = false;
```

```
            pi.innerHTML = "Skipping first Resume.";
        } else {
            //Get the current date
            endTime = new Date();
            timeDiff = (endTime - startTime) / 1000;
            //Update the screen
            pi.innerHTML = "Paused for " + timeDiff + " seconds.";
        }
    }

</script>
</head>
<body onload="onBodyLoad()">
    <h1>Pause Counter</h1>
    <p id="pauseInfo">Waiting for pause.</p>
</body>
</html>
```

As I worked through this example, I learned something about these events that is not documented in the PhoneGap API documentation. An Android or BlackBerry application will fire the resume event as soon as the application starts. On iOS, the resume event is fired only when the application resumes from being suspended in the background. Because of this quirk, I had to create a Boolean variable called firstTime, which is used by the application to control whether the first firing of the resume event is ignored by the program. Also, because of a quirk in the Device API, for a BlackBerry device the application has to look for a number in the device name rather than the word BlackBerry.

```
pName = device.platform;
if ((pName == "Android") || (pName == "3.0.0.100")) {
    firstTime = true;
} else {
    firstTime = false;
}
```

The application registers a listener for the pause event using the following code:

```
document.addEventListener("pause", processPause, false);
```

This indicates that the processPause function should be called before the application transitions to the background. Within the function, the sample application simply updates the screen and stores the current timestamp in a variable. When the application runs on an Android device, you can see the screen update before the application moves to the background. On iOS, the screen update is not visible before the application suspends.

The sample application registers a listener for the resume event using the following code:

```
document.addEventListener("resume", processResume, false);
```

In this case, the processResume function is called when the application activates. The function first checks to see whether it should be skipping the first firing of the resume event by checking, and then resetting if necessary, the value of the firstTime variable. After that, it retrieves the stored timestamp indicating when the application suspended and uses the value to update the screen with the amount of time the application was suspended.

Figure 17-1 shows Example 17-2 running on an Android device.

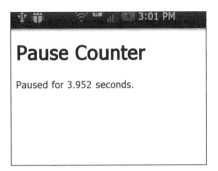

Figure 17-1   Example 17-2 running on an Android device

Network Status Events

Any mobile application that uses network-based resources should in some way monitor network availability and attempt to send or receive data across a network connection only when the network connection is available. An application can manually check the status of the device's network connection using the PhoneGap Connection object (described in Chapter 14) before trying to utilize a network connection.

In other cases, an application will use the PhoneGap online and offline events to listen for changes in a network connection and adjust accordingly. Whenever the device loses its network connection, it will fire the offline event. When a connection becomes available again, the online event will fire. A network-savvy application will use these events to track the status of the connection and queue data for transmission only when the connection is available.

Example 17-3 shows a simple network tracker application that leverages the online and offline events to update the screen as the network comes and goes.

Example 17-3

```
<!DOCTYPE html>
<html>
  <head>
    <title>Example 17-3</title>
    <meta name="viewport" content="width=device-width,
      height=device-height initial-scale=1.0, maximum-
      scale=1.0, user-scalable=no;" />
    <meta http-equiv="Content-type" content="text/html;
      charset=utf-8">
    <script type="text/javascript" charset="utf-8"
      src="jquery.js"></script>
    <script type="text/javascript" charset="utf-8"
      src="phonegap.js"></script>
    <script type="text/javascript" charset="utf-8">

      function onBodyLoad() {
        document.addEventListener("deviceready", onDeviceReady,
          false);
      }

      function onDeviceReady() {
        //Add the online event listener
        document.addEventListener("online", isOnline, false);
        //Add the offline event listener
        document.addEventListener("offline", isOffline, false);
      }

      function isOnline() {
        var d = new Date();
        $('#networkInfo').prepend("Online: " +
          d.toLocaleString() + "<br />");
      }

      function isOffline() {
        var d = new Date();
        $('#networkInfo').prepend("Offline: " +
          d.toLocaleString() + "<br />");
      }
    </script>
  </head>
  <body onload="onBodyLoad()">
    <h1>Network Tracker</h1>
    <p id="networkInfo"></p>
  </body>
</html>
```

The application registers two event listeners, one for each of the network events we're monitoring. The isOnline function is executed when the online event fires, and the isOffline function executes when the offline event fires.

To keep the application as simple as possible, the application uses jQuery to manage appending the network status updates to the top of the networkInfo paragraph tag:

```
$('#networkInfo').prepend("some_value<br />");
```

In this example, jQuery will locate the networkInfo page element and prepend the supplied text to the content that's already there.

Figure 17-2 shows Example 17-3 running on an Android device.

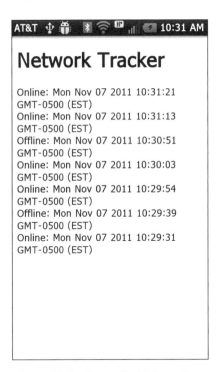

Figure 17-2   Example 17-3 running on an Android device

Button Events

Smartphones typical use physical buttons to allow users to interact more directly with the OS. iOS devices have only a single button (not counting the volume buttons), one that depending on how it's used, either allows the user to return to the OS home screen or opens a list of paused applications. Android and BlackBerry devices, on the other hand, offer the user several buttons and are therefore simpler for more advanced users to operate.

To allow for PhoneGap applications to respond to these buttons, PhoneGap will fire the following events whenever the corresponding buttons are pressed:

- `backbutton`: Fires when the user presses the back button on a device. This is typically the Escape button on Android and BlackBerry devices; iOS devices do not have a back button.

- `menubutton`: Fires when the user presses the device's menu button. iOS devices do not have a menu button.

- `searchbutton`: Fires when the user presses the dedicated search button on an Android device.

- `startcallbutton`: Fires when a BlackBerry user presses the dedicated start call button (located to the left of the BlackBerry menu button).

- `endcallbutton`: Fires when a BlackBerry user presses the dedicated end call button (located to the right of the BlackBerry escape button).

- `volumedownbutton`: Fires when a BlackBerry user presses the device's volume down button.

- `volumeupbutton`: Fires when a BlackBerry user presses the device's volume up button.

To respond to these buttons, simply implement the appropriate event listeners and write the code that executes when the button is pressed.

As you can see from the list, many of the events are device specific; even though volume up and down buttons are available on most smartphones, event listeners are for some reason available only in BlackBerry PhoneGap applications. It's rare in this day in age, with Android and iOS devices much more popular than Black-Berry, for BlackBerry to receive more attention than other platforms when it comes to framework features.

It's important to note that when a PhoneGap application overrides one of these buttons by registering an event listener for the button, the default behavior of the button no longer applies while the listener is in place. For example, on most devices, pressing the escape button causes the application to return to a previous screen or exit the application if on the main screen. When the escape button is overridden (by creating a `backbutton` event listener) as shown in the following code, pressing the escape button causes only the code specified in the onBackButton function to execute.

```
document.addEventListener("backbutton", onBackButton, false);
```

If you want the application to exhibit default behavior when one of the overridden buttons is pressed, then you'll have to implement the code to do so in your application. Using the previous code as an example, the onBackButton function might first do any cleanup required by the application and then call the navigator.app.exitApp() function, as shown here:

```
function onBackButton() {
  //Do whatever you need to do before closing the application
  ...

  //Then close the application
  navigator.app.exitApp();
};
```

This is very important for the escape button as shown but for the menu button as well. Unless your application doesn't need a menu and you're replacing the functionality behind the menu button with something specific to your application, Android and BlackBerry users are used to a menu appearing within an application when the menu button is pressed. If you want your own menu and override the menu button, your application is responsible for creating and displaying the appropriate menu when the button is pressed. The OS-specific menu will not appear when an overridden menu button is pressed.

The call buttons on BlackBerry cause additional problems for the PhoneGap developer. If you override the phone call buttons to use for other purposes in a game, for example, the user would have to leave the application in order to be able to press the phone button to bring up the phone application. This isn't a big deal, but it's important to pay attention to as you design your applications.

Example 17-4 shows a sample application that registers event listeners for each of the supported buttons. It doesn't do much, but it does illustrate how to use these events.

Example 17-4

```
<!DOCTYPE html>
<html>
  <head>
    <title>Example 17-4</title>
    <meta name="viewport" content="width=device-width,
      height=device-height initial-scale=1.0, maximum-
      scale=1.0, user-scalable=no;" />
```

```
<meta http-equiv="Content-type" content="text/html;
  charset=utf-8">
<script type="text/javascript" charset="utf-8"
  src="jquery.js"></script>
<script type="text/javascript" charset="utf-8"
  src="phonegap.js"></script>
<script type="text/javascript" charset="utf-8">

  function onBodyLoad() {
    //alert("onBodyLoad");
    document.addEventListener("deviceready", onDeviceReady,
      false);
  }

  function onDeviceReady() {
    alert("onDeviceReady");

    //Check to see if we've registered any events
    var eventCount = 0;

    //What platform are we running on?
    pName = device.platform;

    if((pName == "Android") || (pName == "3.0.0.100")) {
      eventCount += 2;
      //Android & BlackBerry only events
      document.addEventListener("backbutton", onBackButton,
        false);
      document.addEventListener("menubutton", onMenuButton,
        false);
    }

    if(pName == "Android") {
      eventCount += 1;
      //Android only event
      document.addEventListener("searchbutton",
        onSearchButton, false);
    }

    if(pName == "3.0.0.100") {
      eventCount += 4;
      //BlackBerry only events
      document.addEventListener("startcallbutton",
        onStartCallButton, false);
      document.addEventListener("endcallbutton",
        onEndCallButton, false);
      document.addEventListener("volumedownbutton",
        onVolumeUpButton, false);
      document.addEventListener("volumeupbutton",
```

```
                    onVolumeDownButton, false);
  }

  //did we register any event listeners?
  if(eventCount < 1) {
    //0, must be running on an iOS device
    alert("Must be running on an iOS device, No event
      listeners registered");
  } else {
    //Android or BlackBerry
    alert("Registered " + eventCount +
      " event listeners.");
  }
}

function onBackButton() {
  $('#buttonInfo').prepend("Back button pressed<br />");
  //Do button processing here
};

function onMenuButton() {
  $('#buttonInfo').prepend("Menu button pressed<br />");
  //Do button processing here
};

function onSearchButton() {
  $('#buttonInfo').prepend("Search button pressed<br />");
  //Do button processing here
};

function onStartCallButton() {
  $('#buttonInfo').prepend(
    "Start Call button pressed<br />");
  //Do button processing here
};

function onEndCallButton() {
  $('#buttonInfo').prepend(
    "end Call button pressed<br />");
  //Do button processing here
};

function onVolumeUpButton() {
  $('#buttonInfo').prepend(
    "Volume Up button pressed<br />");
  //Do button processing here
};
```

```
    function onVolumeDownButton() {
      $('#buttonInfo').prepend(
        "Volume Down button pressed<br />");
      //Do button processing here
    };
  </script>
</head>
<body onload="onBodyLoad()">
  <h1>Button Tracker</h1>
  <p id="buttonInfo">Waiting for button press</p>
</body>
</html>
```

In Example 17-4, the code checks to see which platform it's running on before registering the events. While not necessary, there's no reason to try to register an event that will never fire on the mobile device. Of course, since the PhoneGap device.name property returns the BlackBerry platform version rather than the word BlackBerry, the check for BlackBerry is a hack and would have to be updated for production use. As written, it checks only for a particular version of the platform and would not work correctly for other devices.

Figure 17-3 shows Example 17-4 running on an Android device.

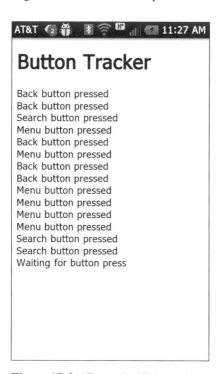

Figure 17-3 Example 17-4 running on an Android device

To restore a button to its default behavior, simply make a call to the JavaScript removeEventListener method, as shown here:

```
document.removeEventListener("backbutton", onBackButton, false);
```

18

File

The PhoneGap File API provides an application with the methods needed to locate, read, write, copy, move, and remove files in both temporary and persistent file storage on a mobile device. PhoneGap's implementation of the File API is based in part on the W3C File API: Directories and System specification (www.w3.org/TR/file-system-api). At this time, not all of the capabilities of the W3C specification have been implemented, but the API provides the essential capabilities a mobile developer will be interested in.

Example Application

A sample application, Example 18-1, was created to help illustrate the features of the File API. Because of the length of the application, however, it was not possible to include the complete application source code in this chapter.

Relevant portions of the application's code and screen shots of the application in action are shown within the chapter, but to see the complete code, you will need to point your browser of choice to the book's web site at www.phonegapessentials.com and look for the example project files in the Code section of the site.

Available Storage Types

A typical smartphone operating system provides applications with two different types of file storage space it can use. To store temporary files, an application should use the temporary storage location. For content and data that is integral to the application's operation and must remain available after the application is closed and restarted, the application should use persistent storage.

In general, an application might use temporary storage for transient data, data that's written to the file system as part of a memory management strategy or as swap space when analyzing or manipulating a large amount of data. With temporary storage, the application can read from and write to the storage area with impunity, creating and deleting files as needed within the available storage limitations of the device. It's even possible that the device will empty temporary storage when the application closes or the device reboots, freeing up storage space for other applications.

Persistent storage is more stable; the device OS protects it during reboots and when the application closes. An application's persistent storage will be emptied by the OS when the application is uninstalled from the device.

Accessing the Device's File System

If an application needs to browse the file system looking for files and directories, the application must first request a handle to it using the following code:

```
window.requestFileSystem(fileSystemConstant, sandboxSize,
  onSuccessFunction, onErrorFunction);
```

In this example, a file system sandbox is created for the application to use. The possible values for the `fileSystemConstant` constant are listed here; these are used to specify which type of storage will be used by the application:

- `LocalFileSystem.PERSISTENT`

- `LocalFileSystem.TEMPORARY`

When calling `requestFileSystem`, the application requests the allocation of storage it thinks it will need using the `sandboxSize` parameter shown in the example. There's really not a lot of information in the documentation or forums about this parameter, but in general, you will want to make sure you allocate enough space for the temporary files your application will be creating. The size requested is checked against the free space on the device to verify there is enough space available. A `FileError.QUOTA_EXCEEDED_ERR` will be returned if there is not enough space available on the device. When an application writes data to files, there is no check performed to make sure you don't use more than the requested space.

To request access to 5 MB of temporary sandbox storage, the application would execute the following code:

```
window.requestFileSystem(LocalFileSystem.TEMPORARY,
  5 * 1024 * 1024, onSuccessFunction, onErrorFunction);
```

You could also use the following code, but for me, the previous example is easier to understand what's happening. This option is of course less work for the application since it doesn't have to do the math every time it runs; it's your call—readability vs. performance.

```
window.requestFileSystem(LocalFileSystem.TEMPORARY,
  5242880, onSuccessFunction, onErrorFunction);
```

The onSucessFunction and onErrorFunction parameters define the functions that are called when the request completes if there is an error encountered during the process. The onSuccessFunction will be executed when the call to requestFileSystem completes. The function is passed a file system object (fs in this case) that can be used to directly interact with the file system, as will be shown in the following section.

```
function onSuccessFunction(fs) {
  alert("Accessing " + fs.name + " storage (" +
    fs.root.fullPath + ")");
  //Do something with the file system (fs) here

}
```

The onErrorFunction is executed when there is an error with most of the methods defined in the File API. The information provided here will be relevant to most of the other examples provided in this chapter. Passed to the onErrorFunction is an error object that can be queried to determine the nature of the problem. The following list of constants define the possible values that can be returned by the File API for file and directory access problems:

- FileError.ABORT_ERR

- FileError.ENCODING_ERR

- FileError.INVALID_MODIFICATION_ERR

- FileError.INVALID_STATE_ERR

- FileError.NO_MODIFICATION_ALLOWED_ERR

- FileError.NOT_FOUND_ERR

- FileError.NOT_READABLE_ERR

- FileError.PATH_EXISTS_ERR

- FileError.QUOTA_EXCEEDED_ERR

- FileError.SECURITY_ERR

- FileError.SYNTAX_ERR

- FileError.TYPE_MISMATCH_ERR

The following is an example of a function that can be used within an application to display an error message to users. In this example, the code uses e.code property to determine the error condition (using the error constants listed earlier).

```
function onFileError(e) {
  var msgText;
  switch(e.code) {
    case FileError.NOT_FOUND_ERR:
      msgText = "File not found error.";
      break;
    case FileError.SECURITY_ERR:
      msgText = "Security error.";
      break;
    case FileError.ABORT_ERR:
      msgText = "Abort error.";
      break;
    case FileError.NOT_READABLE_ERR:
      msgText = "Not readable error.";
      break;
    case FileError.ENCODING_ERR:
      msgText = "Encoding error.";
      break;
    case FileError.NO_MODIFICATION_ALLOWED_ERR:
      msgText = "No modification allowed.";
      break;
    case FileError.INVALID_STATE_ERR:
      msgText = "Invalid state.";
      break;
    case FileError.SYNTAX_ERR:
      msgText = "Syntax error.";
      break;
    case FileError.INVALID_MODIFICATION_ERR:
      msgText = "Invalid modification.";
      break;
    case FileError.QUOTA_EXCEEDED_ERR:
      msgText = "Quota exceeded.";
      break;
    case FileError.TYPE_MISMATCH_ERR:
      msgText = "Type mismatch.";
      break;
    case FileError.PATH_EXISTS_ERR:
      msgText = "Path exists error.";
      break;
    default:
      msgText = "Unknown error.";
  }
  //Now tell the user what happened
  navigator.notification.alert(msgText, null, "File Error");
}
```

When working with individual files, like the image file path information you get back from the Camera (Chapter 11) and Capture (Chapter 12) APIs, you don't need access to the file system directly; you can just work with the file individually.

Reading Directory Entries

Once you have access to the file system (either through the persistent or temporary storage area), you have the ability to process directory entries using the File API's DirectoryReader object. To create a DirectoryReader object, an application must make a call to createReader, as shown in the following function:

```
function onGetFileSystemSuccess(fs) {
  alert("Accessing " + fs.name + " storage (" +
    fs.root.fullPath + ")");
  //Create a directory reader we'll use to list the files in
  //the directory
  var dr = fs.root.createReader();
  // Get a list of all the entries in the directory
  dr.readEntries(onDirReaderSuccess, onFileError);
}
```

In this example, the call to createReader is made in the callback function executed after requesting a file system object as described in the previous section. Here the application uses the file system object to create a DirectoryReader pointing at the root folder of the selected file system. The DirectoryReader (dr in the example) supports only a single method, readEntries, which is used to read all of the entries in the specified folder.

As shown in the following example function, the callback function executed when a DirectoryReader has been successfully created is passed a dirEntries object. This object is an array of FileEntry and DirectoryEntry objects that can be accessed to obtain information about all of the files and directories in the folder.

```
function onDirReaderSuccess(dirEntries) {
  var i, fl, len;
  len = dirEntries.length;
  if(len > 0) {
    fl = '<ul data-role="listview">';
    for( i = 0; i < len; i++) {
      if(dirEntries[i].isDirectory == true) {
        fl += '<li><a href="#" onclick="processEntry(' + i +
          ');">Directory: ' + dirEntries[i].name + '</a></li>';
      } else {
        fl += '<li><a href="#" onclick="processEntry(' + i +
          ');">File: ' + dirEntries[i].name + '</a></li>';
      }
    }
```

```
    fl += "</ul>";
  } else {
    fl = "<p>No entries found</p>";
  }
  //Update the page content with our directory list
  $('#dirEntries').html(fl);
  //Display the directory entries page
  $.mobile.changePage("#dirList", "slide", false, true);
}
```

In this example, the function first checks to see whether any entries were found in the directory and then loops through them building an unordered list of list items (using the HTML <ul>, </ul>, <li>, and </li> tags) that are then added to the page. The application will display different content depending on whether the entry is a file or directory.

In this example, I'm using jQuery Mobile (www.jquerymobile.com) to create a more professional-looking UI for the application, so that's why you'll see the data-role="listview" attribute associated with the <ul> tag in the code. The call to $('#dirEntries').html(fl) at the end of the function is a function of jQuery (www.jquery.com) that provides a quick method for updating the content of the dirEntries <div> on the HTML page I'm using. Finally, the application makes a call to $.mobile.changePage(), which is a jQuery function that switches to a different page within the application.

The capabilities highlighted in the previous paragraph illustrate several of the important reasons why a developer would use jQuery and jQuery Mobile for their applications; it takes away much of the complexity of creating compelling UIs and user experiences. Using the following section of an HTML page, the code we've just discussed will generate the interactive screen shown in Figure 18-1.

```
<section id="dirList" data-role="page" data-add-back-btn="true">
  <header data-role="header">
    <h1>File API Demo</h1>
    <a onclick="writeFile();" data-icon="plus"
      class="ui-btn-right">Write</a>
  </header>
  <div data-role="content">
    <p>File system contents:</p>
    <div id="dirEntries"></div>
    <hr />
    <div id="writeInfo"></div>
  </div>
</section>
```

Figure 18-1   Example 18-1 running on a BlackBerry Torch 9800 simulator

The Write button shown in the figure will be discussed in the section entitled "Writing Files" later in the chapter.

Accessing FileEntry and DirectoryEntry Properties

The FileEntry and DirectoryEntry objects expose several properties an application can use to obtain additional information about a file or directory entry. The properties that can be accessed by an application are as follows:

- fullPath: The complete, absolute path from the root of the file system to the entry

- isDirectory: Returns true for DirectoryEntry objects and false for FileEntry objects

- isFile: Returns true for FileEntry objects and false for DirectoryEntry objects

- name: The file name, excluding path information, for the entry

Before an application can access these properties, it must first have a handle to the entry. In the previous section, the DirectoryReader returned an array of entries, so accessing properties is not that difficult.

To obtain an entry using a file name, use the following code:

```
fs.root.getFile("sample.txt", { create : false },
  processEntry, onFileError);
```

fs refers to a FileSystem object obtained from a call to requestFileSystem described earlier in the chapter. Once you have access to a file or directory entry, you can access the properties as shown in the following function. In this example, the processEntry function was passed as a success callback parameter in the call to getFile, so it's executed automatically as soon as getFile has a handle to the file. The file entry (theEntry in this example) is passed as a parameter to the function.

```
function processEntry(theEntry) {
  var fi = "";
  fi += '<p><b>Name</b>: ' + theEntry.name + '</p>';
  fi += '<p><b>Full Path</b>: ' + theEntry.fullPath + '</p>';
  fi += '<p><b>URI</b>: ' + theEntry.toURI() + '</p>';
  if(theEntry.isFile == true) {
    fi += '<p>The entry is a file</p>';
  } else {
    fi += '<p>The entry is a directory</p>';
  }
  //Update the page content with information about the file
  $('#fileInfo').html(fi);
  //Display the directory entries page
  $.mobile.changePage("#fileDetails", "slide", false, true);
}
```

A file can also have metadata associated with it; accessing the metadata requires another method call and a callback function, as shown in the following example:

```
theEntry.getMetadata(onGetMetadataSuccess, onFileError);
```

After the call to `getMetadata`, the `onGetMetadataSuccess` callback function is executed and passed a `metadata` object containing additional information about the directory or file entry. The File API currently supports only the `modificationTime` property, so you can access the property using the following example:

```
function onGetMetadataSuccess(metadata) {
  alert("File Modification Time:" + metadata.modificationTime);
}
```

To display any number of metadata properties that could be added in the future, the sample application for this chapter uses the following code instead:

```
function onGetMetadataSuccess(metadata) {
  var md = '';
  for(aKey in metadata) {
    md += '<b>' + aKey + '</b>: ' + metadata[aKey] + br;
  }
  md += hr;
  //Update the page content with information about the file
  $('#fileMetadata').html(md);
}
```

When used in conjunction with the `processEntry` function described earlier in this section and the HTML page segment shown next, the application will display a screen similar to the one shown in Figure 18-2.

```
<section id="fileDetails" data-role="page"
  data-add-back-btn="true">
  <header data-role="header">
    <h1>File API Demo</h1>
  </header>
  <div data-role="content">
    <p><em>Directory Entry Information</em></p>
    <hr />
    <div id="fileInfo"></div>
    <hr />
    <p><em>File Metadata:</em></p>
    <div id="fileMetadata"></div>
    <input type="button" value="View File"
      onclick="viewFile();">
    <input type="button" value="Remove File"
      onclick="removeFile();">
  </div>
</section>
```

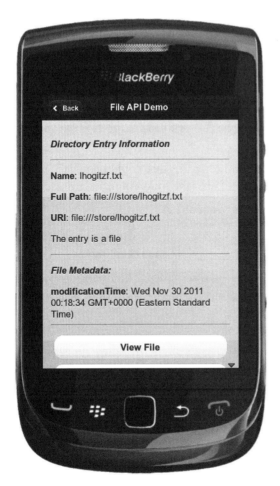

Figure 18-2   Example 18-1: directory entry details

Writing Files

To write data to files in either persistent or temporary storage, an application uses a FileWriter object. To begin the process, the application must first get access to a file object representing the file using the getFile method, as shown in the following example:

```
theFileSystem.root.getFile('appdata1.txt', {create : true},
    onGetFileSuccess, onFileError);
```

After the call to `getFile`, the `onGetFileSuccess` function is executed and passed the `file` object that will be used to create the `FileWriter`, as shown in the following example:

```
function onGetFileSuccess(theFile) {
  theFile.createWriter(onCreateWriterSuccess, onFileError);
}
```

Once again, we have another callback to wait for; once the `FileWriter` has been created, the callback function is executed, and the actual file writing can happen, as illustrated in the following example:

```
function onCreateWriterSuccess(writer) {
  writer.onwritestart = function(e) {
    console.log("Write start");
  };

  writer.onwriteend = function(e) {
    console.log("Write end");
  };

  writer.onwrite = function(e) {
    console.log("Write completed ");
  };

  writer.onerror = function(e) {
    console.log("Write error: " + e.toString());
  };

  writer.write("File created by Example 18-1: ");
}
```

The function is passed a `writer` object, which is used to control the writing of data to the file. The `FileWriter` exposes several events that are triggered during the write process. An application can associate functions with those events and update the screen, a log file, or the browser console with information about the stats of the process. The following list shows the valid event types associated with the `FileWriter`:

- `onabort`: Executed when the write process has been aborted through a call to `writer.abort()`

- `onerror`: Executed when an error occurs during the write process

- `onwrite`: Executed when the write process has completed successfully

- `onwriteend`: Executed when the writer has completed a write request

- `onwritestart`: Executed when the write process starts

There is additional functionality provided by the `FileWriter` object such as the ability to abort a write, seek a certain location within the file, and truncate the file. Refer to the File API documentation at http://docs.phonegap.com for additional information about these capabilities.

In my testing on the BlackBerry platform, the application couldn't execute sequential calls to `writer.write` to write data to the file; only the content from the first write would be written to the file. If I placed calls to `alert()` between my writes to interrupt the flow of the application, all of the content would be written to the file. There's clearly an issue when new calls are made to `write` when previous writes are in process. This is happening because calls to the `FileWriter` are asynchronous; you can't make calls to `write` until the previous write has completed. To get around these issues, one PhoneGap developer has created a useful wrapper that solves the problem; you can find information about the solution here: http://tinyurl.com/bt3kyrl.

Reading Files

The process to read content from files is very similar to what was demonstrated in the previous section. To read files, an application uses a `FileReader` object. To begin the process, the application must first get access to a `file` object representing the file using the `getFile` method, as shown in the following example:

```
theFileSystem.root.getFile('appdata1.txt', {create : false},
  onGetFileSuccess, onFileError);
```

If the application already has a handle to a file entry object pointing to the file, it can use the following code:

```
theEntry.file(onGetFileSuccess, onFileError);
```

In the `onGetFileSuccess` callback function, the application creates the `FileReader` object and then uses it to read the file, as shown in the following example:

```
function onGetFileSuccess(file) {
  var reader = new FileReader();

  reader.onloadend = function(e) {
    console.log("Read end");
    alert(e.target.result);
  };

  reader.onloadstart = function(e) {
    console.log("Read start");
  };
```

```
  reader.onloaderror = function(e) {
    console.log("Read error: " + e.target.error.code);
  };

  reader.readAsText(file);
}
```

As with the `FileWriter`, the `FileReader` object exposes several events that are triggered during the read process. An application can associate functions with those events and update the screen, a log file, or the browser console with information about the stats of the process. The following list shows the valid event types associated with the `FileReader`:

- `onabort`: Executed when the read process has been aborted through a call to `reader.abort()`

- `onerror`: Executed when an error occurs during the read process

- `onload`: Executed when the read has completed successfully

- `onloadend`: Executed when the reader has completed the read request

- `onloadstart`: Executed when the read process starts

In this example, the contents of the file are read as text using a call to `reader.readAsText()`. Once the read has completed, the value stored in `e.target.result` contains the contents of the file. The `FileReader` also supports the `readAsDataURL` method, which reads the file and returns the file's data as a base64-encoded data URL. Don't forget what you learned in Chapter 11—retrieving a large file's contents as raw data may overload the device's JavaScript processor and crash a PhoneGap application.

Deleting Files or Directories

To remove a file from local storage, an application must first obtain a `FileEntry` or `DirectoryEntry` object pointing to the file or directory and then can call the following code to delete it:

```
theEntry.remove(onRemoveFileSuccess, onFileError);

function onRemoveFileSuccess(entry) {
  var msgText = "Successfully removed " + entry.name;
  console.log(msgText);
  alert(msgText);
}
```

When deleting a directory, the directory must be empty or the remove operation will fail. To remove a directory that contains files, use the removeRecursively method, which will empty the directory before removing it.

In my testing of the sample application, I was able to successfully remove files, but the application would call the onFileError function and return a FileError.INVALID_MODIFICATION_ERR error code. In Bryce's testing on an Android device, it worked without error, so there's likely a bug somewhere that needs to be addressed.

Copying Files or Directories

To copy a file or directory, an application must first obtain a FileEntry or DirectoryEntry object pointing to the file or directory and then call the following code to copy it to a new location:

```
theEntry.copyTo(parentEntry, newName, onSuccessFunction,
  onErrorFunction);
```

The parentEntry parameter refers to the directory where the file or directory will be copied. Directory copies are recursive, so the process will copy the directory as well as the contents of the directory.

The newName parameter defines the name for the file or directory in the destination directory. This parameter is optional; if you don't include it, the file or directory's current name will be used. This parameter is required if copying a file to the same directory.

The onSuccessFunction and onErrorFunction used here are the same as you've seen in many other examples; the onSuccesFunction is the function that is executed when the copy process completes, and the onErrorFunction is the function that is executed when an error occurs during the copy process.

The standard limitations you would expect from any file action apply here. When copying a file or directory to the same directory (essentially renaming it), you must supply a new name for the file or directory; otherwise, the copy process will fail. Also, you cannot copy a directory inside itself.

Moving Files or Directories

To move a file or directory, an application must first obtain a FileEntry or DirectoryEntry object pointing to the file or directory and then call the following code to move the file to a new location:

```
theEntry.moveTo(parentEntry, newName, onSuccessFunction,
  onErrorFunction);
```

The `parentEntry` parameter refers to the directory where the file or directory will be moved. Directory moves are recursive, so the process will move the directory as well as the contents of the directory.

The `newName` parameter defines the name for the file or directory in the destination directory. This parameter is optional, if you don't include it, the file or directory's current name will be used. This parameter is required if you are moving a file to the same directory, which is essentially renaming the file.

The `onSuccessFunction` and `onErrorFunction` used here are the same as you've seen in many other examples; the `onSuccessFunction` is the function that is executed when the move process completes, and the `onErrorFunction` is the function that is executed when an error occurs during the move process.

The standard limitations you would expect from any file action apply here. When moving a file or directory to the same directory (essentially renaming it), you must supply a new name for the file or directory; otherwise, the move process will fail. Also, you cannot move a directory to a directory inside itself.

Uploading Files to a Server

The PhoneGap File API includes a `FileTransfer` object that allows applications to upload files to a remote server. An application must first create a new `FileTransfer` object and then call the object's upload method to begin the data transfer to the server. An example of this is illustrated in the following code:

```
var ft = new FileTransfer();
ft.upload(fileURI, serverURL, onUploadSuccess, onUploadError,
  fileUploadOptions);
```

The `fileURI` parameter references the file path pointing to the file that will be uploaded to the server. The `serverURL` parameter refers to the server URL that will be accessed to upload the file. The `onUploadSucess` and `onUploadError` are the callback functions executed on success and failure of the upload activity.

The `fileUploadOptions` parameter refers to an object that defines the following option settings that control the upload process:

* chunkedMode: Boolean value that controls whether streaming of the HTTP request is performed without internal buffering. If this value is not set, it defaults to true. Apparently ColdFusion doesn't like this parameter enabled (http://tinyurl.com/7nbpwb3).

* fileKey: Defines the name of the form element the file is uploaded to on the server. If this value is not set, it defaults to `file`.

- fileName: The file name for the uploaded file on the remote server. If this value is not set, it defaults to image.jpg.

- mimeType: The MIME type of the data you are uploading. If this value is not set, it defaults to image/jpeg.

- params: An optional set of key/value pairs that are included in the HTTP request header.

The onUploadSuccess function is passed a result object that can be used to determine the status of the upload. The result object supports the following properties:

- bytesSent: The number of bytes sent to the server as part of the upload

- responseCode: The HTTP response code returned by the server

- response: The HTTP response returned by the server

The following function illustrates how to access these properties in an application:

```
function onUploadSuccess(ur) {
  console.log("Upload Response Code: " + ur.responseCode);
  console.log("Upload Response: " + ur.response);
  console.log("Upload Bytes Sent: " + ur.bytesSent);
}
```

Currently iOS does not set values for the responseCode and bytesSent properties.

The FileTransfer object passes an error object to the onUploadError callback function; the code property can be queried to determine the cause of the error as illustrated, in the following example:

```
function onUploadError(e) {
  var msgText;
  switch(e.code) {
    case FileTransferError.FILE_NOT_FOUND_ERR:
      msgText = "File not found.";
      break;
    case FileTransferError.INVALID_URL_ERR:
      msgText = "Invalid URL.";
      break;
    case FileTransferError.CONNECTION_ERR:
      msgText = "Connection error.";
      break;
    default:
      msgText = "Unknown error.";
  }
  //Now tell the user what happened
  navigator.notification.alert(msgText, null,
    "File Transfer Error");
}
```

19

Geolocation

The Geolocation API allows an application to leverage the GPS capabilities of a mobile device and determine the device's location on the surface of the earth. Using this API, either an application can manually check the device's current position or it can create a location watch that will cause the application to be periodically notified of the device's physical location.

To use this API, the device running the application must provide geolocation capabilities (by utilizing either a GPS radio and associated software or some alternate mechanism for determining the device's location). While geolocation capabilities in smartphones are regularly enhanced in newer models, an application cannot guarantee that even though the device has geolocation capabilities, it will be able to determine its location. There are many geographical (such as being in a canyon) or mechanical issues (such as being inside a building) that can affect the device's ability to report its location to a PhoneGap application.

Since most HTML 5–compatible mobile browsers provide support for the W3C Geolocation API Specification already (www.w3.org/TR/geolocation-API), PhoneGap applications running on a compatible device can use this API directly today (this is the default behavior for PhoneGap applications). For devices that don't provide a Geolocation API such as BlackBerry devices running Device Software 5 or Android 1.x devices, the PhoneGap development team has included a compatible Geolocation API in the standard PhoneGap JavaScript library. For these devices, to enable a PhoneGap application to use PhoneGap's implementation of the Geolocation API, simply invoke `Geolocation.usePhoneGap()` once the PhoneGap `deviceready` event has fired.

The implementation of this API is structured very similarly to how the Accelerometer (Chapter 10) and Compass (Chapter 13) APIs work. You'll find that the examples provided in this chapter are very similar to what has already been shown in those chapters.

Getting a Device's Current Location

To manually determine the location of a smartphone, an application should execute the following code:

```
navigator.geolocation.getCurrentPosition(onGeolocationSuccess,
  ongeolocationError);
```

The call to `getCurrentPosition` includes the callback functions `onLocationSuccess` and `onLocationError`. The `onLocationSuccess` is executed when the device's location has been successfully measured, and the `onLocationError` function is executed if there is an error measuring the device's location.

An application can also configure options that control the way in which the API measures location, as shown in the following example:

```
var geolocationOptions = {
  timeout : 3000,
  enableHighAccuracy : true
};
navigator.geolocation.getCurrentPosition(onGeolocationSuccess,
  ongeolocationError, geolocationOptions);
```

In this example, a `geolocationOptions` object is passed to the call to `getCurrentPosition`. The available properties for `geolocationOptions` are as follows:

- `enableHighAccuracy`: Boolean value indicating whether the application would like to measure the device's location with a higher degree of accuracy. When enabling this option, the application may obtain more accurate results, but at the same time, it will place a higher load on the device, which may decrease performance and battery life while the application runs.

- `frequency`: Defines in milliseconds how often the location is measured. This option applies only when implementing a location watch (described later in this chapter). This is a PhoneGap-specific setting, and as PhoneGap more closely implements the W3C specification, this property will be removed. Developers should use the `maximumAge` property instead.

- `maximumAge`: Defines the maximum age (in milliseconds) of a cached location value that will be accepted by the application. A smaller value for this property should force the API to only deliver more recent location updates.

- `timeout`: The maximum amount of time (in milliseconds) that is allowed to pass between the call to either `geolocation.getCurrentPosition` or `geolocation.watchPosition` until the `onGeolocationSuccess` callback is executed.

After the API measures the device's location, it executes the `onGeolocationSuccess` callback function. Passed to the function is a location object that exposes `coords` properties an application can use to understand the device's location. The following function illustrates the properties that are exposed through the location object:

```
function onGeolocationSuccess(loc) {
  //We received something from the API, so first get the
  // timestamp in a date object so we can work with it
  var d = new Date(loc.timestamp);
  //Then replace the page's content with the current
  // location retrieved from the API
  lc.innerHTML = '<b>Current Location</b><hr />' +
    '<b>Latitude</b>: ' + loc.coords.latitude +
    '<br /><b>Longitude</b>: ' + loc.coords.longitude +
    '<br /><b>Altitude</b>: ' + loc.coords.altitude +
    '<br /><b>Accuracy</b>: ' + loc.coords.accuracy +
    '<br /><b>Altitude Accuracy</b>: ' +
    loc.coords.altitudeAccuracy +
    '<br /><b>Heading</b>: ' + loc.coords.heading +
    '<br /><b>Speed</b>: ' + loc.coords.speed +
    '<br /><b>Timestamp</b>: ' + d.toLocaleString();
}
```

When an error occurs while measuring the device's location, the `onGeolocation Error` callback function is executed. Passed to the function is an error object that exposes the `code` and `message` properties, as shown in the following example:

```
function onGeolocationError(e) {
  var msgText = "Geolocation error: #" + e.code + "\n" +
    e.message;
  console.log(msgText);
  alert(msgText);
}
```

Example 19-1 illustrates how to use the `getCurrentPosition` method in an application. The application exposes a single button that, when clicked, calls `getCurrentPosition` and updates the screen with the device's current location.

Example 19-1

```html
<!DOCTYPE html>
<html>
  <head>
    <title>Example 19-1</title>
    <meta name="viewport" content="width=device-width,
      height=device-height initial-scale=1.0,
      maximum-scale=1.0, user-scalable=no;" />
    <meta http-equiv="Content-type" content="text/html;
      charset=utf-8">
    <script type="text/javascript" charset="utf-8"
      src="phonegap-1.2.0.js"></script>
    <script type="text/javascript">

      //Location content
      var lc;
      //PhoneGap Ready variable
      var pgr = false;

      function onBodyLoad() {
        //During testing, Let me know we got this far
        alert("onBodyLoad");
        //Add the PhoneGap deviceready event listener
        document.addEventListener("deviceready", onDeviceReady,
          false);
      }

      function onDeviceReady() {
        //During testing, Let me know PhoneGap actually
        // initialized
        alert("onDeviceReady");
        //Get a handle we'll use to adjust the accelerometer
        //content
        lc = document.getElementById("locationInfo");
        //Set the variable that lets other parts of the program
        //know that PhoneGap is initialized
        pgr = true;
      }

      function getLocation() {
        alert("getLocation");
        if(pgr == true) {
          var locOptions = {
            timeout : 5000,
            enableHighAccuracy : true
          };
          //get the current location
          navigator.geolocation.getCurrentPosition(
```

```
                onGeolocationSuccess, onGeolocationError,
                   locOptions);
                //Clear the current location while we wait for a
                //reading
                lc.innerHTML = "Reading location...";
             } else {
                alert("Please wait,\nPhoneGap is not ready.");
             }
          }

      function onGeolocationSuccess(loc) {
          alert("onLocationSuccess");
          //We received something from the API, so first get the
          // timestamp in a date object so we can work with it
          var d = new Date(loc.timestamp);
          //Then replace the page's content with the current
          // location retrieved from the API
          lc.innerHTML = '<b>Current Location</b><hr />' +
             '<b>Latitude</b>: ' + loc.coords.latitude +
             '<br /><b>Longitude</b>: ' + loc.coords.longitude +
             '<br /><b>Altitude</b>: ' + loc.coords.altitude +
             '<br /><b>Accuracy</b>: ' + loc.coords.accuracy +
             '<br /><b>Altitude Accuracy</b>: ' +
             loc.coords.altitudeAccuracy +
             '<br /><b>Heading</b>: ' + loc.coords.heading +
             '<br /><b>Speed</b>: ' + loc.coords.speed +
             '<br /><b>Timestamp</b>: ' + d.toLocaleString();
      }

      function onGeolocationError(e) {
          alert("Geolocation error: #" + e.code + "\n" +
             e.message);
      }
    </script>
  </head>
  <body onload="onBodyLoad()">
    <h1>Geolocation API Demo #1</h1>
    <p>
      Click the button to determine the current location.
    </p>
    <input type="button" value="Refresh Location"
      onclick="getLocation();">
    <hr />
    <p id="locationInfo"></p>
  </body>
</html>
```

Figure 19-1 shows Example 19-1 running on a BlackBerry Torch 9800 simulator.

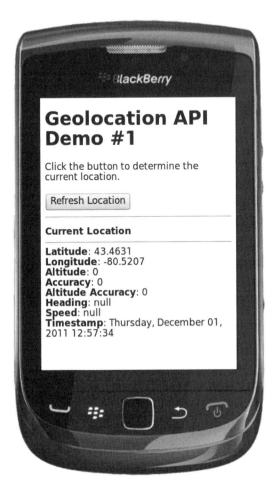

Figure 19-1   Example 19-1 running on a BlackBerry Torch 9800 simulator

Watching a Device's Location

Instead of checking the device's location manually, an application can define a geolocation watch that causes the device's location to be passed to the program periodically.

Setting a Watch

To create a location watch, an application should execute the following code:

```
watchID = navigator.geolocation.watchPosition(
  onGeolocationSuccess, onGeolocationError);
```

In this example, a `watchID` variable is assigned to the result of the operation; an application can use the `watchID` at a later time to cancel the watch. As with other PhoneGap APIs, the method is passed the names of two functions, the `onGeolocationSuccess` and `onGeolocationError` functions, which are executed after the device's location has been successfully measured and when there is an error measuring the device's location.

As with the call to `getCurrentLocation`, the `watchPosition` method can accept a `geolocationOptions` object to control configuration parameters for the watch. In the following example, the `geolocationOptions` object is configured to ignore cached values older than 10 seconds (10,000 milliseconds), to time out if a response isn't received within 5 seconds (5,000 milliseconds), and to try to measure with higher accuracy when determining the device's location.

```
var geolocationOptions = {
  maximumAge : 10000,
  timeout : 5000,
  enableHighAccuracy : true
};
//get the current location
watchID = navigator.geolocation.watchPosition(
  onGeolocationSuccess, onGeolocationError, geolocationOptions);
```

The `onGeolocationSuccess` function is passed a geolocation object, `loc` in this example, which exposes the same geolocation properties described in the previous section.

```
function onGeolocationSuccess(loc) {
  //We have a new location, so get the timestamp in a date
  // object so we can work with it
  var d = new Date(loc.timestamp);
  //Replace the page's content with the current
  //location retrieved from the API
  $('#locationInfo').html('<b>Latitude</b>: ' +
    loc.coords.latitude + '<br /><b>Longitude</b>: ' +
    loc.coords.longitude + '<br /><b>Altitude</b>: ' +
    loc.coords.altitude);
  $('#timestampInfo').prepend(d.toLocaleString() +
    '<br />');
}
```

In this example, a subset of the location information is built into some HTML markup for cleaner rendering on the application screen and then added to the `locationInfo` division of the page using the `$()` function from jQuery (www.jquery.com). The application also maintains a reverse chronological (newest at the top) history of timestamp information in the `timestampInfo` division of the page (you can see the HTML markup for the page and the complete application code in the listing for Exercise 19-2 later in the chapter). When the application runs, it will display a screen similar to the one shown in Figure 19-2.

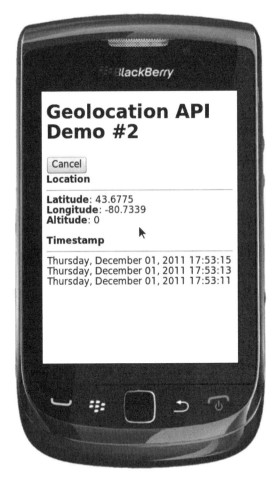

Figure 19-2   Exercise 19-2 running on a BlackBerry Torch 9800 simulator

As you can see from the figure, the onGeolocationSuccess function is being executed every two seconds, even if the device hasn't moved. When I first started working with this API, I expected that some sort of trigger could be defined that could be used to minimize the number of times the onGeolocationSuccess function would be fired, but that turned out to not be the case. No matter what values I entered for maximumAge and timeout, the watch returns geolocation information every two seconds.

If you think about it, querying for geolocation every two seconds will likely put a big load on the device and likely affect both application and overall device performance plus reduce battery life. To help reduce the impact on performance, I rewrote the function so it captures the previous longitude and latitude values and updates the location information on the screen only when there's been a change, as shown in the following example:

```
function onGeolocationSuccess(loc) {
  //We have a new location, so get the timestamp in a date
  // object so we can work with it
  var d = new Date(loc.timestamp);
  //Has anything changed since the last time?
  if(lastLat != loc.coords.latitude ||
    lastLong != loc.coords.longitude) {
    //Then replace the page's content with the current
    // location retrieved from the API
    $('#locationInfo').html('<b>Latitude</b>: ' +
      loc.coords.latitude + '<br /><b>Longitude</b>: ' +
      loc.coords.longitude + '<br /><b>Altitude</b>: ' +
      loc.coords.altitude);
    $('#timestampInfo').prepend(d.toLocaleString() +
      '<br />');
    lastLat = loc.coords.latitude;
    lastLong = loc.coords.longitude;
  } else {
    $('#timestampInfo').prepend('Skipping: ' +
      d.toLocaleTimeString() + '<br />');
  }
}
```

Depending on your application, you could easily modify this approach so it takes into consideration how much the location has changed before updating the screen or doing something time-consuming or processor-consuming within the application. Figure 19-3 shows the same application with that fix implemented; in other words, it shows the geolocation information being updated only when the values actually change.

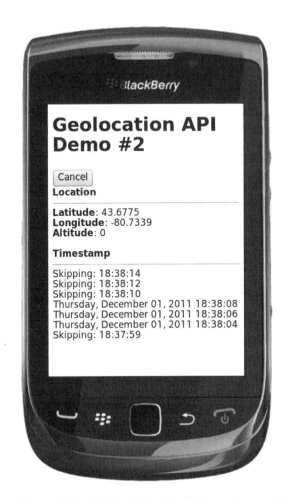

Figure 19-3 Updated Exercise 19-2 running on a BlackBerry Torch 9800 simulator

The onGeolocationError function is the same as the one used in the previous section:

```
function onGeolocationError(e) {
  var msgText = "Geolocation error: #" + e.code + "\n" +
    e.message;
  console.log(msgText);
  alert(msgText);
}
```

Canceling a Watch

Once a watch has been created, it can be canceled using the saved `watchID` variable and the following code:

```
navigator.geolocation.clearWatch(watchID);
```

There's no callback function required, but you could do a little extra work to help out your user, as shown in the following function example:

```
function cancelWatch() {
  //Clear the watch
  navigator.geolocation.clearWatch(watchID);
  //Clear the watch ID (just because)
  watchID = null;
  //Let the user know we cleared the watch
  alert("Location Watch Cancelled");
}
```

In the example, I clear the watch and then null out the `watchID` variable just to make sure it's not available in case the program accidently tries to clear the same watch later. We don't have an `onGeolocationError` function to execute if this fails, so it might even be better if you wrap the call into a `try/catch` block and deal with any errors that might occur directly.

Example 19-2 lists the complete HTML markup and application code for the application illustrated in Figure 19-3.

Example 19-2

```
<!DOCTYPE html>
<html>
  <head>
    <title>Example 19-1</title>
    <meta name="viewport" content="width=device-width,
      height=device-height initial-scale=1.0,
      maximum-scale=1.0, user-scalable=no;" />
    <meta http-equiv="Content-type" content="text/html;
      charset=utf-8">
    <script type="text/javascript" charset="utf-8"
      src="jquery-1.7.1.js"></script>
    <script type="text/javascript" charset="utf-8"
      src="phonegap.js"></script>
    <script type="text/javascript">

      var watchID, lastLong, lastLat;

      function onBodyLoad() {
        //Add the PhoneGap deviceready event listener
        document.addEventListener("deviceready", onDeviceReady,
```

```
      false);
}

function onDeviceReady() {
  //Create the watch
  startWatch();
}

function startWatch() {
  //Clear out the previous content on the page
  $('#locationInfo').empty();
  $('#timestampInfo').empty();
  //Show and hide the appropriate buttons
  $('#btnStart').hide();
  $('#btnCancel').show();
  //Geolocation Options
  var locOptions = {
    maximumAge : 10000,
    timeout : 5000,
    enableHighAccuracy : true
  };
  //get the current location
  watchID = navigator.geolocation.watchPosition(
    onLocationSuccess, onLocationError, locOptions);
}

function onLocationSuccess(loc) {
  //We have a new location, so get the timestamp in a date
  // object so we can work with it
  var d = new Date(loc.timestamp);
  //Has anything changed since the last time?
  if(lastLat != loc.coords.latitude ||
    lastLong != loc.coords.longitude) {
    //Then replace the page's content with the current
    // location retrieved from the API
    $('#locationInfo').html('<b>Latitude</b>: ' +
      loc.coords.latitude + '<br /><b>Longitude</b>: ' +
      loc.coords.longitude + '<br /><b>Altitude</b>: ' +
      loc.coords.altitude);
    $('#timestampInfo').prepend(d.toLocaleString() +
      '<br />');
    lastLat = loc.coords.latitude;
    lastLong = loc.coords.longitude;
  } else {
    $('#timestampInfo').prepend('Skipping: ' +
      d.toLocaleTimeString() + '<br />');
  }
}
```

```
    function onLocationError(e) {
      alert("Geolocation error: #" + e.code + "\n" +
        e.message);
    }

    function cancelWatch() {
      //Clear the watch
      navigator.geolocation.clearWatch(watchID);
      //Clear the watch ID (just because)
      watchID = null;
      //Hide the cancel button so they can't cancel it again.
      $('#btnCancel').hide();
      $('#btnStart').show();
      //Let the user know we cleared the watch
      alert("Watch Cancelled");
    }
  </script>
</head>
<body onload="onBodyLoad()">
  <h1>Geolocation API Demo #2</h1>
  <input type="button" value="Cancel"
    onclick="cancelWatch();" id="btnCancel">
  <input type="button" value="Start"
    onclick="startWatch();" id="btnStart">
  <br />
  <b>Location</b>
  <hr />
  <div id="locationInfo"></div>
  <br />
  <b>Timestamp</b>
  <hr />
  <div id="timestampInfo"></div>
</body>
</html>
```

20

Media

The Media API provides applications with the ability to record and play audio files. With this API, there is some overlap with the capabilities of the Capture API described in Chapter 12. Essentially, this API has limited capabilities as compared to the Capture API, and it's likely that not much will be done with this API going forward. The documentation for the Media API even kicks off with a warning to developers reminding them that the API doesn't align with the W3C specification for media capture and that future development will revolve around the Capture API.

That being said, the Media API is still useful. Even though the Capture API allows you to capture audio files, duplicating the same functionality provided in the Media API, the Capture API doesn't provide a mechanism to play audio files, so you'll need the Media API to do that. The API is limited in that it offers support only for Android, iOS, and Windows Phone devices today. Any application you build using this API would not work on a BlackBerry device, for example.

This API works differently than any of the other PhoneGap APIs covered so far. As you'll see in this chapter, the way the API exposes information about the media file creates some challenges for the PhoneGap developer.

The Media Object

The following sections describe how to work with the Media object in your PhoneGap applications.

Creating a Media Object

Before a PhoneGap application can play an audio file, it must first create a Media object that points to the audio file. Once the object has been created, methods are exposed through the object that allow the application to play the file plus pause and stop playback. These capabilities are essential for gaming applications that need the ability to play audio clips during play.

To create a Media object that can be used to play an audio file, at a minimum, an application would use the following code:

```
theMedia = new Media(mediaFileURI, onSuccess);
```

In this case, we're creating a new theMedia object that application will interact with. The Media object's constructor is passed a file URI pointing to the audio file being opened plus an onSuccess function that will be executed when the Media API completes playing or recording an audio clip.

 Note: The onSuccess function doesn't execute when this call completes; it executes every time the object completes playing or recording an audio file.

When this process completes, you have a new Media object to work with, but nothing is known about the audio clip. The object you've created exposes methods your application will use to play the audio clip or record a new audio clip, but the application has not accessed the media file yet. As you'll see later, there are methods you can use to determine the duration of a clip and read or set the current position within the clip, but none of those operations have any value unless the clip is currently being played.

File URI

The mediaFileURI passed to the constructor points to the audio clip that will be accessed. This could be a file located on a file server, as you'll see in the example code shown later in the chapter. It could also point to a file on the local file system. In this case, the application could use the File API described in Chapter 18 to obtain access to the local file system and browse for and access files.

An application can also package the audio files it needs into the PhoneGap application and access them directly from within the application. The beauty of this approach is that the files will be guaranteed to be there when the application needs them without having to connect to a remote server to play them or rely upon the files being in a particular location in temporary or persistent storage (explained in Chapter 18). The drawback of this approach is that depending on the mobile platforms you support with your application, you will find the files in different locations on the device.

When you include media files in an application on Android, those files can be accessed from the `android_asset` folder, as shown in the following example:

```
theMedia = new Media("/android_asset/thefile.mp3", onSuccess);
```

On iOS, the files are accessible directly from the / folder, as shown in the following example:

```
theMedia = new Media("/thefile.mp3", onSuccess);
```

The previous, just in case you're interested, resolves to the www folder within the private folder structure created for each installed application on iOS.

```
Applications/08B5D45E-1128-4FA1-97D6-1CD092B16CD7/myapp.app/
  www/thefile.mp3
```

So, if you're building applications for multiple mobile device platforms, you'll have to determine which platform the application is running on and pull the files from the appropriate folder depending on the mobile device.

Callback Functions

This is where things start to get weird with the Media API. The `onSuccess` function being passed in to the constructor doesn't identify the code that will be executed when the creation of the new Media object completes successfully; instead, you're specifying the function that will be executed when the playing or recording of audio clips completes successfully. Even though the documentation clearly said this, I didn't understand it properly until I got my application working and saw what was really happening. You'll see how this impacts your applications in a little while.

The Media constructor supports additional, optional callback functions, as shown in the following example:

```
theMedia = new Media(mediaFileURI, onSuccess, onError,
  onStatus);
```

The optional `onError` function is executed whenever an error occurs during playing or recording audio. As with the other PhoneGap APIs, the `onError` function is passed an object an application can use to understand and report the nature of the error as shown. With many of the other PhoneGap APIs, only an error code is returned, so it must be compared to a list of error constants to determine the source of an error; the Media API makes this easier by also including an error message, as shown in the following example:

```
function onMediaError(e) {
  var msgText = "Media error: " + e.message + "(" + e.code +
    ")";
```

```
    console.log(msgText);
    navigator.notification.alert(msgText, null, "Media Error");
}
```

The API also provides the following error constants, which can be used to identify each error type:

- MediaError.MEDIA_ERR_ABORTED

- MediaError.MEDIA_ERR_DECODE

- MediaError.MEDIA_ERR_NETWORK

- MediaError.MEDIA_ERR_NONE_SUPPORTED

So, an application can respond directly to each type of error using an approach similar to the following one:

```
function onMediaError(e) {
  switch(e.code) {
    case MediaError.MEDIA_ERR_ABORTED:
      //Do something about the error

      break;
    case MediaError.MEDIA_ERR_NETWORK:
      //Do something about the error

      break;
    case MediaError.MEDIA_ERR_DECODE:
      //Do something about the error

      break;
    case MediaError.MEDIA_ERR_NONE_SUPPORTED:
      //Do something about the error

      break;
    default:
      navigator.notification.alert("Unknown Error: " +
        e.message + " (" + e.code + ")", null, "Media Error");
  }
}
```

The optional onStatus function is periodically executed during and after playback to indicate the status of the activity. The following function illustrates the onSuccess function in action:

```
function onMediaStatus(statusCode) {
  console.log("Status: " + statusCode);
}
```

The supported values for statusCode are as follows:

- 0: Media.MEDIA_NONE

- 1: Media.MEDIA_STARTING

- 2: Media.MEDIA_RUNNING

- 3: Media.MEDIA_PAUSED

- 4: Media.MEDIA_STOPPED

Current Position

An application can determine the current position within a playing audio clip using the getCurrentPosition method, which uses a callback function to deliver the current position to the application, as shown in the following example:

```
function updateUI() {
  theMedia.getCurrentPosition(onGetPosition, onMediaError);
}

function onGetPosition(filePos) {
  console.log('Position: ' + Math.floor(filePos) + ' seconds');
}
```

This value applies only to an audio clip that is currently being played. If the clip is paused or has not yet been played, the method will return a value of -1.

Since the method doesn't work unless the clip is playing and, as you'll see later, the Media object's play method doesn't provide a callback function, in order to be able to update its UI with information about playback progress, your application will need to fire off a timer immediately after calling the play method and have that timer query getCurrentPosition and update the application's UI accordingly. This is performed through a call to the setInterval method, as shown in the following example:

```
Var theTimer = window.setInterval(updateUI, 1000);
```

The application will need to suspend updates before playback is paused or stopped. Refer to the source code listing for Example 20-1 for an example of one way to implement this approach.

Duration

An application can determine the length of a playing audio clip using the getDuration method, as shown in the following example:

```
console.log('Duration: ' + theMedia.getDuration() + ' seconds');
```

getDuration will report a -1 if the audio clip is not currently playing. Unlike getCurrentPosition, the getDuration method will return the clip length even if playback is paused.

Releasing the Media Object

When an application is finished with an audio clip, it should release the memory allocated to the Media object using the following code:

```
theMedia.release();
```

Performing this step is especially important on Android devices because of the way Android allocates resources for audio playback.

Playing Audio Files

To work with audio files, an application using the Media API will first create a Media object, as shown earlier, and use methods on that object to control audio playback. The following sections will illustrate how to use each of the options available when playing audio files using this API.

Play

To play the audio clip associated with a Media object, an application should simply call the object's play method, as shown in the following example:

```
theMedia.play();
```

The method does not support any input parameters or any callback functions. It simply starts playing the audio clip (if it can) and allows the application to continue. If your application needs to update the UI to indicate progress, it will need to use the setInterval method as described previously to create a timer that is fired periodically to update the UI and perform whatever additional housekeeping tasks are required.

When the play method is invoked, the application will open the file URI provided in the constructor for the Media object. This is the first time your application will have actually tried to access the media file. If the file is not available or is somehow not playable on the device, an error will be generated, and the application will have to do whatever it can to recover. If the file resource is stored on a remote server, there will be a delay in playback while the application first downloads the file before attempting playback.

This is a risky situation for any application. Since you won't know whether the audio clip will play until you actually try to play it, your application will have to do extra work to ensure success or at least recover gracefully on failure.

Pause

To pause a playing audio clip, an application should call the Media object's pause method, as shown in the following example:

```
theMedia.pause();
```

If an application invokes pause on a Media object that is not currently playing, no error will be reported to the application.

Stop

To stop playback of an audio clip, an application should call the Media object's stop method, as shown in the following example:

```
theMedia.stop();
```

If an application invokes stop on a Media object that is not currently playing, no error will be reported to the application.

Seek

An application can programmatically seek to a specific position within an audio clip using the seekTo method of the Media object, as shown in the following example:

```
theMedia.seekTo(3600);
```

The method takes a single input parameter: a numeric value indicating the position within the audio file in milliseconds. So, in the example shown, playback will skip to a position 3,600 milliseconds (3.6 seconds) from the beginning of the audio clip.

Recording Audio Files

To record audio files, an application must first create a media object as shown earlier and use methods on that object to control the audio recording process. The following sections will illustrate how to use options available for recording audio using this API.

Note: The audio recording capabilities offered by the PhoneGap Capture API are much better suited for audio recording; I recommend you utilize that API instead.

Start Recording

To begin recording audio, an application should call the `startRecord` method of a `Media` object, as shown in the following example:

```
theMedia.startRecord();
```

This method doesn't support any direct callback functions, but the `onError` function that was defined when the `Media` object was created will fire if there's an error creating the recording. If you want to indicate that the application is recording and update the application's UI with the recording status (recording length, for example), you will have to do it manually using the `setInterval` method described previously.

Stop Recording

To discontinue recording audio, an application should call the `stopRecord` method of a `Media` object, as shown in the following example:

```
theMedia.stopRecord();
```

This method doesn't support any direct callback functions, but the `onError` function that was defined when the `Media` object was created will fire if there's an error.

Seeing Media in Action

To illustrate how different aspects of the Media API are used within an application, I created Example 20-1, which highlights one way to manage audio clip playback using this API.

Figure 20-1 shows the application at startup. Notice how the audio clip's duration is set to -1; this was discussed earlier in the chapter. Even though the application has created a `Media` object, the `getDuration` method does not return a value unless the clip is actually playing.

As with some of the other examples in this book, this application uses jQuery (www.jquery.com) and jQuery Mobile (www.jquerymobile.com) to create the application's UI. The application doesn't use many features of jQuery Mobile as some other examples; I wanted the buttons to fit together cleanly and an unobtrusive mechanism for updating page content, so I took this approach. Where you see HTML attributes `data-role` and `data-icon`, those are instructions to jQuery

Mobile to help clean up the UI. The `$().html` functions you see peppered throughout the code are simply a shortcut notation for updating the HTML content of page elements. Beyond that, everything is straight HTML and JavaScript.

Figure 20-1   Example 20-1 at startup

Example 20-1

```
<!DOCTYPE html>
<html>
  <head>
    <title>Example 20-1</title>
    <meta name="viewport" content="width=device-width,
      height=device-height initial-scale=1.0,
      maximum-scale=1.0, user-scalable=no;" />
    <meta http-equiv="Content-type" content="text/html;
      charset=utf-8">
    <link rel="stylesheet" href="jquery.mobile1.0b3.min.css" />
    <script type="text/javascript" charset="utf-8"
```

```
      src="jquery1.6.4.min.js"></script>
<script type="text/javascript" charset="utf-8"
  src="jquery.mobile1.0b3.min.js"></script>
<script type="text/javascript" charset="utf-8"
  src="phonegap.js"></script>
<script type="text/javascript" charset="utf-8"
  src="main.js"></script>
<script type="text/javascript">

  var fileDur, theMedia, theTimer;

  function onBodyLoad() {
    //Add the PhoneGap deviceready event listener
    document.addEventListener("deviceready", onDeviceReady,
      false);
  }

  function onDeviceReady() {
    //Get our media file and stuff
    init();
  }

  function init() {
    var fileName = "http://server/folder/file_name.mp3 ";
    console.log(fileName);
    //Create the media object we need to do everything we
    // need here
    theMedia = new Media(fileName, onMediaSuccess,
      onMediaError, onMediaStatus);
    //Update the UI with the track name
    $('#track').html("<b>File:</b> " + fileName);
    $('#pos').html('Duration: ' +
      Math.round(theMedia.getDuration()) + ' seconds');
  }

  function onMediaSuccess() {
    console.log("onMediaSuccess");
    window.clearInterval(theTimer);
    theTimer = null;
  }

  function onMediaError(e) {
    var msgText;
    console.log(msgText);
    navigator.notification.alert(msgText, null,
      "Media Error");
  }
```

```
   function onMediaStatus(statusCode) {
     console.log("Status: " + statusCode);
   }

   function doPlay() {
     if(theMedia) {
       //Start the media file playing
       theMedia.play();
       //fire off a timer to update the UI every second as
       //it plays
       theTimer = setInterval(updateUI, 1000);
     } else {
       alert("No media file to play");
     }
   }

   function doPause() {
     if(theMedia) {
       //Pause media play
       theMedia.pause();
       window.clearInterval(theTimer);
     }
   }

   function doStop() {
     if(theMedia) {
       //Kill the timer we have running
       theTimer = null;
       //Then stop playing the audio clip
       theMedia.stop();
     }
   }

   function updateUI() {
     theMedia.getCurrentPosition(onGetPosition,
       onMediaError);
   }

   function onGetPosition(filePos) {
     //We won't have any information about the file until
     //it's actually played. Update the counter on the page
     $('#pos').html('Time: ' + Math.floor(filePos) + ' of '
       + theMedia.getDuration() + ' seconds');
   }
 </script>
</head>
<body onload="onBodyLoad()">
  <section id="main" data-role="page" >
    <header data-role="header">
      <h1>Example 20-1</h1>
```

```
      </header>
      <div data-role="content">
        <p id="track"></p>
        <p id="pos"></p>
        <div data-role="controlgroup">
          <a onclick="doPlay();" id="btnPlay"
            data-role="button" data-icon="arrow-r">Play</a>
          <a onclick="doPause();" id="btnPause"
            data-role="button" data-icon="grid">Pause</a>
          <a onclick="doStop();" id="btnStop"
            data-role="button" data-icon="delete">Stop</a>
        </div>
      </div>
    </section>
  </body>
</html>
```

When the user clicks play, the UI will update showing playback status, as shown in Figure 20-2, as the clip plays through the device speakers.

Figure 20-2   Example 20-1 playing an audio clip

To make the application work with a server-based audio clip on iOS, I had to configure the ExternalHosts array, as shown in Figure 20-3. This property is a list of external hosts that the application is authorized to pull content from.

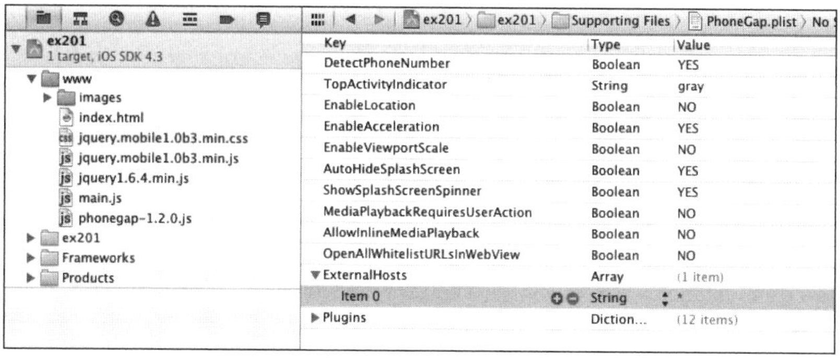

Figure 20-3   Configuring ExternalHosts in Xcode

In my testing, I tried each of the following options for the field:

- `http://server_name/`

- `http://server_name/*`

- `http://server_name/folder_name/`

- `http://server_name/folder_name/*`

- `http://server_name/folder_name/file_name.ext`

None of them worked; I had to use the asterisk, which I thought was a wildcard value authorizing any external resource. What I learned afterward from Bryce is that it's looking for a regular expression here, not a wildcard. He indicated that it would be changing from regular expressions to wildcards in the future, and a recent update to the PhoneGap wiki included "Wildcards are ok. So if you are connecting to 'http://phonegap.com', you have to add 'phonegap.com' to the list (or use the wildcard '*.phonegap.com' which will match subdomains as well)," so it looks like it's already been fixed.

I'm not sure how PhoneGap Build will deal with this restriction. As documented today, Build doesn't currently support configuration options for security settings like this.

21

Notification

The PhoneGap Notification API provides methods that allow an application to provide feedback to a user visually (through pop-up alerts) and through tactile or audible feedback. The methods supported by this API are as follows:

- `notification.alert`
- `notification.confirm`
- `notification.beep`
- `notification.vibrate`

Visual Alerts (Alert and Confirm)

The `alert` and `confirm` methods are each essentially extended versions of the standard JavaScript `alert` function. The JavaScript `alert` method, which works just fine in PhoneGap applications, takes a single parameter, which is the text of the message displayed on the screen, as shown in the following example:

```
alert("You clicked the Click Me button.");
```

This code generates the pop-up dialog shown in Figure 21-1.

Figure 21-1 A standard JavaScript alert

The PhoneGap alert and confirm functions allow a program to control not only the message being displayed but also the title associated with the pop-up dialog, the text displayed on the dialog's button(s), and the function that's executed when the user clicks a button in the pop-up. The difference between alert and confirm is the number of buttons displayed in the dialog; alert displays a single button, and confirm can display one or more buttons.

The following is an example of how to call the PhoneGap alert function:

```
navigator.notification.alert(message_text, callback_function,
  "title", "button_text");
```

The parameters passed to the function are described here:

- message_text: The message text that appears between the title and the button.

- callback_function: The function that is executed when the user clicks the button on the dialog.

- title: (Optional.) The text that appears on the top of the pop-up dialog.

- button_text: (Optional.) The text that appears on the button. If no value is provided, it will default to OK.

The following code shows an example of how to use the PhoneGap alert method:

```
navigator.notification.alert("Figure 21-2", onDoAlert,
  "Sample Alert", "Click Me!");
```

This will generate the pop-up dialog shown in Figure 21-2 and execute the onDoAlert function after the user clicks the button.

Figure 21-2   PhoneGap alert on an Android device

To skip executing a function when the user clicks the button, simply pass in a `null` for the function name, as shown in the following example:

```
navigator.notification.alert("Figure 21-2", null,
  "Sample Alert", "Click Me!");
```

The `confirm` function operates exactly the same as `alert`; the only difference is in the `button_text` parameter passed to the function. Instead of a single text value, `confirm` expects a comma-separated list of values, as shown here:

```
navigator.notification.confirm(message_text, callback_
  function, "title", "button_text_array");
```

If no button values are provided, the function will default to using OK and Cancel.

The following code will generate the pop-up dialog shown in Figure 21-3 and execute the `onDoConfirm` function after the user clicks either of the buttons:

```
navigator.notification.confirm("Figure 21-3", onDoConfirm,
  "Sample Confirmation", "Yes, No");
```

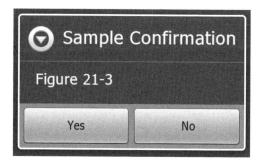

Figure 21-3   PhoneGap `confirm` on an Android device

When the onDoConfirm function is called by confirm, it passes in a button variable that represents the number of the button clicked by the application user. As shown in the following example, a value of 1 is assigned to the first button, 2 to the second, and so on:

```
function onDoConfirm(btnNum) {
  if(btnNum == "1") {
    alert("Thanks for saying yes!");
  } else {
    alert("Too bad, you said no.");
  }
}
```

Beep

To play the mobile device's default beep tone, execute the following code:

```
navigator.notification.beep(beepCount);
```

The beepCount parameter is a numeric value that defines the number of times the beep should play.

Vibrate

To cause the mobile device to vibrate, execute the following code:

```
navigator.notification.vibrate(vibeDuration);
```

The vibeDuration parameter is a numeric value that refers to the number of milliseconds the device should vibrate. A value of 1000 equals one second, 500 is half a second, and so on. To make an application vibrate, pause, and then vibrate again, you will have to manually call vibrate several times and force the required wait between calls; there is no repeat value that can be passed to the vibrate function.

Notification in Action

Example 21-1 shows an application that highlights each of the supported functions in the PhoneGap Notification API.

Example 21-1

```
<!DOCTYPE html>
<html>
  <head>
```

```
<title>Example 21-1</title>
<meta name="viewport" content="width=device-width,
  height=device-height initial-scale=1.0,
  maximum-scale=1.0, user-scalable=no;" />
<meta http-equiv="Content-type" content="text/html;
  charset=utf-8">
<link rel="stylesheet" href="jquery.mobile1.0b3.min.css" />
<script type="text/javascript" charset="utf-8"
  src="jquery1.6.4.min.js"></script>
<script type="text/javascript" charset="utf-8"
  src="jquery.mobile1.0b3.min.js"></script>
<script type="text/javascript" charset="utf-8"
  src="phonegap.js"></script>
<script type="text/javascript" charset="utf-8">

  function onBodyLoad() {
    //alert("onBodyLoad");
    document.addEventListener("deviceready",
      onDeviceReady, false);
  }

  function onDeviceReady() {
    //Nothing to do here really
    alert("onDeviceReady");
  }

  function doAlert() {
    msgText = document.getElementById('msgText').value;
    navigator.notification.alert(msgText, onDoAlert,
      "Sample Alert", "Click Me!");
  }

  function onDoAlert() {
    alert("You clicked the Click Me button.");
  }

  function doConfirm() {
    msgText = document.getElementById('msgText').value;
    navigator.notification.confirm(msgText, onDoConfirm,
      "Sample Confirmation", "Yes, No");
  }

  function onDoConfirm(btnNum) {
    if(btnNum == "1") {
      alert("Thanks for saying yes!");
    } else {
      alert("Too bad, you said no.");
    }
  }
```

```
      function doBeep() {
        beepCount = document.getElementById('beepSlider').value;
        navigator.notification.beep(beepCount);
      }

      function doVibe() {
        vibeCount = document.getElementById('vibeSlider').value;
        navigator.notification.vibrate(vibeCount);
      }
    </script>
</head>
<body onload="onBodyLoad()">
  <div data-role="header">
    <h1>Notification Demo</h1>
  </div>
  <div data-role="content">
    <div data-role="fieldcontain">
      <label for="msgText">Message Text:</label>
      <input type="text" name="msgText" id="msgText"
        value="This is a message" />
      <div data-role="controlgroup" data-type="horizontal">
        <input type="button" value="Alert"
          onclick="doAlert();">
        <input type="button" value="Confirm"
          onclick="doConfirm();">
      </div>
    </div>
    <div data-role="fieldcontain">
      <label for="beepSlider" >Number of Beeps</label>
      <input type="range" name="beepSlider" id="beepSlider"
        value="1" min="1" max="3" />
      <input type="button" value="Beep" onclick="doBeep();">
    </div>
    <div data-role="fieldcontain">
      <label for="vibeSlider" >Vibrate Duration</label>
      <input type="range" name="vibeSlider" id="vibeSlider"
        value="100" min="100" max="1000" step="100" />
      <input type="button" value="Vibrate"
        onclick="doVibe();">
    </div>
  </div>
</body>
  </html>
```

The application makes use of HTML sliders to allow the user to more easily select beep counters or vibration duration. It also uses the capabilities provided by jQuery Mobile (www.jquerymobile.com) to make the application more visually appealing. All of those `div` containers you see in the code with the `data-role` and `data-type` attributes are instructions to jQuery Mobile. Figure 21-4 shows the application running on an Android smartphone.

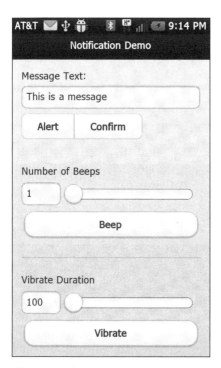

Figure 21-4   Example 21-1 running on an Android device

22

Storage

Most HTML 5–compatible browsers provide web applications with the ability to read and write key/value pairs from/to a local storage facility and to read and write data from/to a local SQL database. Neither of those capabilities is a direct functions of HTML but instead something typical browsers made available to JavaScript code running within the browser.

These capabilities were originally delivered through implementations of the W3C Web SQL Database Specification (www.w3.org/TR/webdatabase) and the W3C Web Storage API Specification (www.w3.org/TR/webstorage). The Web Storage API is still valid, but the W3C has stopped work on the Web SQL specification, and instead developers typically work with the SQLite (www.sqlite.com) database engine included with most modern smartphone browsers.

A PhoneGap application can easily leverage the browser container's storage capabilities directly from within their applications; this is not anything PhoneGap-specific. For older mobile devices that have not implemented HTML 5 or either storage option directly, the PhoneGap team implemented the W3C Web SQL Database Specification and the Web Storage API into the PhoneGap API.

If a mobile platform includes support for these storage options, the `phonegap.js` file for the particular platform will just omit the objects, properties, and methods for the storage option. If not supported by the device, the PhoneGap JavaScript library will include the implementation of the storage capabilities and the appropriate supporting code to make it work on the mobile device.

Since the capabilities provided by this PhoneGap API are based upon standards that have been available for a while and are used heavily by developers today, this chapter will not cover the API in great detail.

Example Application

A sample application has been created to help illustrate the features of the PhoneGap Storage API. Example 22-1 illustrates how to build a simple mileage tracker application using both Web Storage and Web SQL capabilities.

Because of the length of the application, it was not possible to include the application source code in this chapter. Relevant portions of the application code and screen shots of the application in action are shown within the chapter, but to see the completed application, code you will need to point your browser of choice to the book's web site at www.phonegapessentials.com and look for the example project files in the Code section of the site.

Local Storage

The local storage capabilities of PhoneGap allow an application to persist data as key/value pairs stored with the application. The W3C Web Storage API includes support for both session and local storage, but the current release of PhoneGap seems to have support for the local storage option. Session storage is for transient values that are needed only during a particular session with the application; it is designed to allow the application to make use of the storage area while the application is running, but the data values stored there will be erased when the application closes. The local storage option is designed to support data that needs to be available between sessions—maintained when the application closes and available when the application launches again. The best use case for local storage would be for the storage of configuration settings for an application; this is something you would want available every time the application executed.

Data stored using local storage is maintained in key/value pairs. To write a value to local storage, an application would use the following code:

```
window.localStorage.setItem("key_name", value);
```

If the application wanted to store a value for a purge interval configuration setting for example, it would use the following code:

```
thePurgeInterval =
  document.getElementById("purgeInterval").value;
window.localStorage.setItem("purgeInterval",
  thePurgeInterval);
```

To retrieve a value from local storage, an application would use the following code:

```
purgeInterval = window.localStorage.getItem("key_name");
```

To retrieve the value for the purge interval configuration setting, an application would use the following code:

```
thePurgeInterval = window.localStorage.getItem("purgeInterval");
```

That's it—that's all there is to this part of the API. When working with an application that leverages this API, you can use the debugging capabilities of your browser to view the settings for local storage, as shown in Figure 22-1. In this example, I worked out the kinks of the application using the desktop browser and then switched over to the mobile device once I knew everything was working. In the figure, the key/value pair for `purgeInterval` is highlighted.

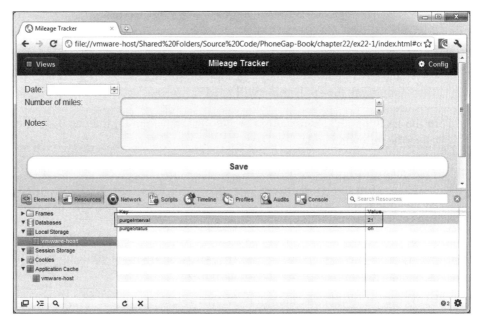

Figure 22-1 Example 22-1 running in the desktop browser debugger

SQL Database

The Storage API implements a simple database an application can read from and write to using Structured Query Language (SQL). To use this API, an application must first open the database using the following code:

```
theDB = window.openDatabase(db_name, db_version,
  db_display_name, db_size);
```

In this example, the call to openDatabase simply creates a database object that exposes some methods an application can use to manipulate the database. There are no callbacks functions that need to be implemented. The openDatabase method takes the following parameters:

- db_name: The name of the database. This will be the file name for the database when it's written to device memory.

- db_version: The version number for the database. An application can query this version number and upgrade the database schema as needed using the changeVersion method of the database object.

- db_display_name: The display name for the database.

- db_size: The amount of space allocated for the database in bytes. When allocating space, keep in mind that mobile devices may have limitations on the size of databases they can support, so allocate only the amount of space you think the application will need.

In the Example 22-1 application created for this chapter, the database is opened using the following code:

```
theDB = window.openDatabase("mtDB", "1.0", "Mileage Tracker",
  3 * 1024 * 1024);
```

At this point, the application has access to a database object, and space has been allocated for the database in persistent storage on the device. From this point forward, everything you do with the database is performed using SQL statements. For this example, I allocated 3 MB of storage, although there is no way this particular application will need that much space.

Using this API, an application must wrap its SQL statements within a transaction. Transactions allow a database engine to process multiple SQL statements sequentially and recover gracefully (back to the starting point if possible) if an error occurs while they are processing the statements. Transactions are most useful when performing actions against a database that have parts that must all be executed for the action to be complete. The best example of this would be a banking transaction: When transferring money from one account to another, you will want the transaction to roll back (cancel cleanly) if the money is successfully taken from your account but then cannot be credited to another.

To create a transaction that can be used to execute one or more SQL statements against a database, an application will use the following code:

```
theDB.transaction(createTable, onTxError, onTxSuccess);
```

In this example, a function called `createTable` is passed to the transaction; this is the function that will execute the SQL statement used to create the database table used by the application. There are also two callback functions: the `onTxError` and `onTxSuccess` functions that are passed to the method. Please note that the callback functions are passed in a different order than they are for any other API in this book.

Note: The `transaction` method of the `database` object is the only example in this book where an error function is passed as a parameter to a method before the success callback function. In every other example in the book, the success function has always been first, followed by the error function. In this case, the success function is optional and the error function is required, so that's why the error function comes first.

I have to admit that this caused me quite a bit of trouble as I built the sample application. Everything was working, but I couldn't figure out why the transaction's `onError` function fired every time the application wrote to the database. Yes, I had the parameters switched and listed the success function first like I had for every other example. Let my mistake save you some time: Be sure to pay attention to the order of callback functions when using this API.

Let's talk about the callback functions before we dig into the `createTable` function.

The `onTxError` function is passed two objects. One is a transaction object, `tx`, which as you'll see in a minute can be used to execute SQL statements against the database. The other is an error object that exposes an error code and error message that can be used to help identify and possibly correct the error that occurred. The following function shows how a simple function can be constructed that displays an error to the user. When this function executes, the application can assume that the transaction has rolled back and any changes that were made as part of this transaction have been discarded.

```
function onTxError(tx, err) {
  var msgText;
  if(err) {
    //Tell the user what happened
    msgText = "TX: " + err.message + " (" + err.code + ")";
  } else {
    msgText = "TX: Unknown error";
  }
  console.error(msgText);
  alert(msgText);
}
```

The `onTxSuccess` function is simply a way to let the application know the transaction completed. In most cases, there's really nothing to do, so you may not even implement the function in your applications. The function is not passed any values, so all the function can really do is write a status update to the console or update the application's UI, as shown in the following example:

```
function onTxSuccess() {
  console.log("TX: success");
}
```

Passed to the transaction is a function that's executed to perform whatever updates are needed on the database. The first thing an application should do after opening a database is create or open one or more tables the application needs to store its data. Fortunately, the SQL statement that creates a table will simply open the table if it already exists. The following code is the example createTable function that is used to create the table required by the application. The function is passed a transaction object, tx, that can be used by the application to execute SQL statements, as shown here:

```
function createTable(tx) {
  var sqlStr = 'CREATE TABLE IF NOT EXISTS MILEAGE
    (tripDate INT, miles INT, notes TEXT)';
  console.log(sqlStr);
  tx.executeSql(sqlStr, [], onSqlSuccess, onSqlError);
}
```

In this example, the SQL statement creates a MILEAGE table consisting of three columns (tripDate, miles, and notes). The statement is executed through a call to tx.executeSql, which takes the following parameters:

- **SQL statement**: The SQL statement that will be executed against the database object the transaction is associated with

- **Values**: An array of values that are passed to the SQL statement (this will be described later)

- **Success function**: The name of the function that will be executed after the SQL statement has executed successfully

- **Error function**: The name of the function that will be executed if there is an error executing the SQL statement

Note: Note the order of the callback functions; in this case, the success callback precedes the error callback (as it has been for most of the APIs in this book).

The success callback function is passed two parameters: a transaction object (which can be used to execute additional SQL statements) and a results object, which contains the results of the operation. The results object exposes the following properties:

- `insertId`: The row ID for the row of data that was added to the table if the SQL statement executed contained an `INSERT` statement.

- `rowAffected`: The number of table rows that were changed by the SQL statement. A value of zero indicated that no rows were affected.

- `rows`: An object containing the rows returned by the SQL statement. The object will be empty if the SQL statement returns no rows.

The following code shows a sample success function. The function writes some information about the result set to the console and then loops through the results.

```
function onSqlSuccess(tx, res) {
  if(res) {
    console.log("Insert ID: " + res.insertID);
    console.log("Row affected: " + res.rowAffected);
    if (res.rows) {
      var len = res.rows.length;
      if(len > 0) {
        for(var i = 0; i < len; i++) {
          //Do something with the row data

        }
      } else {
        alert("No records processed.");
      }
    }
  } else {
    alert("No results returned.");
  }
}
```

The `onSqlError` function operates the same as the `onTxError` function described earlier; they both do the same thing, only at a different part of the process. The function is passed transaction and error objects, as shown in the following example:

```
function onSqlError(tx, err) {
  var msgText;
  if(err) {
    msgText = "SQL: " + err.message + " (" + err.code + ")";
  } else {
    msgText = "SQL: Unknown error";
  }
  console.error(msgText);
  alert(msgText);
}
```

After all of this processing has completed, the application displays a screen similar to the one shown in Figure 22-2. At this point, the user can start to populate the MILEAGE table with data by filling out the form shown in the figure and clicking the Save button.

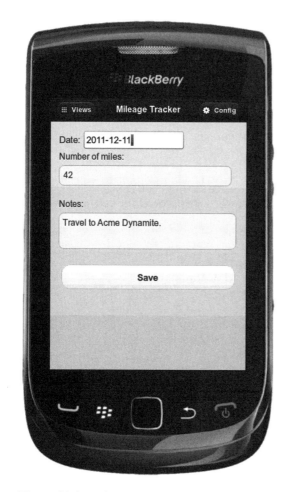

Figure 22-2   Mileage tracker running on a BlackBerry Torch 9800

At this point, all the application needs to do is execute another SQL statement to add the user-provided data to the table. To do this, the application fires off another transaction, as shown in the following code:

```
theDB.transaction(insertRecord, onTxError, onTxSuccess);
```

The application's `insertRecord` function does the work to add the data to the table. The following code shows a simplified version of the function that has the table row values hard-coded into the function:

```
function insertRecord(tx) {
  var sqlStr = 'INSERT INTO MILEAGE (tripDate, miles, notes)
    VALUES ("2011-12-09", 42, "Travel to Acme Dynamite")';
  tx.executeSql(sqlStr, [], onSuccess, onError);
}
```

The application uses dynamic values as shown in the following code. The function first pulls some values from the form and then passes the values to the SQL statement. Since the application is recording date values and needs to be able to retrieve mileage records by date and ordered by date, the date value needs to be stored in the table in numeric format. To accomplish this, I used a free JavaScript library called `Date.fromString()` from Joey Mazzarelli (http://joey.mazzarelli .com/2008/11/25/easy-date-parsing-with-javascript) that allows the application to take the inputted date string directly into a JavaScript `Date` object. Once the `Date` object is available, the application uses the `valueOf()` method to get the date value in numeric format as needed.

```
function insertRecord(tx) {
  //Create a new date object to hold the date the user entered
  var tmpDate = new
    Date.fromString(document.getElementById("editDate").value);
  var tmpMiles = document.getElementById("editNumMiles").value;
  var tmpNotes = document.getElementById("editNotes").value;
  var sqlStr = 'INSERT INTO MILEAGE (tripDate, miles, notes)
    VALUES (?, ?, ?)';
  console.log(sqlStr);
  tx.executeSql(sqlStr,
    [tmpDate.valueOf(), tmpMiles, tmpNotes],
    onSqlSuccess, onSqlError);
}
```

Remember how the call to `executeSQL` could take an array of values as a parameter? In the example shown, the SQL statement includes a VALUES parameter and a parenthetical group of question marks, as shown in the following example:

```
INSERT INTO MILEAGE (tripDate, miles, notes) VALUES (?,?,?)
```

Each question mark refers to a particular field value in the INSERT statement. The table row values for `tripDate`, `miles`, and `notes` are then passed into the SQL statement as an array of values, as shown in the following example:

```
tx.executeSql(sqlStr, [tmpDate.valueOf(), tmpMiles, tmpNotes],
  onSqlSuccess, onSqlError);
```

Getting data out of the table requires yet another SQL statement. The following function fires off a transaction to query the MILEAGE table; the processing of the results of the query is done in the onQueryResults function that follows:

```
function openView(viewType) {
  var sqlStr = "SELECT * FROM MILEAGE ORDER BY tripDate ASC";
  theDB.transaction(function(tx){tx.executeSql(sqlStr, [],
    onQuerySuccess, onQueryFailure);
  }, onTxError, onTxSuccess);
}
```

In this example, I broke with one of the conventions I've used throughout most of the book. In general, I've broken out all functions in order to make the code more readable. In the openView function, the full function (not shown) does some work to create the appropriate page heading and SQL statement depending on which view was selected. The application then needed to pass the appropriate SQL statement to the transaction function, and the cleanest way to do that was just to pass in the function's code as an anonymous function to the call to tx.executeSql. I've simplified the JavaScript code in the example function, showing only how to generate the SQL statement for one of the views, but when you look at the full example application, you'll see how the use of anonymous functions makes this code simpler although harder to read.

In the onQuerySuccess function, the code takes the results returned from the execution of the SQL statement and generates a page similar to the one shown in Figure 22-3. The table column values are returned in the results array; the application uses results.rows.item(i).ColumnName to retrieve values for each column and then build the appropriate HTML content before assigning it to the page.

```
function onQuerySuccess(tx, results) {
  if(results.rows) {
    console.log("Rows: " + results.rows);
    var len = results.rows.length;
    if(len > 0) {
      var htmlStr = "";
      for(var i = 0; i < len; i++) {
        var theDate = new Date(results.rows.item(i).tripDate);
        htmlStr += '<b>Date:</b> ' + theDate.toDateString() +
          '<br />';
        var numMiles = results.rows.item(i).miles;
        if(numMiles > 1) {
          htmlStr += '<b>Miles:</b> ' + numMiles +
            ' miles<br />';
        } else {
          htmlStr += '<b>Miles:</b> 1 mile<br />';
        }
        //Check to see if there are any notes before writing
        // anything to the page
        var theNotes = results.rows.item(i).notes;
```

```
        if(theNotes.length > 0) {
          htmlStr += '<b>Notes:</b> ' + theNotes + '<br />';
        }
        htmlStr += '<hr />';
      }
      //Use JQuery's $() to assign the content to the page
      $("#viewData").html(htmlStr);
      //Then open the View page to display the data
      $.mobile.changePage("#dataView", "slide", false, true);
    } else {
      alert("No rows.");
    }
  } else {
    alert("No records match selection criteria.");
  }
}
```

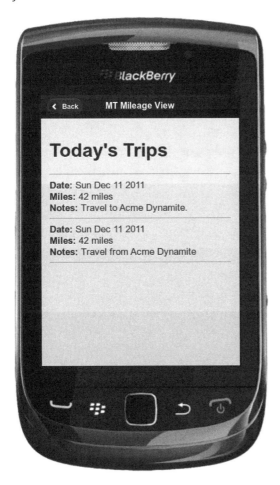

Figure 22-3   Example 22-1 displaying query results

Most of what's covered here is related to SQL statements and how to work with database tables; there's not much that's really PhoneGapish. As shown, once you have the database opened, it's all executing SQL statements and writing callback functions.

As older devices drop out of use, I expect the PhoneGap development team to simply drop this API and let applications use the native SQLite capabilities available in most modern smartphones.

A

Installing the PhoneGap Files

Installing PhoneGap is a pretty straightforward process. Point your browser of choice to www.phonegap.com, and then click the Download icon in the upper-right corner of the landing page, as highlighted in Figure A-1. You should be redirected to a page, and the most recent version of PhoneGap will automatically begin downloading in a few seconds. If the download does not start automatically, simply click the download link provided on the page to download the files directly.

Figure A-1 The PhoneGap project landing page

The PhoneGap project files are distributed in a standard zip archive. To install PhoneGap, simply extract the downloaded files to the folder of your choice on your local hard drive or on a network server (in cases where the files will be shared with other developers or between multiple systems).

Because many Java applications on Windows used to have issues with spaces in folder names, I typically install the PhoneGap files off of the root of the system's hard drive, as shown in Figure A-2. In this case, I extracted the files and then renamed the root PhoneGap folder to the version of PhoneGap, as shown in the figure. This approach has saved me some grief with other tools in the past. The files you will used to build PhoneGap applications are located in the lib folder.

As you can see, the PhoneGap project files include a separate folder for each supported mobile device platform. Those folders contain the specific project files and associated PhoneGap JavaScript libraries for each target operating system.

It's important to note that PhoneGap source files differ greatly between each target OS. You can't use the PhoneGap JavaScript libraries for one mobile platform in a project for another mobile platform. This is one of the issues that makes PhoneGap development complicated and creates the need for PhoneGap Build (described in Chapter 9).

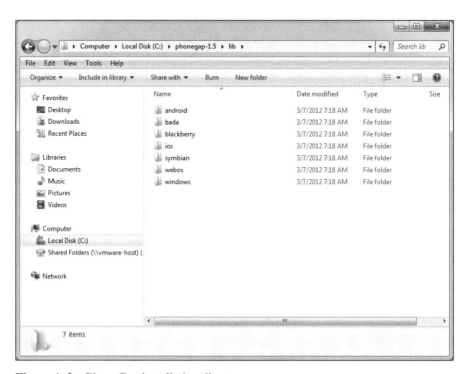

Figure A-2   PhoneGap installation directory

Preparing for Samsung bada Development

For some reason, the PhoneGap JavaScript source code files for bada are distributed as separate JavaScript files for each API category instead of consolidated into a single file as they are for other platforms. Before you can use the PhoneGap JavaScript APIs in your PhoneGap applications for bada, you must first generate the consolidated source code file phonegap.js. To do this, open a Windows command prompt, navigate to the PhoneGap installation's bada/Res/PhoneGap folder, and execute the phonegap.bat file located in the folder. The batch file will copy each of the source JavaScript files into a single phonegap.js file and display the output shown in Figure A-3.

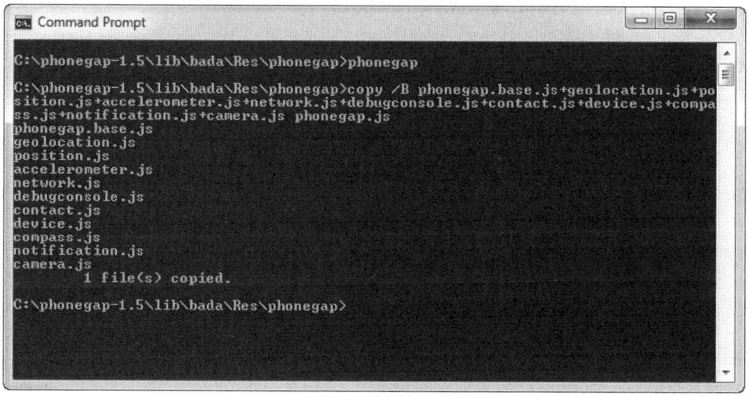

Figure A-3   Generating the bada phonegap.js file

If you look in the folder, you will see a new file there called phonegap.js, all ready to be used in your PhoneGap applications. Any time you modify any of the source JavaScript files, you will need to repeat this process to generate an updated phonegap.js file for your projects.

Preparing for iOS Development

For iOS development with PhoneGap, you must perform an additional installation step to configure Xcode, Apple's development environment for iOS, for PhoneGap development. In Finder, navigate to the iOS folder within the PhoneGap installation files folder, as shown in Figure A-4. Double-click the Cordova-1.5.0.dmg file to start the installation process.

Figure A-4 PhoneGap iOS file folder

Finder will extract the files and then open a window similar to the one shown in Figure A-5. Double-click the `Cordova-1.5.0.pkg` file to install the PhoneGap files into the Xcode IDE.

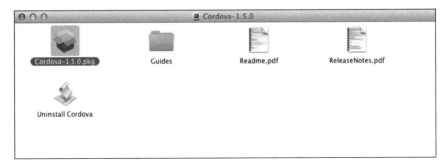

Figure A-5 PhoneGap installation package

Once this step has been completed, Xcode will have an additional project template (PhoneGap) to select from when creating new projects.

Preparing for Windows Phone Development

To simplify PhoneGap development on Windows Phone, the PhoneGap project includes a plug-in to Microsoft Visual Studio that allows Visual Studio to create complete PhoneGap projects with a few clicks of the mouse.

Open Windows Explorer, and navigate to the folder where you extracted the PhoneGap files. In the `WP7` folder, copy the `GapAppStarter.zip` file to Visual

Studio's project templates folder. The destination folder should be located under the Windows Documents folder for the currently logged in user. The folder should be located here:

```
c:\users\user_name\Documents\Visual Studio 2011\Templates\
ProjectTemplates\
```

In this example, `user_name` refers to the user-specific profile folder for the logged-in user. For example, for my developer workstation running Windows 7, the folder is located here:

```
c:\users\John M. Wargo\Documents\Visual Studio 2011\Templates
ProjectTemplates\
```

After the zip file is copied, the folder contents should look similar to what is shown in Figure A-6. Alternatively, you can place the `GapAppStarter.zip` file in the Visual C# folder instead; it seems to work in that location as well.

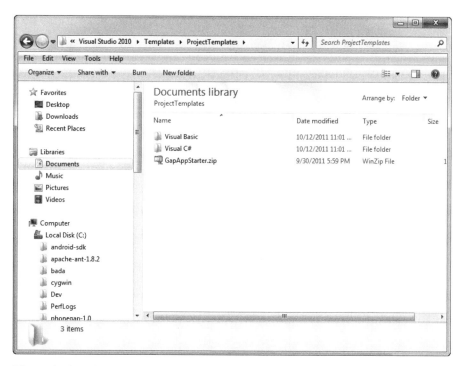

Figure A-6 Visual Studio `ProjectTemplates` folder

B

Installing the Oracle Java Developer Kit

The Android and BlackBerry development tools use Oracle's Java Developer Kit (JDK) to build (compile) Java applications for Android. Apple's Mac OS will either already include the JDK or install it automatically when you run your first Java program, so if you're installing on a Macintosh computer, you can skip this appendix and move on.

Downloading the JDK

To obtain the JDK, point your browser of choice to http://java.oracle.com, and then click the Get Java button on the landing page. On the page that appears, scroll down and click the Download button for the appropriate JDK version to download.

At this time, Oracle is shipping version 7 of the JDK, but the Android development tools support only versions 5 and 6. Be sure to check to see that the version of the JDK you download is compatible with the Android tools before downloading and installing the software.

 Note: The Java download site contains different flavors of Java for you to download. The most common options are the Java Runtime Environment (JRE) and the Java Developer Kit (JDK). The JRE is the client-side runtime environment used to run Java applications you may have downloaded over the Internet or installed on your local workstation.

The JDK contains the tools needed to compile Java code into executable applications and applets. To use the Android developer tools, you must install the JDK, not the JRE. So that you can execute Java applications, the JDK includes the JRE, so you'll be covered for both.

Figure B-1 shows the download options for the JDK. For each supported operating system, there's a different download depending on whether you're running a 32-bit or 64-bit operating system. When selecting the files to download, be sure to match the download to both the processor and the operating system running on your development machine, as described in Table B-1.

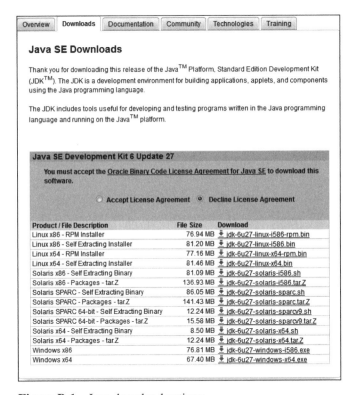

Figure B-1   Java download options

Table B-1   Determining the JDK to Download

Processor Bit Depth	Operating System Bit Depth	JDK Download
32-bit	32-bit	x86
64-bit	32-bit	x86
64-bit	64-bit	x64 or 64-bit

Installing the JDK

Once the JDK has been downloaded, launch the downloaded file to begin the installation. You can simply accept the default installation options to complete the installation. Some installation options may not be needed for your installation (such as source code and Java DB) and can be omitted (as shown in Figure B-2); all the other components are required and cannot be disabled.

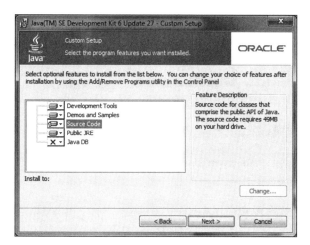

Figure B-2   Java installation wizard

Configuring the Windows Path

Once the installation has completed, the Windows Path environment variable must be updated to point to the JDK's `bin` folder. This allows the Java tools to be executed by any program on the computer such as the Android developer tools, without specifically pointing to the folder where the JDK is installed. By default the JDK executables will be installed in the Windows `Program Files` folder (`C:\ Program Files\Java\jdk#\bin`, where the # refers to the version of the JDK installed). To modify the Path variable, open the Windows Control Panel and then select System or right-click My Computer and select Properties.

In the System Properties application, click the Advanced System Settings tab, as shown in Figure B-3, and then click the Environment Variables button on the bottom of the window. In the "System variables" area of the Environment Variables window, select Path then click the edit button. In the window that appears (also shown in Figure B-3), modify the variable value field by appending a semicolon at the end of the existing value and adding the full path to the JDK `bin` folder (`C:\Program Files\Java\jdk1.6.0_27`, as shown in the figure) to the end of the value that is already there. Do not replace the contents of the variable value field; simply append a semicolon and the JDK path to the end of the value that's already there. Click OK repeatedly to close the windows that have been opened during this process.

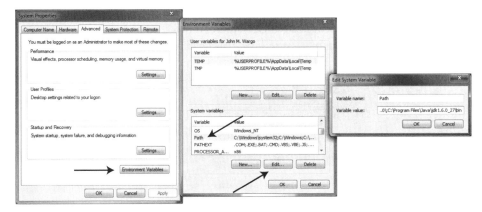

Figure B-3 Setting the Windows Path environment variable

Confirming Installation Success

To confirm that the Path variable has been set correctly, open a Command Prompt window (shown in Figure B-4), type `javac` at the prompt, and press Enter. If the path has been correctly configured, the Command Prompt window will fill with instructions on how to use the Java compiler (javac, one of the programs included with the JDK), as shown in the figure. If you receive an error message such as "bad command or file name" or "'javac' is not recognized as an internal or external command, operable program or batch file," then the path has not been configured correctly, and you will need to fix the configuration before continuing.

```
Command Prompt

C:\Users\John M. Wargo>javac
Usage: javac <options> <source files>
where possible options include:
  -g                         Generate all debugging info
  -g:none                    Generate no debugging info
  -g:{lines,vars,source}     Generate only some debugging info
  -nowarn                    Generate no warnings
  -verbose                   Output messages about what the compiler is doing
  -deprecation               Output source locations where deprecated APIs are u
sed
  -classpath <path>          Specify where to find user class files and annotati
on processors
  -cp <path>                 Specify where to find user class files and annotati
on processors
  -sourcepath <path>         Specify where to find input source files
  -bootclasspath <path>      Override location of bootstrap class files
  -extdirs <dirs>            Override location of installed extensions
  -endorseddirs <dirs>       Override location of endorsed standards path
  -proc:{none,only}          Control whether annotation processing and/or compil
ation is done.
  -processor <class1>[,<class2>,<class3>...]Names of the annotation processors t
o run; bypasses default discovery process
  -processorpath <path>      Specify where to find annotation processors
  -d <directory>             Specify where to place generated class files
```

Figure B-4 Testing the JDK configuration on Windows

C

Installing Apache Ant

The Android and BlackBerry development tools use Apache Ant to automate command-line build tasks. Ant is an open source project within the Apache Software Foundation's suite of products. Ant is a Java-based build tool and therefore requires a Java Runtime Environment (JRE). Refer to Appendix B for instructions for installing the Java Developer Kit (JDK), which includes the JRE.

Macintosh Installation

For Macintosh users, Mac OS X includes a version of Ant preinstalled. You will need to verify that the version installed is compatible with the mobile development SDKs you will be working with (for example, at the time of this writing, the Android SDK requires version 1.8 and newer). To determine the installed version, open a terminal window, and issue the following command:

```
ant -version
```

Ant will respond with the currently installed version information, as shown in Figure C-1.

If a more recent version is needed, let the Macintosh OS software update process install its updates, and then try again. To perform a software update, open the System Preferences application, select Software Updates, and then click Check Now.

Figure C-1 Verifying the Ant version on Macintosh

Windows Installation

To install Ant on a system running Microsoft Windows, point your browser of choice to http://ant.apache.org, and click the home page link to download the latest version of the project's files. Once the download has completed, extract the files to a folder off of your system's root folder. Figure C-2 shows an example of an Ant installation in Windows using the default zip file name (which includes the Ant version information) as the installation folder location.

Once the files have been extracted, you must update the Windows Path environment variable to point to the Ant installation's bin folder. This allows Ant to be executed by any program on the computer such as the Android developer tools, without specifically pointing to the folder where Ant is installed. To modify the Path variable, open the Windows Control Panel and then select System or right-click My Computer and select Properties. In the System Properties application, click the Advanced System Settings tab, and then click the Environment Variables button on the bottom of the window. In the "System variables" area of the Environment Variables window, select Path, and then click the Edit button. In the window that appears, modify the variable value field by appending a semicolon at the end of the existing value and adding the full path to the Ant `bin` folder (`C:\apache-ant-1.8.2\bin`, as shown in Figure C-2) to the end of the value that is already there. Do not replace the contents of the variable value field; simply append a semicolon and the Ant bin path to the end of the value that's already there. Click OK repeatedly to close the windows that have been opened during this process. An example of this process is illustrated in Figure B-3 in Appendix B.

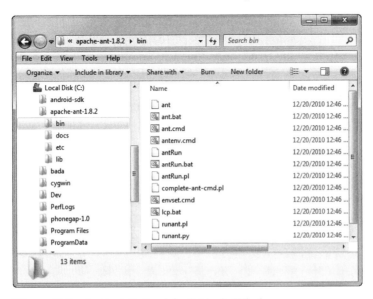

Figure C-2   Ant installation `bin` folder in Windows

Once the process has completed, verify the successful installation and configuration by checking the Ant version using the instructions provided in the previous section.

Index

A

Accelerator API
  overview of, 157–158
  querying device orientation, 158–161
  watching device orientation, 161–164
addresses array, specifying contact
  properties, 225–226
Adobe, in history of PhoneGap, 5
Alerts
  debugging PhoneGap applications and,
    37–38
  Notification API and, 307–310
allowEdit property, Camera API, 180
Android
  accelerator determining device
    orientation, 157–158, 164
  Apache Ant and, 337
  application status events, 253–254
  building PhoneGap applications, 13–14
  button events, 257–258, 261
  camera simulators, 170
  Capture API example on, 200–204
  Compass API example on, 209
  configuring PhoneGap Build for mobile
    platforms, 143–145
  contact information, 231
  debugging PhoneGap applications, 41–43
  device object running on, 245
  Eclipse plug-in and, 19
  errors related to contact information,
    229–230
  geolocation support, 279

JDK (Java Developer Kit) and, 333–334
Media API support, 293
media files, 295
network status events, 256
operating systems supported by
  PhoneGap, 3
PhoneGap API support, 9
PhoneGap Build support, 141
picture capture process, 168–169,
  173–175
releasing Media objects, 298
searching for contact information, 235
testing applications created with
  PhoneGap Build, 152
testing applications on physical devices,
  36–37
watchHeading function on, 213
Android development tools
  AVD (Android Virtual Device) for testing
    PhoneGap applications, 60–64
  configuring Eclipse development
    environment, 64–66
  creating PhoneGap project, 67–69
  creating PhoneGap project with Eclipse,
    73–74
  installing SDK on Macintosh OSs, 60
  installing SDK on Windows OSs, 58–59
  making changes to Java source files,
    70–72
  managing PhoneGap projects from
    command-line, 74–77
  options for creating PhoneGap projects,
    66–67

Android development tools (*cont.*)
　steps in installation of, 57–58
　testing PhoneGap applications, 77–79
Android Virtual Device (AVD), testing
　PhoneGap applications with, 60–64, 78
Antenna Volt, types of hybrid
　applications, 21
Apache
　Cordova Git repository. See Git
　　repository
　history of PhoneGap and, 5
Apache Ant
　BlackBerry development environment
　　and, 97
　building PhoneGap applications, 76–77
　installing on Macintosh OSs, 337
　installing on Windows OSs, 338–339
APIs (application programming interfaces)
　capturing settings from another
　　application and adding to bada
　　project, 93
　consistency as cross-platform issue,
　　50–51
　defining application version in bada,
　　88–90
　PhoneGap APIs. See PhoneGap APIs
　PhoneGap supported, 10
　running web applications within
　　PhoneGap container, 8
　suite in PhoneGap, 3
Appcelerator Titanium, types of hybrid
　applications, 20
Apple
　development environment. See iOS
　　development environment
　iOS. See iOS
　iPhone. See iPhone
　PhoneGap and, 11
　registering as Apple developer, 113–114

Application container, designing for, 11–13
Application development
　on Android. See Android development
　　tools
　on bada. See bada development
　　environment
　on BlackBerry. See BlackBerry
　　development environment
　on iOS. See iOS development
　　environment
　with PhoneGap Build. See PhoneGap
　　Build
　with Symbian. See Symbian development
　　environment
　Windows OSs. See Windows
　　development environment
Application Manager, bada
　creating application ID, 88
　creating application profile, 86–88
　defining application version, 88–90
　defining platform version, 90–93
　selecting target devices, 93–94
Application profile, creating for bada
　development project, 86–88
Application status events, 251–254
Applications, PhoneGap. See also Web
　applications
　architecture of, 6–7
　building, 13–16, 27
　cross-platform issues, 49–53
　debugging. See Debugging PhoneGap
　　applications
　Hello, World! example, 23–25
　hybrid. See Hybrid applications
　initialization, 25–28
　leveraging PhoneGap APIs, 28–30
　running on physical device, 36–37
　running on simulators, 29–30, 33–34,
　　35–36

testing. See Testing PhoneGap applications

user interface enhancements, 30–35

Web 1.0 approach to building, 11

Web 2.0 approach to building, 11–12

Arrays, specifying contact properties, 225–226

AT&T WorkBench, 21

Audio

  callback functions, 295–297

  capture on Android devices, 202

  capture with Capture API, 186, 198–199

  creating `Media` objects, 294

  determining current position while playing, 297

  determining duration of playback, 297–298

  example of use of Media API, 300–305

  `mediaFileURI`, 294–295

  playing clips, 298–299

  recording, 299–300

AVD (Android Virtual Device), testing PhoneGap applications with, 60–64, 78

B

bada development environment

  adding manifest file to PhoneGap project, 94–95

  capturing API settings from another application, 93

  configuring application security, 90, 92

  creating application ID, 88

  creating application profile, 86–87

  creating PhoneGap project, 82–86

  defining application version, 88–89

  defining platform version, 90–92

  defining unique name for application, 87–88

  downloading/installing PhoneGap files, 80–82

  overview of, 79–80

  preparing PhoneGap for, 329

  selecting target devices, 93–94

  testing PhoneGap applications, 95–96

bada (Samsung), PhoneGap supported operating systems, 4

Beep, in Notification API, 310

BES (BlackBerry Enterprise Server), 109

BlackBerry

  accelerator determining device orientation, 157–158

  accelerator support and, 161

  adding/saving contacts, 232–233

  Apache Ant and, 337

  application status events and, 253

  build issues, 151

  building PhoneGap applications, 14–15

  button events, 257–258, 261

  Capture API on, 196, 204

  configuring camera options, 178, 180

  configuring PhoneGap Build for mobile platforms, 143–145

  debugging PhoneGap applications, 40–41

  device object running on simulator, 245–246

  E/S (emulator/simulator) and, 35–36

  errors related to contact information, 229–230

  `FileWriter` object and, 274

  geolocation support, 279

  getting current location of device, 284

  HelloWorld application on, 29–30, 34

  JDK (Java Developer Kit) for building applications, 333

  Media API support, 293

  mileage tracker example, 322

  PhoneGap API documentation, 51

BlackBerry (*cont.*)
  PhoneGap API support, 8–9
  PhoneGap Build support, 141
  PhoneGap supported operating systems, 4
  picture capture process, 168, 170–172
  reading directory entries, 269–272
  running contacts example on, 231
  searching for contact information, 234
  signing keys, 99
  storing contact information, 228
  testing applications created with
    PhoneGap Build, 152
  testing applications on physical device,
    36–37
  watching location of device,
    286, 288
  WebWorks. See WebWorks
BlackBerry development environment
  build process, 104–107
  building PhoneGap applications,
    107–109
  `config.xml` file, 100–103
  creating PhoneGap project, 99–100
  installing WebWorks SDK, 98–99
  overview of, 97
  testing PhoneGap applications on device,
    111–112
  testing PhoneGap applications on
    simulator, 109–111
BlackBerry® Development Fundamentals
  (Wargo), xxiv, 21, 40, 97, 105, 107
BlackBerry Enterprise Server (BES), 109
BlackBerry Mobile Data System (MDS)
  overview of, 106–107
  testing PhoneGap applications on,
    109–111
BlackBerry WebWorks. See WebWorks
Build process. See also PhoneGap Build
  accessing contact information and, 230

in BlackBerry development environment,
  104–107
building applications for BlackBerry,
  107–109
PhoneGap applications, 13–16
in PhoneGap Build, 148
`build.xml file`, 109
Button events
  event listener for, 258–262
  list of button types, 257
  overriding button behavior, 257–258
  overview of, 256–257
  running on Android, 261

C

Callback functions
  Capture API, 187–188
  Contacts API, 236, 242
  `DirectoryReader` object and, 267
  File API, 270–271, 273–274, 277–278
  Geolocation API, 280–281
  how PhoneGap works and, 9
  Media API, 295–297
  Notification API, 308–309
  SQL database, 321–322
  Storage API, 319–320, 326
Camera API
  accessing pictures on devices, 165–166
  `allowEdit`, 180
  Android example, 173–175
  BlackBerry example, 171–172
  Capture API compared with, 185
  configuring camera options, 176
  dealing with issues related to,
    182–184
  default options, 166–167
  `destinationType`, 178–179
  `encodingType`, 181

inconsistencies between device platforms, 168–170

iOS example, 169–170

iPhone example, 167–168

mediaType, 181–182

optic quality and, 177–178

overview of, 165

sourceType, 179–180

targetHeight and targetWidth, 181

Cameras, testing PhoneGap applications via, 152–153

Capture API

audio and video capture, 198–199

Camera API compared with, 185

configuring capture options, 189–191

image preview on iOS, 197–198

inconsistencies between device platforms, 195–196

Media API compared with, 293

overview of, 185

running on Android device, 200–204

running on BlackBerry device, 204

running on iPhone, 191–195

using, 186–189

Chrome (Google), 44–45

clone method, contacts and, 242

Cloud

building PhoneGap applications in, 141

packaging PhoneGap applications, 14

Command-line tools

development on BlackBerry and, 98

managing projects with, 74–77

testing applications, 77–79

Compass API

overview of, 205

querying device orientation, 205–206

running on iPhone, 206–208

watchHeading function, 210–213

watchHeadingFilter function, 213–215

watching device orientation, 209

Compression, JPEG format, 177

config.xml file

BlackBerry projects, 100–103

PhoneGap Build and, 16

PhoneGap Build projects, 145–146, 150

confirm method, in Notification API, 307–310

Connection object

example, 219–220

overview of, 217–219

running on Android device, 220

console object, JavaScript, 38–39

Contacts API

adding/saving contact on BlackBerry, 232–233

cloning contacts, 242

creating contacts, 224

example, 226–230

overview of, 223

removing contacts, 242

running on Android device, 235

running on BlackBerry device, 231

running on iOS device, 235

searching for contact information on BlackBerry, 234

searching for contact information on iPhone, 237

searching for contacts, 235–241

specifying contact properties, 224–226

Contacts API, W3C, 223

Copying files or directories, 276

Cordova Git repository. See Git repository

createTable function, SQL database, 319–320

Cross-platform applications
  building native applications, 3
  development issues, 49–53
CSS (Cascading Style Sheets)
  building cross-platform native
    application, 3
  running web applications within
    PhoneGap container, 7
Cygwin, building Symbian applications on
  Windows OS, 126–128

D

Dalvik Debug Monitor Server (DDMS),
  42–43
`database` object, `transaction` method
  of, 319
DDMS (Dalvik Debug Monitor Server),
  42–43
Debug mode, in PhoneGap Build, 153–154
Debugging camera problems, 183–184
Debugging PhoneGap applications
  leveraging debugging capabilities, 37–43
  overview of, 35
  in PhoneGap Build, 153–154
  RMEE (Ripple Mobile Environment
    Emulator) for debugging, 44–46
  on Symbian, 134
  third-party tools, 43–44
  Weinre (Web Inspector Remote) for
    debugging, 46–49
  on Windows Phone, 139–140
`destinationType` property, Camera API
  settings, 178–179
Developers
  adding developer tools to Eclipse, 65–66
  registering as Apple developer, 113–114
  tools for, 55
Development environments
  Android. See Android development tools

bada. See bada development environment
  BlackBerry. See BlackBerry development
    environment
  iOS. See iOS development environment
  PhoneGap Build. See PhoneGap Build
  Symbian. See Symbian development
    environment
Device APIs and Policy (DAP) Working
  Group, W3C (Worldwide Web
  Consortium), 10
Device location
  canceling a watch, 289–291
  getting current location, 280–284
  setting a watch, 285–288
  watching location of, 284
Device object
  `device` properties, 244
  overview of, 243
  running on Android, 245
  running on BlackBerry, 245–246
  running on iPad, 246–248
  running on iPhone, 246
Device orientation, in Accelerator API
  overview of, 157–158
  querying device orientation, 158–161
  watching device orientation, 161–164
Device orientation, in Compass API
  querying device orientation, 205–206
  `watchHeading` function, 210–213
  `watchHeadingFilter` function,
    213–215
  watching device orientation, 209
`device` properties, device object, 244
`deviceready` events, 250–251
Devices, physical. See Physical devices
Digital signing, configuring PhoneGap Build
  for mobile platforms, 143–145
Directories
  accessing, 264

copying, 276

deleting, 275–276

errors accessing, 265

moving, 276–277

properties, 269–272

reading directory entries, 267–269

DirectoryEntry object

copying directories, 276

deleting directories, 275–276

moving directories, 276–277

properties, 269–272

DirectoryReader object, 267–269

Documentation, PhoneGap API, 17–18, 51

Dojo Mobile, 31

Downloads

bada SDK, 80–82

installing PhoneGap and, 327

JDK (Java Developer Kit), 333–334

Droid (Motorola), Capture API example on, 201

Drupal, PhoneGap plug-ins, 19

Duration, audio playback, 297–298

duration property, Capture API, 190

E

E/S (emulator/simulator)

camera simulators, 170

contacts example on BlackBerry simulator, 231

device object running on BlackBerry simulator, 245–246

device object running on iPad simulator, 246–248

launching PhoneGap project in iPhone simulator, 120

onCameraError on iOS simulator, 183

running PhoneGap applications, 35–36, 78

testing BlackBerry applications, 109–111

testing PhoneGap application in bada emulator, 95–96

testing PhoneGap application in iPhone simulator, 123

testing PhoneGap application with AVD, 60–64

testing PhoneGap Build applications, 152

Windows Phone Emulator, 136

Eclipse

configuring development environment for, 64–66

creating PhoneGap project with, 67–74

LogCat window, 41–42

Package Explorer, 70–71

PhoneGap plug-ins, 19

testing PhoneGap applications, 36–37, 77

Workbench, 65

Emulator Web Application, testing application in bada emulator, 95–96

encodingType property, Camera API settings, 181

Enterprises, iOS development and, 114

Errors

build issues, 150–151

camera problems, 182–183

Capture API, 188–189

Compass API, 206

Contacts API, 228–230

database transactions, 319–321

directory access, 265

file and directory access, 265–266

geolocation, 281

Media API, 295–296

Event listeners

for application status events, 251–253

creating, 249–250

for deviceready events, 250–251

Event Log application, BlackBerry, 40–41

Events API
  application status events, 251–254
  button events, 256–262
  creating event listeners, 249–250
  `deviceready` events, 250–251
  network status events, 254–256
  types of events supported by
    PhoneGap, 249
ExternalHosts, configuring in Xcode, 305

F

Facebook, PhoneGap plug-ins, 18
File API
  accessing file system, 264–267
  copying files or directories, 276
  deleting files or directories, 275–276
  `FileEntry` and `DirectoryEntry`
    properties, 269–272
  moving files or directories, 276–277
  overview of, 263
  reading content from files, 274–275
  reading directory entries, 267–269
  storage types, 263–264
  uploading files to servers, 277–278
  writing data to files, 272–274
File API:Directories and System
  specification, W3C (Worldwide Web
  Consortium), 263
File system, accessing, 264–267
`FileEntry` object
  copying files, 276
  deleting files, 275
  moving files, 276–277
  properties, 269–272
`FileReader` object, 274–275
`FileTransfer` object, 277–278
`FileURI`, for `Media` object, 294–295
`FileWriter` object, 272–274

Folders
  installing PhoneGap and, 328
  location for iOS project, 118
4G networks, connection object
  and, 218

G

Geolocation API
  canceling a watch, 289–291
  getting current location of device,
    280–284
  overview of, 279–280
  setting a watch, 285–288
  watching device location, 284
Geolocation API specification, W3C
  (Worldwide Web Consortium), 279
Git repository
  delivering application files to build
    server, 147
  downloading/installing files for bada
    development project, 80–81
Google Android. See Android
Google Chrome, 44–45
Google Groups, 19
GPS capabilities. See Geolocation API
Graphics. See Images

H

HP/Palm webOS. See webOS
HTML (Hypertext Markup Language)
  building cross-platform native
    applications, 3
  HTML5 approach to building PhoneGap
    applications, 11–13
  HTML5 support for geolocation, 279
  HTML5 support for storage, 315
  running web applications within
    PhoneGap container, 7

Web 1.0 (traditional) approach to building applications, 11

Web 2.0 approach to building applications, 11–12

Hybrid applications
    defined, 3
    frameworks of, 19–20

Hypertext Markup Language. See HTML (Hypertext Markup Language)

I

IBM, in history of PhoneGap, 4–5

IBM Worklight, 22

Icons
    creating iOS projects, 119
    creating PhoneGap Build projects, 145–146
    as cross-platform issue, 53

IDEs (integrated development environments)
    bada as, 82–86
    Eclipse as, 64

Image capture. See Camera API; Capture API

Images
    accessing on mobile devices, 165–166
    accessing pictures on devices, 165–166
    displaying image file URI, 169–170
    mediaType property, 182
    rotating graphics with jQuery Rotate, 212

index.html
    creating PhoneGap project with Eclipse, 73–74
    delivering application files to build server, 146

Infuse 4G device (Samsung), 204

Initialization, of PhoneGap applications, 25–28

INSERT statement, SQL database, 323–324

Installing PhoneGap. See PhoneGap installation

Integrated development environments (IDEs)
    bada as, 82–86
    Eclipse as, 64

iOS
    accessing media files, 295
    application status events, 251, 253
    building PhoneGap applications, 15
    button events, 256–257
    camera simulators, 170
    Capture API example on, 197
    configuring camera options, 180
    configuring PhoneGap Build for mobile platforms, 143–145
    device object running on iPad simulator, 246–248
    displaying image file URI, 169–170
    Hello, World! application on, 26
    image preview on, 197–198
    Media API support, 293
    onCameraError in iOS simulator, 183
    PhoneGap API documentation, 51
    PhoneGap API support, 9
    PhoneGap Build support, 141
    PhoneGap plug-in for Drupal, 19
    PhoneGap supported operating systems, 3
    picture capture process, 168–169
    searching for contact information, 235
    testing applications on physical device, 36
    uploading files to server and, 278

iOS development environment
    accessing web content for project, 119–122
    creating PhoneGap project, 116–117
    folder location for projects, 118
    installing Xcode, 114–116

iOS development environment (*cont.*)
  naming projects and defining project
    locations, 117–118
  overview of, 113
  preparing PhoneGap for, 329–330
  registering as Apple developer, 113–114
  testing PhoneGap applications, 122–123
  versioning, 118–119
iPad
  device object and, 246–248
  PhoneGap support, 3–4
iPhone
  accelerator support and, 159
  Camera API example, 167–168, 191–195
  configuring camera options, 180
  device object, 246
  inconsistent implementation of PhoneGap
    APIs, 30
  launching PhoneGap project in, 120
  PhoneGap support, 3
  running HelloWorld application on
    iPhone simulator, 26
  searching for contact information, 237
  testing PhoneGap application in, 123
iPhoneDevCamp, 4

J

Java API, RIM (Research In Motion), 246
Java Developer Kit. See JDK (Java
  Developer Kit)
Java, making changes to source file using
  Eclipse, 70–71
JavaScript
  `alert` method, 307
  bada source code files, 329
  build cross-platform native applications, 3
  building PhoneGap applications, 13–14
  `console` object, 38–39
  cross-platform issue, 51
  loading JavaScript library, 27
  running web applications within
    PhoneGap container, 7–8
  Web 2.0 approach to building
    applications, 11–12
  WebWorks providing JavaScript
    methods, 246
JDK (Java Developer Kit)
  Android development and, 57
  bada and, 80
  BlackBerry development and, 97
  configuring Windows Path environment,
    335–336
  confirming installation of, 336
  downloading, 333–334
  installing, 334
  JRE (Java Runtime Environment)
    included in, 337
JPEG format
  compression, 177
  images, 181
  `mode` property of Capture API, 190
jQuery
  `$()` function, 212
  reasons for using, 268
  rotating graphics with, 212
jQuery Mobile (jQM)
  as application interface, 192, 200
  creating interface for directory
    reader, 268
  creating interface for media application,
    300–301
  creating interface for notification
    application, 313
  searching for contact information, 237
  use in application development, 30–35
JRE (Java Runtime Environment),
  333–334, 337

K

Key/value pairs, local storage and, 316

L

Launch screens, creating iOS PhoneGap
   project, 119
LG Thrill device
   device object on, 245
   video capture on, 202–203
`limit` property, Capture API, 190
Linux OSs
   building Symbian PhoneGap applications
      on, 125
   configuring Eclipse development
      environment, 64
   launching Unix applications from
      command line, 75
   options for PhoneGap development on
      Android, 57
Local storage, Storage API, 316–317
LogCat window, Eclipse, 41–43

M

Macintosh OSs
   bada development tools and, 79
   building Symbian PhoneGap applications
      on, 125–127
   configuring Eclipse development
      environment, 64
   development environment. See iOS
      development environment
   installing Android SDK on, 60
   installing Apache Ant on, 337
   Installing BlackBerry WebWorks SDK,
      98–99
   JDK (Java Developer Kit) and, 333
   launching Unix applications from
      command line, 75

   options for PhoneGap development on
      Android, 57
   packaging Symbian PhoneGap
      projects, 131
   testing Symbian PhoneGap projects, 132
   Windows Phone development and, 135
Magnetic poles, device orientation
   and, 206
Make utility
   installing, 126–127
   packaging PhoneGap projects, 131–132
Makefiles, 126, 131–132
Manifest file, adding to PhoneGap project in
   bada, 94–96
Media API
   callback functions, 295–297
   creating `Media` objects, 294
   determining current position while
      playing media files, 297
   determining duration of playback,
      297–298
   example of use of, 300–305
   `FileURI`, 294–295
   overview of, 293
   playing audio clips, 298–299
   recording audio, 299–300
   releasing `Media` objects, 298
Media Capture API, W3C (Worldwide Web
   Consortium), 185
Media files, using Capture API, 186–187
`Media` objects
   creating, 294
   releasing, 298
`mediaType` property, Camera API settings,
   181–182
Memory cards, 61
Microsoft Windows. See Windows OSs
Mobile browsers. See also Web
   browsers, 279

Mobile Data System (MDS)
   BlackBerry and, 106–107
   testing PhoneGap BlackBerry
      applications on, 109–111
mode property, Capture API, 190–191
Motorola Droid, Capture API example
   on, 201
Moving files or directories, 276–277

N

Names
   defining unique name for application,
      87–88
   iOS PhoneGap project, 117
   PhoneGap Build project, 145
Navigation, as cross-platform issue, 52
Navigator object, instantiating APIs
   from, 28
Network status events, 254–256
Networks, connection object and, 217–218
New project dialog, PhoneGap Build,
   147–148
Nitobi
   history of PhoneGap and, 4–5
   support offered by, 19
Nokia
   Symbian. See Symbian
   Web Tools, 125–126
Notification API
   beep, 310
   example application of, 310–313
   overview of, 307
   vibrate, 310
   visual alerts, 307–310

O

offline events, network status events, 254
online events, network status events, 254

onStatus function, media playback and,
   296–297
Open source frameworks
   PhoneGap as, 3
   support and, 19
Optic quality, cameras and, 177
Oracle JDK. See JDK (Java Developer Kit)
organizations array, specifying
   contact properties, 226
OSs (operating systems)
   application requirements as cross-
      platform issue, 52
   bada. See bada (Samsung)
   configuring Eclipse development
      environment, 64
   emulator/simulators and, 35–36
   installing Apache Ant on, 337–339
   JDK (Java Developer Kit) and, 334
   Linux OSs. See Linux OSs
   Macintosh OSs. See Macintosh OSs
   PhoneGap supported, 3–4
   Windows OSs. See Windows OSs
OTA (over the air)
   deploying applications to BlackBerry
      smartphones, 108–109
   testing PhoneGap applications, 152

P

Packaging PhoneGap projects
   cloud-based service, 14
   with Symbian, 131–132
Palm webOS (HP). See webOS
pause events, application status events,
   251–254
pause method, Media objects, 298–299
Persistent storage, file storage options,
   263–264
PhoneGap APIs
   accelerometer. See Accelerator API

camera. See Camera API

capture. See Capture API

capturing API settings from another application and adding to bada project, 93

compass. See Compass API

connection. See Connection object

contacts. See Contacts API

defining application version in bada, 88–90

devices. See Device object

events. See Events API

files. See File API

geolocation capabilities. See Geolocation API

leveraging, 28–30

media. See Media API

notifications. See Notification API

responding to JavaScript calls, 27–28

storage. See Storage API

supporting multiple mobile platforms, 8–9

PhoneGap Build

build process, 148

building applications with, 27

cloud-based packaging service, 14

configuring, 143–145

configuring projects, 148–150

config.xml file, 16

creating accounts, 142–143

creating application for, 145–146

creating projects, 146

dealing with build issues, 150–151

debugging applications, 153–154

delivering application files to build server, 146–147

development environments compared with, 142

need for, 328

new project dialog, 147–148

overview of, 141

testing applications, 152–153

PhoneGap installation

overview of, 327–328

preparing for bada development, 329

preparing for iOS development, 329–330

preparing for Windows Phone development, 330–331

PhoneGap, introduction to

building applications, 13–16

designing for application container, 11–13

history of, 4–5

how it works, 6–10

hybrid application frameworks, 19–22

limitations of, 17–18

overview of, 3–4

plug-ins, 18–19

reasons for using, 5–6

support options and resources, 19

Photos. See Images; Pictures

Physical devices

testing accelerator on, 158

testing applications created with PhoneGap Build, 152

testing BlackBerry applications on, 111–112

testing Eclipse applications on, 78–79

testing PhoneGap applications on, 36–37

Pictures. See also Images

accessing on devices, 165–166

mediaType property, 182

play method, Media object, 298–299

Playback, of media files

determining current position, 297

determining duration of, 297–298

playing audio clips, 298–299

Plug-ins
  Eclipse, 64
  jQuery Rotate, 212
  for use with PhoneGap, 18–19
PNG format, 181, 190
Properties
  connection object, 217–218
  contact, 224–226
  device object, 244–245
  `FileEntry` and `DirectoryEntry`, 269–272
  geolocation, 280–281

Q

`quality` property, Camera API settings, 177–178
Queries, SQL databases, 324–325

R

Raw images, 178–179
Reading
  content from files, 274–275
  directory entries, 267–272
Recording audio, 299–300
`remove` method, contacts, 242
Research In Motion. See RIM (Research In Motion)
`resume` events, application status, 251–254
RIM (Research In Motion)
  BlackBerry. See BlackBerry
  emulator/simulators and, 35–36
  Java API, 246
  PhoneGap supported operating systems, 4
  RMEE (Ripple Mobile Environment Emulator), 44–46
RMEE (Ripple Mobile Environment Emulator), 44–46

S

Samsung
  bada development environment. See bada development environment
  Infuse 4G device, 204
  PhoneGap supported operating systems, 4
SDKs (software development kits)
  downloading/installing bada SDK, 80–82
  installing Android SDK on Macintosh OSs, 60
  installing Android SDK on Windows OSs, 58–59
  installing BlackBerry WebWorks SDK, 98–99
  Nokia, 125–126
  PhoneGap Build compared with, 142
  testing PhoneGap applications, 78–79
  Windows Phone 7.1, 135–136
Searches, for contacts, 235–241
Security
  configuring in bada development environment, 90, 92
  PhoneGap Build projects and, 145
`seekTo` method, `Media` objects, 298–299
Sencha Touch, use in application development, 31
Servers
  BES (BlackBerry Enterprise Server), 109
  DDMS (Dalvik Debug Monitor Server), 42–43
  delivering application files to build server, 146–147
  uploading files to, 277–278
Session storage, local storage, 316
Signing keys
  BlackBerry applications, 99
  configuring PhoneGap Build for mobile platforms, 143–145

Simulators. See E/S (emulator/simulator)

Smartphones
    application status events, 251
    button events, 256
    Capture API example on, 201
    connection object, 217
    current location of, 280
    deploying applications to, 108–109
    device object example, 245
    emulator/simulators and, 35–36
    file storage options, 263–264
    geolocation capabilities, 279
    how PhoneGap works, 6
    memory cards, 61
    mimicking native applications, 31
    Ripple emulator and, 46
    running HelloWorld application on,
        24–25
    specifying contact properties and, 226
    SQLLite and, 315, 326
    testing PhoneGap applications, 152–153
    Web 1.0 and Web 2.0 technologies, 12

`sourceType` property, Camera API
    settings, 179–180

Splash screens, PhoneGap Build projects,
    145–146

SQL databases
    creating transactions, 317–318
    example of mileage tracker
        application, 322
    executing SQL statements, 320–324
    opening, 317
    passing functions to transactions,
        319–320
    querying SQL statements, 324–325

SQL (Structured Query Language), 317

SQLLite database engine, 315, 326

`stop` method, `Media` object, 298–300

Storage API
    creating database transactions, 317–318
    executing SQL statements, 320–324
    local storage, 316–317
    mileage tracker example on BlackBerry
        Torch 9800, 322
    opening SQL database, 317
    overview of, 315
    passing functions to transactions,
        319–320
    querying SQL statements, 324–325
    SQLLite and, 326

Storage types, files, 263–264

Strings, specifying contact properties,
    224–225

Strobe, types of hybrid applications, 22

Structured Query Language (SQL), 317

Symbian
    building PhoneGap applications, 15
    cross-platform issues, 51
    PhoneGap Build support, 141
    supported operating systems, 4

Symbian development environment
    configuring application settings,
        129–130
    creating PhoneGap project, 128–129
    installing Make utility, 126–127
    installing Nokia Web Tools, 125–126
    modifying HelloWorld application for,
        130–131
    overview of, 125
    packaging PhoneGap projects, 131–132
    testing applications created with
        PhoneGap Build, 152
    testing PhoneGap applications, 132–134

T

Tables, SQL database, 319–320

Tablets, support for WebWorks tablet
    applications, 103

targetHeight/targetWidth
properties, Camera API settings, 181

Temporary storage
accessing temporary sandbox storage, 264–265
file storage options, 263–264

Testing PhoneGap applications
on Android emulator, 78
on AVD (Android Virtual Device), 60–64
in bada development environment, 95–96
in BlackBerry development environment, 109–112
in iOS development environment, 122–123
overview of, 35
in PhoneGap Build, 152–153
on physical device, 36–37, 78–79
on simulator, 35–36
in Symbian development environment, 132–134
in Windows development environment, 139–140

Tiggr, types of hybrid applications, 22

Titanium Appcelerator, 20

Torch simulators. See also BlackBerry
contacts example running on, 231
getting current location of device, 284
HelloWorld application running on, 29–30
mileage tracker example, 322
reading directory entries, 269–272
watching location of device, 286, 288

transaction method, of database object, 319

type property, connection object, 217–218

U

UIs (user interfaces). See also jQuery Mobile (jQM)
cross-platform issues related to, 52
enhancements, 30–35

Universities, iOS development and, 114

Uploading files
to build server, 146–147
to servers, 277–278

URI
Camera API and, 165
camera destinationType properties, 177–178
camera quality properties, 177–178
capture process and, 173–175
configuring camera options, 176
FileURI for media objects, 294–295
iOS example displaying image file URI, 169–170

USB
running PhoneGap applications on physical device, 78
testing PhoneGap BlackBerry applications, 111

User interfaces (UIs). See also jQuery Mobile (jQM)
cross-platform issues related to, 52
enhancements, 30–35

V

Versions, in bada development project
defining application version, 88–89
defining platform version, 90–92

Versions, in iOS development project, 118–119

Vibrate, in Notification API, 310

Video capture
on Android devices, 202–204
with Capture API, 186, 198–199
Video, `mediaType` property, 182
Virtual machines (VMs)
developing applications for Windows
Phone, 135
running Windows OS on Macintosh, 79
Visual alerts, in Notification API, 307–310
Visual Studio 2010 Express
creating Windows Phone project,
136–139, 330
testing Windows Phone project, 139–140
VMs (virtual machines)
developing applications for Windows
Phone, 135
running Windows OS on Macintosh, 79
Voice recorders, audio capture on Android
devices, 202–203

W

W3C (Worldwide Web Consortium)
Contacts API, 223
Device APIs and Policy (DAP) Working
Group, 10
File API:Directories and System
specification, 263
Geolocation API specification, 279
Media API and, 293
Media Capture API, 185
Web SQL Database Specification, 315
Web Storage API Specification, 315
Widget Packaging and XML
Configuration specification, 145
widget specification, 125
`watchHeading` function, Compass API,
210–213
`watchHeadingFilter` function,
Compass API, 213–215

`watchID` variable, geolocation API
canceling a watch, 289–291
overview of, 284
setting a watch, 285–288
Web 1.0, 11
Web 2.0, 11–12
Web App Simulator
Nokia Web Tools for Windows OSs, 126
packaging Symbian PhoneGap
projects, 126
testing Symbian PhoneGap projects,
132–134
Web applications
building into PhoneGap application, 25
building PhoneGap applications,
13–16
PhoneGap application types and, 37
running within PhoneGap container,
7–8
Web browsers
geolocation support, 279
running web applications within
PhoneGap container, 7–8
storage and, 315, 317
Web content
accessing for iOS PhoneGap project,
119–122
adding to Windows Phone PhoneGap
project, 138
creating PhoneGap project using
PhoneGap Build, 145–146
folder structure as cross-platform
issue, 51
Web Inspector, debugging Symbian
PhoneGap projects, 134
Web Inspector Remote (Weinre)
debugging applications created with
PhoneGap Build, 154
debugging PhoneGap applications,
46–49

Web Runtime (WRT) widgets
 configuring application settings for
  PhoneGap project on Symbian, 129–130
 running PhoneGap applications on
  Symbian as, 125–126
Web sites, PhoneGap resources, 19
Web SQL Database Specification, W3C
 (Worldwide Web Consortium), 315
Web Storage API Specification, W3C
 (Worldwide Web Consortium), 315–316
Web Tools, Nokia, 125–126
Web views, rendering, 7
webOS
 building PhoneGap applications, 14–15
 PhoneGap Build support, 141
 PhoneGap supported operating
  systems, 3
 testing applications created with
  PhoneGap Build, 152
WebSDKSimulator
 Nokia Web Tools for Mac OSs, 126
 testing Symbian PhoneGap projects, 132
WebWorks. See also BlackBerry
 accessing contact information and, 230
 build process, 104–107
 creating PhoneGap project, 99–100
 debugging web content, 37
 installing SDK, 98–99
 JavaScript methods provided by, 246
 overview of, 21
Weinre (Web Inspector Remote)
 debugging applications created with
  PhoneGap Build, 154
 debugging PhoneGap applications,
  46–49
.wgz files, packaging PhoneGap
 projects, 131
Wi-Fi networks, connection object and,
 217–218

Widget Packaging and XML Configuration
 specification, W3C (Worldwide Web
 Consortium), 145
Widgets
 configuring application settings for
  PhoneGap project on Symbian, 129–130
 running PhoneGap applications on
  Symbian as, 125
Wikis, PhoneGap resources, 19
Windows development environment
 creating PhoneGap project, 136–139
 installing Windows Phone development
  tools, 135–136
 overview of, 135
 testing PhoneGap applications, 139–140
Windows OSs
 bada development tools and, 79
 building Symbian PhoneGap applications
  on, 125–126
 configuring Eclipse development
  environment, 64–65
 installing Android SDK on, 58–59
 installing Apache Ant on, 338–339
 Installing BlackBerry WebWorks SDK,
  98–99
 options for PhoneGap development on
  Android, 57
 packaging Symbian PhoneGap
  projects, 131
 testing Symbian PhoneGap projects,
  132–134
Windows Path environment
 configuring for use with JDK, 335–336
 installing Apache Ant on Windows OSs,
  338–339
Windows Phone
 building PhoneGap applications, 15
 creating PhoneGap project for,
  136–139

installing development tools, 135–136

PhoneGap supported operating systems, 3

preparing PhoneGap for, 330–331

support for, 135

Windows Phone Emulator, 136, 140

Workbench. See AT&T WorkBench

Worklight, types of hybrid applications, 22

Worldwide Web Consortium. See W3C (Worldwide Web Consortium)

Writing data, to files, 272–274

WRT (Web Runtime) widgets

    configuring application settings for PhoneGap project on Symbian, 129–130

    running PhoneGap applications on Symbian as, 125–126

X

X coordinates. See Device orientation, in Accelerator API

Xcode

    accessing web content for iOS project, 119–122

configuring ExternalHosts, 305

creating iOS project, 116–122

installing, 114–116

naming projects and defining project locations, 117–118

new project window, 117

preparing PhoneGap for iOS development, 329

welcome screen, 116

XHTML, 11

Y

Y coordinates. See Device orientation, in Accelerator API

Z

Z coordinates. See Device orientation, in Accelerator API

Zip archives

    options for delivering application files to build server, 146

    packaging PhoneGap projects, 131

    PhoneGap files distributed via, 328

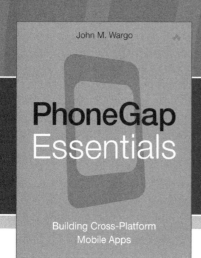

PhoneGap Essentials

John M. Wargo

Building Cross-Platform
Mobile Apps

FREE
Online Edition

Safari
Books Online

Your purchase of *PhoneGap Essentials* includes access to a free online edition for 45 days through the **Safari Books Online** subscription service. Nearly every Addison-Wesley Professional book is available online through **Safari Books Online**, along with thousands of books and videos from publishers such as Cisco Press, Exam Cram, IBM Press, O'Reilly Media, Prentice Hall, Que, Sams, and VMware Press.

Safari Books Online is a digital library providing searchable, on-demand access to thousands of technology, digital media, and professional development books and videos from leading publishers. With one monthly or yearly subscription price, you get unlimited access to learning tools and information on topics including mobile app and software development, tips and tricks on using your favorite gadgets, networking, project management, graphic design, and much more.

Activate your FREE Online Edition at
informit.com/safarifree

STEP 1:   Enter the coupon code: YLGJQZG.

STEP 2:   New Safari users, complete the brief registration form.
Safari subscribers, just log in.

If you have difficulty registering on Safari or accessing the online edition,
please e-mail customer-service@safaribooksonline.com